# Cultured Violence

## Narrative, Social Suffering, and Engendering Human Rights in Contemporary South Africa

Postcolonialism across the Disciplines 7

# Postcolonialism across the Disciplines

*Series Editors*
Graham Huggan, University of Leeds
Andrew Thompson, University of Leeds

Postcolonialism across the Disciplines showcases alternative directions for postcolonial studies. It is in part an attempt to counteract the dominance in colonial and postcolonial studies of one particular discipline – English literary/cultural studies – and to make the case for a combination of disciplinary knowledges as the basis for contemporary postcolonial critique. Edited by leading scholars, the series aims to be a seminal contribution to the field, spanning the traditional range of disciplines represented in postcolonial studies but also those less acknowledged. It will also embrace new critical paradigms and examine the relationship between the transnational/cultural, the global and the postcolonial.

# Cultured Violence

Narrative, Social Suffering,
and Engendering Human Rights
in Contemporary South Africa

**Rosemary Jolly**

Liverpool University Press

First published 2010 by
Liverpool University Press
4 Cambridge Street
Liverpool L69 7ZU

*British Library Cataloguing-in-Publication data*
A British Library CIP record is available


ISBN 978-1-84631-213-7

Typeset in Amerigo by Koinonia, Manchester
Printed and bound in the UK by Bell & Bain Ltd, Glasgow

# Contents

For Alan H. Jeeves

# Acknowledgements

This book is the culmination of a decade's worth of interaction with colleagues, friends, students and participants drawn from the literary critical and health spheres of my teaching, research and community engagement. My gratitude to them does not mean to imply their support of my readings, for which I alone am responsible.

I am grateful to Derek Attridge for his generous encouragement and input from start to finish; and to my literary critical colleagues across three continents: Margaret Lenta and Margaret Daymond in Durban, who have been such kind hosts in times of stress, and whose careers in the South African academy these many years manifest an intellectual tenacity and grace to which I can only hope to aspire; Rosanne Kennedy and Gillian Whitlock in Australia, who facilitated my work with them on 'The Limits of the Human' project and generously read the manuscript in its entirety to advise me on its development; and David Attwell in the UK, a companion South-North intellectual migrant whose friendship I greatly value. Marta Straznicky has created a departmental environment in English at Queen's, welcoming of me and my interdisciplinary pursuits – no easy task in the current academic environment; and thanks to Shelley King, whose intelligence and common sense are anything but common. Julie Salverson has been a staunch friend, colleague and force for sanity in my life. Thank you.

On the medical research side I would like to thank Steve Reid, Chair, Primary Healthcare Directorate, University of Cape Town; Jim Muller of the Pietermaritzburg Hospital Complex; Fritse Miller, whose work at RapeCrisis/ Lifeline Pietermaritzburg has truly been heroic; and Gcina Radebe, District Health Manager of Sisonke through challenging times. Bill Cameron in Ottawa has been a stalwart and practical supporter of my HIV/AIDS-related research, always believing in the interdisciplinary approach. It is difficult for me to thank adequately my colleagues Alan Jeeves and Stevenson Fergus; they are indefatigable scholars, courageously interdisciplinary, and generous in the extreme. Long may we remain collaborators.

Thanks to my graduate student friends and supporters over the years, most particularly Lori Pollock in English, and Jessica Cowan Dewar and Lauren McNicol in Health Studies. Also to my sister, Nomusa Mngoma, thank you.

Special thanks to Miriam Tlali, who sat through TRC hearings with me; and to 'Tauhali', 'Palesa' and 'Thandi'; also to the amazing home-based care-workers of the Centocow Development Programme, and to Bishop Stanley and Father Ignatius; also to Yazir Henri and Mmatshilo Motsei; and to Marjorie Jobson for e-troducing me to Mmatshilo and her work; I hope to meet her in person soon.

Without the friendship of Ellen Hawman and Marg Holland it is doubtful this material would have made it into book form at all. In gratitude for ensuring that I was never lonely in my violent imaginings, thanks to J. M. Coetzee and Philip Grobler overseas; and Eve D'Aeth and Chris Whynot at home.

In acknowledgment of all the uniquely non-human animal enjoyment a being could offer, I celebrate the inestimable ridgeback dog, known to his capacious circle of friends and admirers as Thabo, but to his Winnipeg 'Mum' as Stalkmoor's King's Cross.

To both sets of anonymous readers, thank you: your input has been invaluable. Thanks also to editor Andrea Nattrass and the creative vision of UKZN Press: publishing the novels of Siphiwo Mahala, Sandile Memela, Phaswane Mpe and Futhi Ntshingila made the final chapter and conclusion of this book possible.

To Postcolonialism across the Disciplines Series Editor, Graham Huggan; the ever-patient and encouraging Managing Director at Liverpool University Press, Anthony Cond; and the meticulous Helen Tookey, many thanks.

Thanks to my family and especially to Chris McMullen, who has adopted South Africa wholeheartedly and without whose support of all kinds, from providing amazing meals to serious crisis control, many aspects of the field research would have been simply impossible.

This work has been supported financially by the Office of Research Services, Queen's University; the Science and Humanities Research Council of Canada; and the Canadian Institutes of Health Research. For hosting me to present work from this manuscript, I thank Derek Attridge, University of York and the Leverhulme Foundation, UK; Christine Roulston and the University of Western Ontario; Rosanne Kennedy and Debjani Ganguly of the Research School of the Humanities, Australian National University, Canberra; the Institute for Advanced Studies in the Humanities, University of Edinburgh; Graham Huggan, Leeds University; Len Findlay, University of Saskatchewan; Cynthia Kros, Deborah Posel and the Wits Institute for Scientific and Economic Research, University of the Witwatersrand; Pumla Gobodo-Madikizela and Chris van Wyk, University of Cape Town; and Jane Poyner and Warwick University.

An extracted, earlier version of Chapter 3 was published by the *Canadian Journal of African Studies* 38.3: 622–637 (2004) © Canadian Association of African Studies; and subsequently republished in Greg Cuthbertson's and Alan Jeeves' edited collection, *Fragile Freedom* (2009) © University of South Africa; and an earlier version of Chapter 1 in Jane Poyner's edited collection, *J. M. Coetzee and the Idea of the Public Intellectual* (2006), © University of Ohio Press.

INTRODUCTION

# Testifying in and to Cultures of Spectacular Violence

## Narrative Vision in Times of Violence

It is a sad irony that while South Africa's Truth and Reconciliation process has been widely studied and used as a resource internationally, and while South Africa's remarkable post-apartheid Constitution guarantees rights to its citizens that are radical in their scope, life on the ground in the 'Rainbow Nation' is, for the majority of its citizens, (still) characterized by high rates of poverty, morbidity and violence. Marking the failure of the promise offered by a post-apartheid era in a poignant way is the fact that, fifteen years after the end of apartheid, in May 2008, the army was called out to assist police in controlling South African citizens. At issue was attacks against foreign nationals, migrants from other countries in sub-Saharan Africa who have fled impossible economic and political conditions in their various states of origin, seeking a better life in South Africa.

The return of the army to the townships of South Africa is haunting for those who experienced, with dread, their presence on the streets during the apartheid decades. Another haunting image is that of citizens standing by cheering on the xenophobic attacks, some of which have included necklacing – taking a car tyre and setting it on fire around the neck of the victim. This form of 'punishment' was exercised during the apartheid-era struggle against persons perceived to be sell-outs to the apartheid regime. The attacks have been accompanied by the singing of an erstwhile liberation song in which the singers call for *umshimi wami*, 'my machine gun'.[1] Such haunting speaks to the continuation of the past into the present, in a way that disturbs the attempts to contain South Africa's history into neatly demarcated apartheid and liberation eras.

---

1   I discuss the redeployment of this anti-apartheid song by the supporters of Jacob Zuma in Chapter 4.

The *Guardian Weekly* has commented on these events in an editorial entitled 'Is this the end of the Rainbow nation?' playing on Archbishop Desmond Tutu's vision of the Rainbow Nation as having been betrayed not simply by the phenomenon of xenophobic violence, but also by the causes for it, which are primarily identified in the article as 'the government's lack of delivery on social welfare to the black majority' (*Guardian Weekly*, 2008). This betrayal is significant in its highlighting of the juxtaposition between the then of the heroic narrative and the now of the less glamorous struggle, in which the enemy is not the apartheid government – a relatively discrete and easily named adversary – but the simultaneous legacies of colonization, apartheid and global inequity.

Without denying the heroism of the struggle for liberation, one can acknowledge that the tropes of heroes and villains tend to become entrenched. The centrality of these tropes to our thinking about violence is marked by the fact that we often appeal to them to deny, rather than express, violent relationships. In the case of former President F. W. de Klerk's urging South Africa to look at the future, not the past, in the interests of national unity, we see the attempt of the last National Party (NP) president to rewrite history, casting himself and his party as at worst innocent bystanders and at best, eager and willing negotiators – and thus heroes in some sense – of a post-apartheid future. In the first report made by de Klerk on behalf of the NP to the Truth and Reconciliation Commission (TRC), he claimed that neither he nor his cabinet had authorized gross human rights violations, including torture and death. In the NP's second submission to the TRC – in consequence of the TRC posing specific questions to the NP – de Klerk maintained that he was shocked by the actions of what he called 'maverick elements', who carried out acts of murder and torture that de Klerk maintained had never been government policy (Graybill 2002).[2]

Such denials are not one-sided, as we were made aware when the first post-apartheid government under Mandela refused to accept the final report of the TRC, because of the negative implications it might have had for the contemporary powers; and the scandalous refusal of the South African government to make the reparations called for by the TRC to victims and their families.[3]

---

2   Here, de Klerk's rhetoric of denial operates in much the same way as P. W. Botha's, as I have argued (Jolly 2001).

3   On 28 October 1998 the ANC, represented by Deputy Secretary-General Thenjiwe Mtintso (the same Thenjiwe Mtintso who spoke so movingly of the difficulties of women testifying before the TRC; see Chapter 3) announced that the ANC government would seek an injunction to suppress the TRC's Final Report, in order to suppress the TRC's findings that the ANC had committed gross human rights violations (GHRVs) in its fight against apartheid. For the full text of the submission of the ANC to the TRC in reply to its section 30(2) notification of findings against the ANC see African National Congress 1998. For a sense of how the TRC Report was received by the government of South Africa, see James and van der Vijver 2000; 2001; and, in particular, Boraine 2000; 2001; and Nyatsumba 2000; 2001. While the TRC Report made recommendations to the government for reparations, their recommendations were not binding in any way. This led to a generally acknowledged failure to render the reparations policy operational, or the basic reparations adequate. As with the matter of the reception of the TRC's Final

Recognition of the 'deafness' of various narratives in response to certain calls for accountability or reciprocity allows for the analysis of such failures beyond simple examples of hypocrisy. If we understand that listening is a key capacity of narrative, such an analysis presents an opportunity to extend our modes of listening. The narratives of F. W. de Klerk and Nelson Mandela are obviously motivated by political expediency in support of their respective parties. However, the use of more complex narratives in negotiating South Africa's political transition are less easy to judge: they can and do exhibit a social vision that is self-consciously ethically informed, yet still remain deaf to key aspects of others' narratives of alienation. The TRC has been viewed in this light.

South Africa was so keen to hear testifiers' stories of gross human rights violations (GHRVs) that it created an institutional space for these stories to be told and heard through the TRC. However, certain aspects of survivor-narrators' stories form less desirable material, such as their demands for reparations. These elements of their narratives do not have ready listeners. While the TRC made recommendations to the government for reparations for victim-survivors, as was its task, the government has fallen short dramatically in its delivery of reparations to victim-survivors. This has led the survivors' group, Khulumani, to seek reparations costs internationally, in the State of New York. By arguing that the South African state has taken care of victim-survivors through its own processes and mechanisms the current government of South Africa has aligned itself with those companies that did business with the apartheid state, from which Khulumani is seeking reparations.[4]

While they may be perceived as making belated claims by officials and members of the broader national and international public, the claimant testifiers themselves speak of and represent an (unspeakable) continuity between past and present. The TRC was intended to represent a break with the injustices of the past. However, there is a glaring dissonance between the ethics of accountability and reciprocity symbolized in the TRC and enshrined in South Africa's democratic Constitution on the one hand, and on the other the state's inability to ensure that the rights enshrined in the Constitution are transformed for the majority from the realm of the aspirational into that of the actual. These features include the initial refusal and subsequent delay in providing key services to citizens suffering from HIV/AIDS; and the failure to diminish some of the highest rates of violence in the world, notably in the area of violence against women and children. It is telling that the survivors' group Khulumani issued a strong and clear appeal to fellow South Africans to cease enacting violence against foreign residents of South Africa during the recent xenophobic riots, in the name of the vision of post-apartheid South Africa proposed by the nation's

---

Report, there are many texts that document the failure of the reparations programme and the struggle of TRC victim-survivors for justice more fully than I could ever do here; see, for example, Colvin 2000; Kayser 2001; Hamber et al. 2000; Buur 2003; see also Graybill 2002, especially 'The Rest of the Story', pp. 145–61; Villa-Vicencio and Verwoerd 2000; and particularly Orr 2000 and Walaza 2000.

4   For information on this case see Bohler-Muller 2008; Bond 2008.

own constitutional provisions, of which the TRC was part and parcel.

Embedded in these challenges is what Mamphela Ramphele, in a speech to the TRC Ten Years After Conference held at the University of Cape Town in November 2006, identifies as the defining ethical, social and political challenge facing contemporary South Africa: how to disrupt the continuance of poverty experienced by the majority of blacks under apartheid and in the contemporary era. This challenge she links most particularly to the post-apartheid betrayal of TRC victim-survivors in terms of reparations. For Ramphele, this failure of the post-TRC ethos is manifest in and symbolized by the intolerable refusal of successive post-apartheid governments to follow through with the reparations policy outlined by the TRC in the interests of its victim-survivor testifiers, some of whom, together with Archbishop and TRC Chairperson Desmond Tutu, were present at her address:

> South Africa is not a poor country. For us not to have placed priority on the issue of reparations as a way of restoring dignity to people who were so deeply wounded, and yet who were so generous as has been demonstrated this evening – the level of generosity defies any description; it's actually rude to even refer to it. And yet we found money to do a whole lot of other things, including things that have got us into trouble, like the arms deal [...].[5]
>
> *The least we can do is to move out of denial* and recognise that we made a mistake in terms of addressing the socio-economic injustices with the same vigour that we addressed the political injustices.
>
> We have dealt admirably with our political wilderness, and thanks to uTata [Desmond Tutu] and the A-Team that led us through that process. But we need to think very seriously as a nation about how we are going to heal this growing divide between those who are poor, who are getting poorer, and those who are wealthy, or comfortable, who are getting more and more comfortable. ('Reconciliation is not Enough', see Ramphele 2006; emphasis added)

Apart from the ethical failures entailed in this poor sequel to the TRC, the story demonstrates that survivor-narrators, who make demands not considered to be in the public interest, are rendered unable to command ready listeners for what they may have to say about the undesirability of the *current* cultural, social and political order in South Africa.

Denialism has emerged as a way of maintaining an unbroken heroic narrative of the anti-apartheid struggle and its requisite counterpart, an unmitigated successful transformation, expressed in the vocabulary of the Rainbow Nation, or the African Renaissance, or the capitalist triumphalism of the Black Economic Empowerment (BEE) initiative, to name but a few of the images that fit this bill. A primary example here is President Mbeki's notorious stance in the face of the AIDS epidemic, a phenomenon that I revisit in detail in Chapter 4 of this book. Rhetoric that is willing to parade the heroic narratives of the anti-apartheid era

---

5  For more on the infamous deal in which South Africa spent millions on arms just after the transition in particularly shady circumstances see Arms Deal Virtual Press Office, The, n.d.

without acknowledging, let alone addressing, current, deep, social inequities overlooks the fact that denial of victim-survivors' critical experiences, reflections and demands may have devastating effects not just for those survivors; such denial jeopardizes the project of a different future for the country as a whole.

A trope most often used to express the centrality of this unfinished business to South Africa's contemporary situation is the one of haunting, invoked above in my description of the 2008 riots. Mamphela Ramphele's *Laying Ghosts to Rest: Dilemmas of the Transformation in South Africa* (2008) is another case in point. Ramphele's book deals with these dilemmas of transformation through a socio-political approach to naming and framing the challenges. I take a different, but complementary, approach to naming and conceptualizing these dilemmas. I claim that the creative and critical realm of narrative is privileged in its potential to proffer ways of registering what has become deniable, and therefore unspeakable, within a given cultural context. Narrative analysis can enable us to understand harm done that exceeds the limitation of the verifiable in legal terms and the limitation of the accountable in terms of that which is socially sanctioned. Further, narrative has the potential to accommodate a dynamic of reciprocity that frames stories of wrongdoing as offering possibilities, for their narrators and listeners, of complicity and of transformation.

Critical narrative vision is crucial to tracing the disturbing continuities between South Africa's past and present, and rhetorical structures that encourage denial of those continuities. Such vision enables us to critique narratives as forms of listening that can 'hear' or capture certain subjects within the contemporary social, political and cultural moment, while remaining constitutionally 'deaf' (a revealing pun) to others. Such 'deafness' renders those others literally inconceivable. This book proposes that the narrative forms we use to describe the past and to relate it to the here and now can be seen as forms of listening that hear or capture certain aspects of the narrative of transition, but can remain deaf to, or ignore, others. This is what I term 'deaf listening'; and it obtains in different modes of what I shall define as entrenched, or cultured, violence. An analysis of cultured violence in South Africa leads us to an understanding of the remarkable gap between the constitutional provisions protecting human rights in contemporary South Africa, and the apparent lag effect of the lack of the experience of those rights by a vast number of the country's inhabitants. Finally, this analysis suggests why framing this dilemma as one of practices on the ground simply needing to 'catch up' to the Constitution may be inadequate to the task of what I call 'unculturing' violence.

Here, I attempt both to characterize and to diagnose violence in South Africa by attempting to trace its cultural formations in a nexus of narratives that structure, implicitly, that which is (non-human) animal, that which is female, that which is child, and that which is diseased, as targets of entrenched and allowable violence – narrative structures that, I hasten to add, may have specifically South African formulations but are in no way confined to South Africa per se. I attempt this task by juxtaposing narratives of different sorts: personal narratives, narratives formally accorded the status of testimony, and creative narratives. These narratives together provide the cultural fabric of an analysis that does not limit itself to the material, sociological, or narrowly political.

I shall begin by tracing the challenge of linking representations of actual and fictional violence and the disciplines we use to describe violent phenomena to the conceptual frameworks by which we organize these phenomena. I shall then explore the operations of cultured violence by tracing the relationships between Pierre Bourdieu's concept of symbolic violence and the ways in which we have become habituated to representing and understanding violence spectacularly. The remainder of this Introduction addresses the specific challenges of testifying to violence in ways that illustrate audiences' and readers' unwitting complicity in interpretive strategies, including some forms posed by trauma theory, that tend towards disabling the voice of the testifier as she attempts to bear witness to her violation and the structures that enabled it. I explore the motivation behind this unwitting complicity and the related alienation, or disembodiment, of the victim-survivor, that ensues from this subtle denial of her testimony. By understanding the processes of such deaf listening, we can begin to see our complicity in ways of framing victim-survivors and their suffering as strange. To point out the absurdity of structures of meaning that abstract meaningfulness from the experience of the victim-survivor is to begin to envisage and potentially inhabit an uncomfortable world *with* the victim-survivor who testifies, rather than being complicit in the one from which she is estranged.

## A Methodological Note on Actual and Fictional Violence: Thinking across the Disciplines

The subject of violence as a subject – one that is always already in some sense gendered – highlights the *danger* of making a watertight division between actual violence and the stories we use to represent and understand that violence. As a critic of narrative, I view as crippling contemporary attempts to maintain a conceptual 'apartheid' between representations of violence in narrative form and the acts of violence to which those narratives refer. The reluctance of intellectuals to look at the relationships between the making and reading of fiction and the making and reading of ourselves as subjects, often stems from a desire to recognize the differential status that historical events on the one hand – say, Auschwitz – and fictional events on the other – say, Aeneas's love affair with Dido in Virgil's *Aeneid* – hold for us. (Bear with me in my pairing of these two very different phenomena; it is their ontological difference I wish to explore as a resource in my subsequent reading of them.) Yet we can look at these events comparatively, without losing sight of the fact that one is historical fact and the other fictional event. We can say, for example, that both have to do with the exclusivity and racialized sense of identity that tend to accompany nationalist enterprises; and that both have to do with a feminization of the racialized group that threatens nationalist purity. Hitler wishes to 'purify' the German nation by massacring the Jews en masse, rendering them powerless and thus in some sense 'feminine'[6]; the nationalist rhetoric of the *Aeneid* calls for Aeneas to turn his back on Dido, since she is associated with the African state of Carthage, and has been allied, sexually, with the African prince, Iarbus. The inferior African blood of Dido – weak because she is feminine, weak because she is racially tainted, feminized because she is racially tainted and black because she is feminized – must be rejected, the threat she represents conquered in favour of the true, European blood of Lavinia in order for the nation of Rome to be put on a firm foundation.[7] We can recognize these elements of similarity without collapsing into one another the status of Auschwitz as a historic event of proportions that may exceed our best efforts at sympathetic imagination (but not, importantly, our critical faculties), and the status of the tragedy of Aeneas's betrayal of Dido as a fictional event.

If we censor work on the relations between actual events and their various representations in fiction, we censor, at the same time, work that links the narratives available in a given society for us to inhabit with the forms of violence prevalent in that society. Censorship of critical examinations of relations between the phenomena we perceive in our actuality – particularly violent phenomena – and their representations in fictional form, even when made for the best of moral reasons, has its own negative impact. Such censorship denies the ability of subjects to read and interpret narratives for themselves, and thus obscures the very operation of the ideologies which govern our individual behaviours by rendering them consequent upon necessity, rather than shaped by ideological constructs; it also thereby renders us complicit in a sort of systemic violence that Bourdieu terms 'symbolic violence', a process I shall describe in detail below.

In addition to those boundaries that mark the division between the actual and the fictional, there is another set of borders that we also need to traverse in order to understand the processes by which violence is cultured. This time it is not the conceptual division between the fictional and the real, but the well-policed boundaries between disciplines. If we are to look at the actual and the fictional in relation to one another, we are already involved in crossing the borders between drama, art, English and other literature departments on the

---

6   On the long history of the feminization of the Jews see Horowitz 1998; Gilman 1991 and 1993; Mosse 1985.

7   This betrayal of Dido is not seen as a betrayal in the text, of course. Certainly, Aeneas and Dido have a relationship that is consummated in the cave. But the relationship falters on an illegitimacy that is attributed to Dido in the text. After the death of her husband, Dido is supposed to have taken a vow of chastity to ensure her service to the Carthaginians as queen. Yet as she 'seduces' Aeneas away from his national duty, the rebuilding of Carthage falters and Dido is portrayed as an inadequate sovereign: after all, she is African, a woman, and a 'fallen woman' at that. (About the fact that in the European imagination all African women are always already fallen, I shall have more to say later.) Ultimately, then, the *Aeneid* proposes that Aeneas's betrayal of Dido is proof of his dedication to the project of nation-building. He needs to go on to found Rome; and his departure is in the best interests of the Carthaginians anyway. Dido is left to Africa, just as the snakes of the Medusa's head are supposed to have become the serpents of Libya, after Perseus managed to behead the Gorgon.

one hand, and history, sociology, psychology and so on, on the other. Notice the disciplinary division between the discursive analyses of societies on the one hand – the examination of the stories they tell to make sense of the world – and on the other, the phenomenological analysis of those societies – the examination of the phenomena that make up their historical, sociological and psychological profile.

Of course, this disciplinary division is not complete. For example, the process of writing a play about an aspect of specific responses to the Holocaust in Germany, such as Julie Salverson's *The Haunting of Sophie Scholl* (2001),[8] requires detailed historical research as part of an artistic interpretation of historic events. Similarly, many words that we use all too frequently – including 'violence' – have become so tired that they require interpretation in specific contexts to regain their meaning. One cannot regain the meaning of such words in an intellectual context in which discursive and phenomenological analysis remain in a relation of 'apartheid' to one another. Violence may be described through specific kinds of sociological, psychological and political observations about South African civil society and government; but without discursive analysis – an analysis of the narratives the society produces to explain and create the meanings of those words – our understanding of what they mean in relation to South Africa will be weak, impoverished, untenable.

I come – primarily – from the tradition of literary criticism: a discipline that has a long history of leaving phenomena such as 'violence' to the disciplines of political science and sociology. This is because the relationship between politics and aesthetics can be an uncomfortable one. Even unethical narratives may have effective and interesting aesthetics, such as those of Nazi Germany, or US foreign policy, or apartheid South Africa. Furthermore, the act of reading in and of itself is not inherently ethical, nor does it necessarily produce ethical effects. This constitutes the unspeakable vulnerability of a discipline such as English, whose investments in the idea of culture tend not to extend to an explicit acknowledgement of the fact that both writers and readers can be complicit in culturing violence, even as they demonstrate their technical competence, even brilliance, in the discipline.

Yet to take up the responsibility of literary criticism in this day and age – of having the skills to analyse narratives through an examination of their rhetorical effects in relation to their context, both current and historical – means to understand that our skills can and should be used to make sense of the broader role of narratives, fictional or otherwise, in their construction of the ideologies by which we live and through which we live out our lives. This does not mean that we ignore the differential status of narratives such as 'fiction', or what we call 'life narratives', or testimony, or political commentary. It does mean that we bring these narratives into a dialogue with one another, in order to get a fuller picture of what 'violence' may mean.

8   As yet, there is no published text for the play. See http://www.queensu.ca/drama/production_programs.htm for its performance record (accessed 9 April 2010).

This project includes exploring what the term may mean 'symptomatically' within a given society – what it may mean with reference to what we consider to be its effects, or its phenomenonology. However, it also includes exploring how the term came to have recognizable effects, that is, how folks on the ground perceived and perceive of violence and its related concepts. Specifically, then, we need to explore how 'violence' comes to be *conceived* of in a particular context, and what those processes of conception can tell us, both phenomeno-logically and critically, about the narratives we may use to construct the term 'violence' within our own contexts. Employing this methodology, we can utilize our critical facility to see how what we conceive of as violent can tell us *how* we can see some subjects as having been violated and how we may implicitly render some subjects available for violation: how, in fact, we culture violence. In the chapters that follow I demonstrate the need to make such culturing of violence visible; and I attempt to render cultured violence specifically enacted against non-human animals, children, women and men visible.

I propose that self-consciously evaluating the options open to us of different ways of being in the world, and thus of reshaping our world, depends upon our utilizing the capacity involved when we read and write texts. We both inhabit and create stories by which we live our lives. To the extent to which we can train ourselves to become aware of and consciously evaluate the stories we inhabit as if by default, stories that we assume are the conventions of the social and political context into which we are born, we *can* take responsibility for 'authoring' ourselves. That is to say, unless we undertake the process of 'reading' these conventions critically, and creating new stories for ourselves to inhabit should we find the ones we have inherited dubious, we cannot effectively name violence without understanding our complicity in such violence.

## Spectacular Violence and its relation to Symbolic Violence: Judgement and Complicity

Naming violence as an act usually entails judgement on behalf of s/he who narrates the violent act; and a distancing of the narrator from an act that s/he judges to be wrong from an ethical standpoint. The narrator, the namer of the violence, does not usually see himself or herself as in any way complicit in the act s/he condemns. However, complicity is not always recognized by the complicit; further, there is often an element of systemic or structural violence from which it is difficult to separate oneself. If one is a white who speaks against apartheid during the apartheid era from within South Africa, one positions oneself outside the fold of the perpetrators, despite the fact that one's material and cultural life are lived within the very conditions structured by apartheid: conditions of privilege from which there is no clause for opting out, as Albert Memmi has pointed out in the relevant case of what he terms the 'reluctant colonizer' (Memmi 1991).

We would like representations of violence to speak an *inherent* truth about the nature of the violation that is portrayed: its obscenity, we feel, should be self-evident. We may think, especially in the case of violence towards people or some animals – dogs, say, but not snakes – that there is a supposedly natural sense within all human beings that enables them to sense the wrongness of such violence. Yet this assumption denies context. In a context in which life itself – the life of human beings, the life of non-human animals – has become cheap, undervalued, valueless, what may appear to some to be inexcusable acts of violence represents to others a way of life – or death-in-life.

This situation is further complicated by our desire not only for acts of violence to be readily registered and understood but also by our concomitant desire for acts of violence to be attributable to an identifiable individual or group of individuals whom we can name and hold accountable for their acts. And that accountability should in no way come back to be visited upon us as the narrator or narrators of the violent act, since the very naming of the act as violent is somehow seen to be proof of our non-complicity in that act. What is obscured in this naming of violent acts from a supposed moral high ground is the assumption that violence lies outside our quotidian experience, and separated from the pleasure it offers narrator and audience as an act of scapegoating.

The 'truth' of violence represented and read in this framework is characterized as self-evident: the act is immoral; those responsible are acting amorally; and the narrator-as-judge is not complicit. The naming itself, we assume, requires no judgement other than that inherent within it; the event can be understood within its (isolated), apparently self-evident reiteration: no further contextualization is needed to elicit our moral condemnation, if we are worthy citizens, up to the task of confronting violence. Here, truth is viewed as having an obvious, determinable and predetermined content: truth is a reality-effect, a commodity. Spectacular violence works this way, presenting itself as self-evident by eliding the difference between violent act and representation altogether, erasing the narrator from the screen and offering the pleasure of 'obvious' judgement to the audience, where such judgement can, in addition, mask voyeuristic pleasure in the spectacle of violence.

The collapse of the moment when the image of a violent act first strikes the eye, and our judgement of that violence as having no meaning other than its own status as an abomination, is a crucial turning point. It can obscure a refusal on our part to imagine the context and consequences of that violence: a refusal that, in the end, means that our designation of the violence as an abomination is not necessarily well enough considered to understand what is abominable about it, precisely; and this refusal may represent a strategic reluctance to face the systemic, or structural, motivations for and consequences of violent acts, as well as our role in them.[9]

9    Njabulo Ndebele (1991) makes a related argument about the spectacular specifically in connection with apartheid-era black fiction in his essay collection, *The Rediscovery of the Ordinary*. Here I draw on his argument, conceptualizing the spectacular specifically in relation to representations of violence; and I extend the scope of the spectacular explicitly to extra-literary judgement. For more on Ndebele's argument, see Chapter 3.

Dependence upon a morality that is assumed to be self-evident is a form of fundamentalist reading that excludes the imaginative capacity for interpretation of events. Entrenched in this way of reading, we 'make' events mean what we think they ought to mean according to our predetermined belief and desire. Reading events in this way becomes mere confirmation of a world view that we already hold and refuse to modify, even in the face of contradictory evidence. In extraordinary circumstances, we may even seek to 'remould' the evidence so that it 'fits' our world view, if we have the opportunity and means at our disposal. Such an assumed morality – one that underpins a world view that is presented as self-evident – also pre-empts dialogue. If we assume that moral value is self-evident 'within', as it were, a certain event, text, or any other phenomenon, not only do we exclude varieties of ways of understanding moral values but we also reduce ourselves to the form of thinking employed by, among other fundamentalist 'readers', racists and sexists.

To a racist, black identity represents a threat to the self, a threat that is manifested in the labelling of the black body as inferior. This inferiority is expressed variously as dirt, ungodliness, promiscuity or any other of a range of stereotypical racist 'properties' attributed to the black body. To a sexist, the female represents a similar threat, also expressed in images that attribute moral and other types of inferiority to the female body. Yet when we assume that a violent act – say, the torturing of an African National Congress (ANC) resistance worker during the apartheid era, or (and this is another way of phrasing the same event, an event I shall discuss in some detail later) the slamming of a woman's breast in a desk drawer to entrench male dominance – represents exclusively the consummate evil of its perpetrator, we assume that we can limit the responsibility for that racialized and simultaneously sexualized violence to the perpetrator; and we ignore the political, social and cultural context in which the perpetrator was encouraged and supported in his world view. We ignore, then, the role of culture in initiating, empowering and directing – or managing – violence. It is in this sense that I argue that we overlook violence as cultured, rather than as exclusively an interaction between perpetrators and victims.

To avoid the spectacularization of violence, consideration and examination – free of moral convention – need to take place in the interstice between initial perception of a violent event and our subsequent judgement of it. The collapse of these two moments into the moment of an event's occurrence – the fiction of the simultaneity, for example, of the planes crashing into the World Trade Center towers, our perception of those events and our rendering of the perpetrator(s) and the events as self-evident proof of the evil of both perpetrator(s) and events – does not allow for such ethical thought. In the case of spectacular violence, we appear to want to be constantly surprised by the actual occurrence of violence; as I indicated above, we desire to be offended by it. At first glance the desire to experience such offence may seem an integral aspect of an ethical approach to evidence of violence that we need to deal with on a daily basis. However, such desire has a less attractive underside. It implies that we believe that we, the observers, can understand any act of violence

11

without seeking to understand anything further about the specific context in which that act of violence took place. In other words, we assume that we can interpret acts of violence within our own, implicit framework of assumed moral conventions, rather than reflected-upon ethical constructs. These conventions tend to represent our own sense of customary value, and not necessarily that of those involved in the violent act.

This becomes a particularly fraught issue when we realize that our own sense of propriety is more often than not constructed in relation to a life of relative privilege compared to the lives of those whose violent acts we seek to condemn. When those of us who are relatively privileged seek to distance ourselves from violence by judging those who perpetrate it according to our own scheme of values, we often fail to imagine the systemic context in which violence occurs. In this instance, a lack of self-reflection means that our instantaneous judgement of the perpetrators of violence constitutes, in actuality, a kind of mental laziness, a refusal to imagine conditions in which we ourselves might be brought to exercise violence. Such laziness can have its motivation in a subconscious desire to refuse to recognize the economics of consumption. If the inequity of resource distribution – poverty – is fed by the gross consumption power of First World economies, it is in our interest, as First World consumers, to reject our possible complicity in creating the conditions of poverty in which violence and war proliferate with such determined energy.

The challenge, then, is that in order to develop the capacity for explicit, critical discourse, one needs to question the very fabric of life in which one is immersed. The line South Africa fed its white youth during the 1970s, the decade during which I was a teenager in Bloemfontein, South Africa, was its arrogant but ultimately insecure assertion of the inhumanity and threat of black (non)people. This was not, when explicitly stated, that difficult to understand as a lie. But the South Africa of the 1970s was learning *not* to be explicit. Apartheid made up the very texture of our daily life, but it was rarely referred to explicitly. By the 1970s one had become aware that by naming the foundational political policy of the South African Nationalist government for what it was, one was in some sense naming the unspeakable, in the sense that one was naming (an assumed) necessity but also, simultaneously and unavoidably, an unspeakable vulnerability. This unspeakable vulnerability was symbolically represented by events such as the infamous Soweto children's riots of 1976, when children were killed for demonstrating against the apartheid government; the actual vulnerability of apartheid lay in its dependence on the self-deception to which such events as the schoolchildren's riots gave the lie. It is worth mentioning that this vulnerability did not just belong to strong adherents to the apartheid doctrine but to white liberals as well. That rights were to be assumed by the black majority, rather than whites 'granting' them those rights or even (prosthetically) 'assisting' them to gain those rights, sheds light on the white liberal's unspeakable sense of his own irrelevance.

When I say that a child's growing awareness of the hypocrisy of a society pathologically involved in deceiving itself is disembodying, I use the word *disem-*

*body* quite deliberately. For the process of doublethink starts before one can be cognitively aware of it, as a child. One learns the body language of adults without knowing why; one mimics the grown-ups without realizing that eventually, these adults can be seen – in their unspoken acceptance of certain duplicity – to be adulterous. Ultimately, one can see the betrayal of the grown-ups in the way in which their habitus – to use Bourdieu's term – becomes part of oneself; and how later it may well need to be painstakingly excised in an operation that is never 100 per cent successful.

Bourdieu's habitus speaks to the way in which our individual practices are governed by contexts, laws, rules and ideologies in processes of which we are never completely conscious; and the way in which we (to lesser or greater degrees of consciousness) 'allow' ourselves to conform to the dictates of these contexts, laws, rules and ideologies, because they tend to be our best interest, or we *perceive* such conformity to be to be in our interest. Bourdieu describes our place within the habitus thus:

> The agent engaged in practice knows the world [...] too well, without objectifying distance; he takes it for granted, precisely because he is caught up in it, bound up with it; he inhabits it like a garment [...] he feels at home in the world because the world is also in him, in the form of the habitus. (2000: 142–43)

This 'misrecognition' of what we think is in our interest creates what Bourdieu calls 'symbolic violence': that is, 'the violence which is exercised upon a social agent with his or her complicity' (Bourdieu and Wacquant 1992: 142–43).

White adolescents of the 1970s, like me, are victims in this context only in the sense that we were the subjects of the symbolic violence directed at us by the apartheid state and its habitus; that violence exercised upon us, as social agents, with our complicity, but not necessarily with our conscious complicity. The assumption that knowledge is always conscious and its denial obtains in deliberate hypocrisy ignores the fact that the truth does not lie like a stone beneath the surface, waiting to be discovered. Addiction to a notion of truth as having a determinable, indeed, predetermined content (the prominent apartheid-era South African example being white=good; black=evil) makes trying to conceptualize the cotton-wool blankets of deception and self-deception that sustain unspeakability within the habitus difficult. When, as an adolescent, I started to comprehend the duplicity of what white society had imprinted upon my body, speech and thought patterns, there was no moment of epiphany. Nor does the process of stripping away the self-deception of that white, South African self have a marked beginning or ending. The metaphor of 'uncovering a truth', then, does not necessarily fit the experience of gaining integrity at all.

This is why the Nuremberg challenge is not a simple one to deliver, or to confront truthfully, despite the necessity of doing so. The question, 'How could you keep silent, when you knew this was going on?' implies that knowledge is always conscious and easily accessible for that reason. But knowledge, as Pierre

Bourdieu, among others, has pointed out, is not always conscious. Our bodies can inhabit, act out, conform to, a set of 'truths' that we think we can control: but we do not control our bodies absolutely; our bodies are not totalitarian states. Yet we hesitate to recognize our subconscious complicity.

Bourdieu's symbolic violence is related to spectacular violence in that both have the capacity to obscure complicity by encouraging a lack of self-consciousness about our daily practices that can render our complicity in systemic violence obscure, even to the point of denial. More specifically, spectacular violence can be considered a major tool upon which states and societies depend to inflict the symbolic violence entailed in the enactment of the habitus. This is precisely because, using Bourdieu's conception of symbolic violence, we can argue that to know the world 'without objectifying distance', to '[take] it for granted', means the world itself is assumed to present, on a daily basis, the evidence for the beliefs upon which the practices of the habitus and its fundamental misrecognition are based. If, in spectacular violence, the violation is assumed to be self-evident within the event itself, not requiring critical interpretation for its proper recognition, this rendering of what the harm is assumed to be replicates the fundamental misrecognition of what we assume to be in our interest in terms of our investment in the habitus. 'World' and 'habitus' are mutually constitutive both in the exercise of our daily practices, and in our misrecognition of spectacular violence as that which is always already understood to be a symptom of others' failure to conform to the rules of our habitus for *their* own good, as well as ours.

This reflexivity suggests the resilience of the habitus as a system that is closed to the otherness of a critical gaze. It also suggests to us the formidable power wielded by the effective dimension of culture in the notion of cultured violence. If we hold a certain world view and value system – even if we are to lesser and greater degrees unconscious of these values and therefore of this world view – and we have effective power to assume and therefore actualize that world view (and to do so also with greater and lesser degrees of consciousness), we are complicit in the perpetration of the symbolic violence Bourdieu defines. An example of the ability to make a world view literally materialize concerns the attribution to the black under apartheid of lack of hygiene and an assumption of the failure of blacks to need privacy of any sort. When we observed a black who was, say, urinating on the street or whom we perceived to need a bath, we could easily have seen these attributes as evidence of the tenability of our racist habitus. A critical gaze is required to identify the fact that these assumed 'natural' attributes of lack of hygiene or appropriate actions in public are the consequence of precisely the very racist imagination that masterminded apartheid and was able to manipulate material conditions and deprive blacks of adequate housing, so that blacks would indeed lack privacy and the resources necessary to regular bathing (time, place, water, and so on.) When we assume the habitus, we are encouraged to read events as evidence of our own self-evident right, rather than critically, as potentially bearing witness to the negative effects of the symbolic violence in which we are complicit. In this light we in effect 'culture' violence.

What is required to deconstruct the symbolic violence of the habitus – and the habitus of violence, in which all violence is rendered spectacularly to occlude otherness from the habitus as a whole – is the kind of imaginative reconstruction of as many aspects of the event that we can conceive of to understand it in terms of its uniqueness; its relation to systemic profiles of violence in its contemporary, local context; and its historical and international context. What such an approach does is utilize the same interpretive, critical capacity that fictions – in the sense of creative writing – offer their readers: the opportunity to conceive of the event of the text through positioning themselves in imaginative relation to it. Ethical interpretation, then, entails processes of reading our habitus critically and authoring a story for ourselves as a consequence of that critical reading. This engagement holds the potential to break the closed circuit of the habitus through the deconstruction of spectacular violence and the acknowledgment of our complicity in symbolic violence perpetrated against that which is other to, and othered by, the habitus. Such critical engagement defamiliarizes the habitus; presents our constitution of others within the habitus visible as a process of negation that is violent in and of itself; and in so doing presents us with the project, however fraught with difficulty, of unculturing violence.

## Staging 'deaf listening'

In her analysis of Elie Wiesel's fictional masterpiece, *Night*, Ora Avni presents Wiesel's fiction as an illustration of the phenomenon of what I call 'deaf listening'. This deafness does not occur as a result of premeditated hypocrisy. Instead, it occurs when, despite the listeners' best intentions to be good at their job, their cognitive framework is exceeded by the narrative told them, resulting in incomprehension of crucial aspects of the story. Avni bases her essay on the limitations of psychoanalysis in relation to Shoah testimony with a discussion of the role of Wiesel's character, Moshe the Beadle, in initiating the story of *Night*.

When the town's foreign Jews are deported by the Nazis to an unknown destination, Moshe leaves with them, but he miraculously escapes and returns to warn the townspeople. Avni points out that the novel does not occupy itself with recounting what happened to Moshe during his absence from the town; instead, the opening section of *Night* concentrates on Moshe's faith before the event, and his obsession with warning the townspeople after his traumatic experience:

> [The] opening section calls our attention precisely to the difference between 'before' and 'after,' when after means both *after the event* and *after the telling of the event*. It thus steers toward the scene of narration [...] [of] not only *what* actually and factually happened, but *how it affects* those who come into contact with the story of what happened. In so doing, it moves us toward the

scene of narration of all *Shoah* narratives, towards the effects these narratives had and still have on their readers and listeners, and in turn, towards the narrator's reaction to these effects. (Avni 1995: 204)

Moshe's agony lies in the fact that the townspeople refuse to listen to him. It is not that they think he is lying; it is that they have genuine difficulty believing the magnitude of what he has to say. When offered a narrative that demands a difficult act of listening to its narrator, who enunciates the narrative in the wake of having borne witness to terrible violence, the community proves unable to hear that narrator, despite the fact that he is issuing a warning crucial to their future survival.

Tellingly enough, Avni utilizes speech act theory to underline Moshe's dilemma. Like Judith Butler, she points out that speech acts depend, to some degree, on 'a pre-existing convention shared by the community of listeners' (Avni 1995: 212), or, in Butler's language, the realm of the speakable, in which the speech of the subject 'obeys certain norms governing what is speakable and what is not' (1997: 133). But sometimes, Avni points out, a precise convention for what the speaker has to say does not exist:

> It [the precise convention] has to be inferred and activated out of the stock of beliefs and conventions that both utterer and listeners find workable, plausible, and altogether acceptable. In invoking their shared beliefs, the felicitous speech act thus becomes a *rallying point* for the utterer and the listeners. It binds them together. A community is therefore as much the *result* of its speech acts as the necessary condition for their success. (1995: 212)

Using Avni's terms, then, we can say that Butler's realm of the speakable depends not only upon willing listeners but also upon a successful speech act, which at the same time also *creates* that community of listeners.

Avni is not concerned with Holocaust denial here. The context of her work is one in which listeners are not necessarily hostile to the witness testifying. Instead, the listeners experience difficulty believing the witness because what the witness has to say falls too far outside the conventions of ordinary speech, 'normal' life. Avni argues that while we all have the freedom to choose our expression in terms of words, metaphors, and so on, reflecting our free will, psychological profile, individual experiences – the realm of language choice Saussure calls *parole* – whatever we say is governed by and limited to what is accepted by the community. We cannot, individually, make up private languages and expect to be heard: as Avni says, 'a private language is no language' (Avni 1995: 212); or, in Butler's words, to inhabit, entirely, the realm of unsayable discourse is to produce (what is perceived as) the ramblings of the insane (Butler 1997: 133).[10] In Saussurean terms, then, *langue* – the conventions of syntax and lexical choice I share with my community – limit *parole* to ensure communication with my listeners. Thus the perspective of those who refuse to

10    I examine Butler's discussion of the insane in relation to speech acts I detail in Chapter 3.

listen to Moshe's warnings is not that they think he speaks untruths; it is that they have difficulty facing the challenge of incorporating his *parole* into their *langue*; or, his experience is unspeakable from within their collective habitus, to use Bourdieu's term.

Avni's argument bears strongly on the position of TRC narrator-survivors of testifying to a community of listeners. South African social and cultural language is struggling with an act of communication in which the individual *parole* of each witness needs to interact with the *langue* shared by the community as a whole.[11] In other words, Moshe the Beadle and the survivor-narrator confront a similar dilemma:

> Moshe wants the community to assimilate his story, to take it in and learn its lesson, in the hope that it will allow him a way out of the unbearable solitude into which his experience has cast him, and bridge over the tear that his encounter with the dispassionate force of evil has introduced into his life. In other words, he wants the agrammaticality of his experience, his odd and deviant parole to become part of their langue. The town folk, however, do not want to take up this horror, to make it theirs, to make this story the rallying point between themselves and the narrator, since if they did, his burden would become theirs […]. To integrate Moshe's *parole* into their *langue* would demand such an extensive review of the rules of the *langue* by which they live that it could put its very structure and coherence into question. (Avni 1995: 213)

Mark Sanders has staged this particular moment of possibility, in which the listening community has both the opportunity to deny the witness, by refusing to engage in the extensive review of the rules of *langue* by which they live, and the opportunity to undertake that review: to use the witness's strange *parole* to jeopardize, to re-conceive critically of the rules of, its *langue*. Before I move to a discussion of Sanders' presentation of these possibilities, however, I need to spend some time describing the isolation and risk of the witness who finds herself in the position of Moshe the Beadle.

## The Risks of Victim-Testifiers: Usurpation and Disembodiment

The promise of the TRC was the promise of listening. And as others have remarked long before me, who, how *and* why it recognized victims as such dictated what it was able to hear. As Fiona Ross has pointed out, witnesses can find it damaging to have their subjectivity reduced to their voices as those voices were heard at the TRC, since the subject and the subject's experiences and narratives of those experiences exceed the moment of the TRC (Ross 2003). My project is premised on this excess not only as a resource for the resilience of the witnesses but also as an opportunity for the post-apartheid state to

---

11    For a specific example of how the *parole* of apartheid's dirty tricks operatives has been incorporated into the *langue* of the nation with beneficial effect, see Jolly 2001.

re-envisage (currently stigmatized) victims as subjects who perform, in narratives of various kinds, the critique that enables ethical social vision.

The inability of institutions and institutionalized practices of interpretation to comprehend survivor-narrators and their narratives as exceeding both the duration of the victimization and its stigmatization of them as victims contributes to witnesses' experience of the act of witnessing as disembodying rather than healing. As Ross observes,

> Forcing the self to see the self as though from the outside may feel damaging, and [...] in a context in which voice and dignity are explicitly linked, individuals' lack of control over their testimonies may be experienced as alienation and appropriation. (Ross 2003: 101–102)

The struggle of victims of violence to author their own stories is not merely confined to the question of appropriation in the common sense. If, as Veena Das and Arthur Kleinman suggest, the struggle to testify with beneficial effect resides in the difficulty of making the traumatic a memory through narrative, rather than re-actualizing that event in the present and thus reinvoking the trauma, the stake in sharing one's story through public testimony becomes accordingly extremely high. As those of us from the disciplines of literary interpretation are repeatedly forced to recognize, readers and audiences are notoriously unpredictable. The task is rendered even more challenging by the fact that 'victims of violence as narrators *appear* as those who have already lost the means to author their stories' (Das and Kleinman 2000: 12; emphasis added). In other words, the dice is already loaded, thanks to the stigma of victimization.[12]

Yazir Henri[13] is a TRC testifier who is articulate on the subject of his victimization and on the subject of testifying to that victimization before the TRC. Henri entered the armed struggle against apartheid as a youth, spent two years in exile in Angola as a member of Umkhonto We Sizwe, the armed wing of the African National Congress, returned to South Africa illegally at the age of nineteen, and spent seven months in detention under Section 29 of the then Internal Security Act, before being freed following the signing of the Groote Schuur Minutes of 1990 (Henri 2003). (This agreement between the then apartheid government and the unbanned ANC secured the release of political prisoners.) During the course of his activities, Henri was located by the security police because they had threatened a comrade of his with death until he revealed Henri's whereabouts. Henri, in turn, was forced, through the use of interrogation and torture, to reveal the whereabouts of another comrade, Anton Fransch, who was subsequently killed by the security forces. Yazir Henri's choice was *no choice*: he could either give up Anton Fransch, or, in effect, deliver a death sentence on his own mother and four-year-old nephew.

---

12  I discuss stigma as a phenomenon and its effects upon victim-survivors in detail in Chapter 3.

13  Yazir Henri's surname was originally spelled Henry. As he chose to change the spelling himself, I abide by his wish, using the name under which he publishes his work and by which he wishes to be known.

Henri speaks of the imperative of making individual suffering public, and of the risk of doing so. He clearly relates his restoration as a subject commanding agency to his listeners' ability to return that agency to him through respect for his voice as his, not the disembodied voice of a victim stigmatized as incapacitated, incoherent:

> Since testifying before the HRV Committee I have been called many names, placed within several stories, given several histories and the most harmful of narratives. I have to carry them as they have now become part of my public face. One of these narratives places me within the confines of the agonised confessor or the betrayer who should be pitied and has been constructed, since my testimony, by individual commentators, the media as well as the TRC's Final Report. (Henri 2003: 266)

By citing Henri here I am not suggesting that testimony such as his should not be reproduced and recirculated under any conditions. (This would be impossible to enforce but, more importantly, it introduces the endgame of censorship.[14]) Instead, I propose that we listen to Henri's eloquent account of the negative effects of his TRC experience in terms of the way it interpolated him as a public figure, whose testimony came to sound not his in his own ears; and how this came to be despite the TRC's attempts to create a context in which his telling of his story was intended to accord him agency, not deprive him of it. This allows us to envisage what ideal conditions for testimony might look like.

Yazir Henri possesses sheer determination in his struggle for agency on the part of himself and other victim-survivors, from whom he does not differentiate himself: 'My story is not unique', he says (2003: 262), attempting to pre-empt representations of him that portray him as uniquely young, uniquely traumatized, uniquely betrayed. Henri conveys at one and the same time the emotional, social, ethical and theoretical complexities of his situation as subject of and subject to the TRC processes of witnessing. To understand his dilemma we *do* need to investigate the question of betrayal: not the chain of events put in motion by the agents who extracted information from Henri through torture and the death threats to his family, for one cannot call Henri a betrayer unless one wishes to be complicit with those agents, but, rather, post-apartheid South Africa's betrayal, in narrative terms, of Yazir Henri. Taking into account Henri's bearing witness to the experience of testifying enables us to trace how acts of deaf listening negatively affect not only the testifier but also the society as a whole.

One of the key elements of confronting victims of rape and torture, as Roberta Culbertson has pointed out, is that once the victim-survivor has experienced the violent truncation of her or his ability to control what happens to her or his body – once the sovereignty of the individual over that body has been usurped, violently, by another human being – faith in the notion that this will never happen to one again is impossible to resurrect (Culbertson 1995). To be

14   Official censorship, so infamously deployed during apartheid, has experienced a return of the repressed in the post-apartheid era. I shall discuss the signs of this contemporary censorship in more detail with reference to J. M. Coetzee's *Disgrace,* in Chapter 2.

haunted by this and, at the same time, to have this lack of control repeated in the form of the abduction of one's narrative and its transformation into something quite other than one had intended: this is Yazir Henri's reality as he describes it. How did this second betrayal, the post-apartheid narrative betrayal, of Yazir Henri come about? What does it signify?

When Yazir Henri comments that stories have been imposed upon him, rather than being told by him, he is commenting upon the use made of TRC testimony to perform according to a specific vision of national reconciliation. Many of the appeals to post-apartheid unity that the TRC has occasioned construct forms of listening deeply constrained by the interests of what, in Benedict Anderson's now familiar terms, form the 'imagined community' of the new South African nationalism. In the process of 'manufacturing' the 'legitimacy' of the post-apartheid South African state, Richard Wilson has argued, the TRC led the way in constructing a 'discourse […] linking suffering, the body and the nation':

> [The] nation is conceived of as a physical body, as a generically South African (that is, not generically human) [or, I would add, not an *engendered* human] individual projected onto a national scale.] […].
>
> Seeing the nation as a body is important for nation-builders, as it creates the basis of a new 'we', and it incorporates the individual into a collective cleansing. The TRC constructed a collectivist view of the sick body, which could then be ritually cured in TRC hearings. (Wilson 2001: 14–15)

However, argues Wilson, 'Nations do not have collective psyches which can be healed and to assert otherwise is to psychologize an abstract entity which exists primarily in the minds of nation-building politicians' (2001: 15).

I would not be as hasty as Wilson to suggest that the notion of a collective psyche remains chiefly in the domain of political figures, even if the link between ordinary citizens and their leaders does not conform entirely to the modern state's versions of nationalism. Nor, as I have suggested elsewhere (Jolly 2001), do I dismiss, as he does, the notion of collective memory. However, his point about the ease with which the TRC ascribed a psyche to the nation, and its concomitant envisaging of the nation as a body, is key to understanding the particular deafness the TRC developed in relation to hearing testimony having been produced by embodied individuals – a deafness which, Henri points out, has been replicated by many of the institutions tasked with the responsibility of framing TRC testimony for the public at large, domestically and globally. In this sense, the TRC replaced, rather than *re-membered*, the bodies of the victims with the profoundly metaphorical body of the new nation-state, resting the legitimacy of this move on a metonymical connection between the suffering body of the individual and the 'sick body' of the new nation, in need of healing. Thus when Yazir Henri speaks of the imposition of stories upon him, he is referring to the appropriation of his suffering into a narrative not of his own making. Further, this process represents him as the 'sick body' of the new nation in need of healing, stigmatizing him as a victim in a peculiarly trenchant way. If the nation needs his body and person to act as the metonymical *body part* of the nation that is traumatized and in need of healing, it is very unlikely to be able to envisage him in any other role. Therefore, while institutional bodies such as the TRC claim, in good faith, that their processes are geared towards restoration of the victim, they are imbricated in broader political, social and cultural contexts which are not within their control, and may have devastatingly negative consequences for those they recognize, formally, as witnesses to gross human rights violations.

The restoration of survivor-narrators was emphasized by the TRC in terms of its emphasis on catharsis. Section 3c of the Act that set up the Commission states that one of the Commission's objectives was 'to restore the human and civil dignity of victims by granting them an opportunity to relate their own accounts of the violations of which they are victims' (Truth and Reconciliation Commission of South Africa 1998; 2003a: I, 112). Graybill (2002) has noted that Christianity, with its impetus to forgive and its rhetoric of redemption; psychoanalysis, with its emphasis on the restorative power of truth-telling; and the political ideal of a new, united South Africa, all have a vested interest in what each in its own way perceives to be the healing power of narrative. Yet, as Graybill points out, 'perhaps the cathartic value of testifying and the benefit of having one's sacrifice acknowledged were overemphasized by the media and the commissioners' (2002: 83).[15] This is the case, Henri suggests, in part because the attention to catharsis casts the victim as wounded subject. This wounded subject has listeners whose motivation for listening resembles generosity or charity directed towards the survivor-narrator as an 'other' in need of restoration. The therapeutic dyad is reproduced when the narrator-survivor is viewed exclusively as a victim, rather than one who, in addition to recognition for her suffering, like Moshe the Beadle, needs not only to speak but also to be heard: she has information to convey that, if it remains unheard, threatens the future of the community. In addition to the political discourse of nationalism Wilson outlines, which appropriates the victim's person and body for its own purposes, the therapeutic construction of narration can also contribute, if differently, to the subtraction of the witness's agency. Its focus on the narrator as victim of traumatic event, rather than survivor-narrator as subject of that event and not exclusively to it, is experienced as disempowering and stigmatizing by survivor-narrators.

Theorists of narrative and trauma tend to negotiate between two poles configuring the relationship between narrative and traumatic event. Theories of trauma and narrative that position trauma, atrocity and pain as unable to be adequately represented by language and, occasionally, even more fundamentally, as lying outside language, paradoxically tend to approach language as a remedy for this isolation. Elaine Scarry is a case in point. She has noted (1985) that pain renders language meaningless, marking the separation of the individual-in-pain from the world. As Eckstein has noted (1990: 76), Scarry goes so far as to claim that torture has never produced factual evidence. However, Scarry notes that the process of relating one's story, and observing the fact

15    Wilson (2001) is particularly skeptical of the narrative of sacrifice in the service of the nation.

that one's story is being listened to, reconstitutes the survivor as a subject.[16] The difficulty with placing pain outside language is that it involves a concomitant, implicit tendency to assume that language and the imagination are not involved in constructing the conditions in which humans inflict bodily harm on one another; and that narrative, unlike torture, is never experienced as harmful by those whom it affects.

Further, however, it is the durational aspect of traversing the time between the poles of torturous isolation and the reconstitution of the survivor as subject that itself needs articulation, outside the confines of conventional, clinical renditions of trauma theory. Theories of trauma and narrative originate from the context of the psychoanalyst/counsellor-patient/client dyad. Thus they have a tendency to register traumatic narratives exclusively in relation to the violation suffered by the narrator of the traumatic event. In this scenario, little if any attention is paid to the story the narrator-survivor tells about the inadequacy of the ways of understanding the harm done that is extant at the time the story is told and heard. Furthermore, while trauma theory suggests that trauma works by putting the victim 'back' into the moment of trauma, focusing exclusively on the victim-survivor as in need of therapy overlooks society's role in maintaining the conditions that obtained when the victim-survivor experienced her trauma. The specific form this takes in some theories about narrative and trauma is a confusion of the victim-survivor's experience of trauma with her experience of narrating that trauma. The original experience of trauma and the victim-narrator's telling of the story are two discrete events, related to one another, but discrete nonetheless. As Derek Attridge (2004) has argued in a different context, narration is an event in and of itself; and the narration that describes the survivor-narrator's experience of trauma is a particular kind of narrative event.

Building from (rather than onto) the past requires more than a victim-survivor's therapeutic reintegration into society, it requires the society to reorient its culture to accommodate the survivor-narrator's tale of harm, because the terms by which it has measured harm in the past may well be insufficient to comprehend the survivor-narrator. As Ramphele puts it (2008: 17), 'transcendence requires openness to a radically different frame of reference; it takes one beyond the known into the unknown, demanding courage and a willingness to take risks'. The relation between trauma and narrative can only have ethical and political agency if our understanding of that relation moves beyond the private, clinical dyad of trauma and its correlative in trauma theory: the therapeutic dyad of survivor-narrator as she who needs to be healed through an act of narration; and the reader/listener as he who produces the analysis that renders the act of narration if not wholly therapeutic, at least intelligible in its 'failure' to be so. The social component of this formulation – that which lies beyond

16  Indeed, Scarry's book is organized into two parts around these two poles. In the first part, she describes the way in which pain, in her terms, 'unmakes' the world; and in the second, the way in which imagination and language – 'the nature of material and verbal expressibility' or 'human creation' may 'construct and reconstruct' the world (1985: 3; 161).

the clinical dyad – means that the movement towards healing is not linear, but rather that it constitutes a jagged movement backwards and forwards in terms of the relation between narrator-survivor and the social world. This complex movement cannot be simplified by framing it as always moving towards the closure of the reintegration of the survivor-narrator.

Narrative by definition contains the expectation, the structure, of reciprocity: a listener; a reader. On the other hand, many theories of trauma structure it as, by definition, non-reciprocal, or at the very least, lacking in reciprocity in that the narrator is conceived of as essentially unable to relate her or his story successfully. Yet trauma survivors, as embodied witnesses, hold the potential to testify to the interpersonal violence wrought by socio-political abuse. Narratives attempting to negotiate transition in the wake of extreme violence, then, also navigate the cusp of a theoretical dilemma: How can we negotiate the relationship between trauma and narrative within a *social* framework, one that registers structural violence and entails communal accountability and reciprocity to address that violence?

In order to frame the relations between trauma, narrative and fiction in terms of their transformative potential within a social framework I draw on Mark Sanders' work on testimony and literature. His understanding of the TRC as enacting the role of a good host stages the social dimension of reciprocity (assessments of the success of its performance in that role notwithstanding). Further, his interpretation of the relationship between witness and listener(s) delineates the 'ambiguity' of the imperative to bear witness and the concomitant risk of the failure of that project. Finally, his deployment of the Derridean foreigner in understanding the figure of the witness as one who sees the extant social order otherwise, and his connection of this seeing otherwise to the 'counterfactuality' (2007: 167) of fiction, enables us to see the otherness of the survivor-narrator as that which we can respond to affirmatively, rather than by invoking the debilitating mechanisms of stigma.

## On 'Hospitality': Beyond the TRC

In a chapter entitled 'Literature and Testimony' Mark Sanders indicates that what the operation of the TRC and literature after apartheid share in common are the dynamics and ethics of advocacy. He identifies Antjie Krog's *Country of My Skull* as the *ur*-text in this regard:

> When the poet [Krog] finds wanting her ability to lend form to the testimony she recalls, yet wishes the domain of telling to belong to the witnesses, whose efforts always outdo hers, a way other than memorial reconstruction has to be found of being host to their words. As formulated by Krog, the question of poetry, or literature, after apartheid concerns […] the approach of writers to the facilitation of utterance by others. If the question of literature and law after apartheid is a question of advocacy, of its dynamics and ethics, the commission shares a set of concerns and conditions of possibility with literary

works. Interpreting its public hearings as occasions for advocacy reveals that the structures of identification and substitution, on which it relies when it solicits and elicits the testimony of victims, are as integral to its operations as to a literary work (Sanders 2007: 148)

Sanders' reading of Krog emphasizes the goal of both the TRC and Krog's work in initiating relations of 'hospitality' (Biko cited in Sanders 2007: 164) towards the victim-testifiers as integral to the role of advocacy. If Boraine explains that the TRC should initiate the actions of a benevolent state towards the victim-testifiers, Sanders suggests that we pay attention to the TRC's taking responsibility on itself, on behalf of the perpetrators, for the misdeeds of the past. The ethic of reciprocal listening is expressed as an act of hospitality.

Sanders focuses on Krog's invention of a character other than her husband, a beloved, as a proxy figure necessary for her to articulate what otherwise would remain unarticulated about her displacement – an effect of the secondary trauma of listening to months of TRC testimony – from the quotidian modes of her existence: her family, the ordinary, the non-traumatic. Sanders goes on to argue that the 'dynamics and technics of advocacy, translation, identification and transference' set in place by the TRC comprise the process Krog manifests in her creation of a proxy-listener:

> The process of inventing a proxy figure [...] is essential not only to the process of establishing conditions under which people can relate their stories, but also to its [the TRC's] task [...] of assuming responsibility, in the person of the presiding questioner, on behalf of the perpetrator. Its advocacy engages a transference which releases a ripple effect in which statement-taker, questioner, and translator all absorb, as proxies for the perpetrator, the violence of the victim's anger, anguish or grief [...] The Commission tries to make it possible for the victim to express what otherwise is not, and cannot be, expressed: not only a story, but as current in that story, affect directed at the perpetrator, who may be absent or unknown; or inaccessible, because of amnesty, to impulses such as revenge (2000: 29).[17]

One can take Sanders' argument further: that Krog's creation of a lover-as-proxy figure speaks to the TRC's inability, as an institution, to enact fully the quintessentially interpersonal dynamic of the transference of affect.

In a section of the chapter headed 'Questioning', Sanders cites Jacques Derrida on the subject of the foreigner. Here Sanders frames the witness as the stranger whom Derrida describes as one to whom the host poses a question, but whose very presence puts the host in question. Sanders identifies the Derridean host in the person of the Commissioner, who acts as questioner on behalf of the Commission. This stages the witness, not the Commissioner, as the interrogator:

17 Sanders (2000: 22) makes it clear that he makes this argument based on the oral performance of the testimony between victim-survivor and Commissioner questioning, and not on the written Report, or the (problematically translated) record of TRC testimony in written English.

> [B]efore being a question to be dealt with, before designating a concept, a theme, a problem, a program, the question of the foreigner is a question *of* the foreigner, addressed *to* the foreigner. As though the foreigner were first of all *the one who* puts the first question or *the one to whom* you address the first question…. But also the one who, putting the first question, puts me in question. (Derrida cited in Sanders 2007: 165)

Here we have two related versions of what it means to be a good host. First, the host, composite of questioner, translator, listener(s), is to act as proxy perpetrator for the survivor-narrator, who may then release her anger towards the aggressor through the proxy. This argument would appear to adhere to the TRC's own understanding of the benefit of listening in order to restore human and civil dignity to the testifier. It also takes into account the need for public institutions to represent a corporate social accountability. (The question of the effectiveness of the TRC as such a body is a question of a different order.) Second, Derrida's concept of the foreigner highlights how her presence – the survivor-narrator testifying before the institution – might hold up the host, as the representative of the society's core understandings, for scrutiny. Glossing Sanders' use of Derrida, we may say that the foreigner/survivor-narrator, despite being the one of whom questions are asked, herself puts the host/questioner, and by implication, contemporary social norms, into question *in the first place*. The foreigner/survivor-narrator's very presence produces the need not only for questions to be posed to her, but even before that, the opportunity for the institution and the questions that may ensue from it to put into question its own foundational tenets. The presence of the foreigner/survivor-narrator demands the reconfiguration of our habitus.

Sanders states that more is at stake, then, than the healing of the speaking subject in the poetics of advocacy, or what we might call the therapeutic effect of the survivor-narrator's testimony. Indeed, he claims, the stories told question the arbitrary nature of what we hold to be true – in the sense of verifiable – in that narratives which defy verifiability, such as the narratives of the victim-testifiers, stand

> watch, at times ironically, over the impulse to verify and corroborate tales, and so to falsify others, in the interests of fabricating what the report [...] terms 'the South African story.' It is inviting this unverifiability, in seeking to be host to the word of the other, that the eliciting of testimony too partakes of and with poetry. (Sanders, 2007: 168)

The narratives are unverifiable partly because witnesses to them are not required by TRC processes (and may, indeed, have been unavailable in any event). It is because the authority of the survivor-narrator testifying to her trauma has an authority of its own that the TRC recognized that it exceeded what it called 'factual or forensic truth', and called it instead, 'personal, narrative truth' (Truth and Reconciliation Commission of South Africa 1998; 2003a: I, 111–12).

Narrative truth not only exceeds the verifiable but it also demands listeners who bear witness to narrative by constructing verifiability other-wise. This truth understands that what we may consider necessity does not in and of itself constitute truth; it *is* questionable. Specifically, Sanders' argument suggests that theoretically, *what* the survivor-narrator performs in appearing before the Commission, questions the foundations of the Commission, questions 'the South African story': that story which is narratable in contemporary terms but, in the terms I used above, is insufficient for the (future) restoration of the victim, precisely because it does not underwrite the conditions for transformation that would enable comprehension of the survivor-narrator's experience of harm. Narrative truth, then, has the capacity to reveal the habitus, and the related category of the speakable as an articulation of the habitus, as a construction, not an iteration, of necessity. In this respect, narrative truth can render the habitus arbitrary and the speakable consequently insufficient, if not intelligible.

Sanders uses Krog's reading of Lekotse's testimony to the TRC, entitled 'The Shepherd's Tale' in *Country of My Skull* (Krog 1998) to illustrate how the stranger, in this case Lekotse, can show up the limitations of the conventions that produce the questions directed to him.[18] At one stage Ilan Lax, representing the TRC, asks Lekotse why he did not report the police's abuse of him. He responds, 'How could we report policemen to policemen?' (HRVTRANS 25 June 1997 – LADYBRAND). Lekotse's testimony certainly exposes – through his audience's edgy laughter, the phenomenon related to us by Krog (1998: 213; 215)[19] – the irrelevance of the question to Lekotse's radical experience of displacement. The laughter also exposes, if briefly, any assumptions the TRC might have held that it, in a sense, 'knew' the victim-survivors' stories already, was only providing a space to stage what it already knew and, therefore, could not be surprised in the way that Lekotse surprises it, by victim-survivors testifying to its knowledge.

There are two movements in Sanders' paper that correspond to the two poles of trauma testimony. The first move outlines the 'dynamics' of advocacy involved in the relation of witness testimony and its replication through translation in acts of listening. Sanders' reading of the TRC's act of hospitality as an example of ethically motivated 'hosting', as an instance in which negative affect inhering in the testifier may be transferred to the listener(s) to the benefit of the witness in a pre-eminent example of *ubuntu*,[20] can be aligned to that pole of

18  In the original TRC testimony, Lekotse is called 'Likotsi'; in Krog and Sanders, 'Lekotse'. I have used the last spelling, as it is consistent with Sesotho transliteration into English and because I am working with Krog's and Sanders' readings of Lekotse's testimony.

19  Throughout this work I refer to Krog 1998, the original, South African edition of Krog's book, not Krog 2000, the edition published and heavily revised for a North American audience. For a description and analysis of the revised edition see Sanders 2007 and Moss 2006.

20  *Ubuntu* is the social, ethical and imaginative concept that locates reciprocity as the defining aspect of one's identity. Operative across sub-Saharan Africa, *ubuntu* is translated as 'a person is a person through other people'. The link between *ubuntu* and hospitality has been highlighted by Steve Biko, Desmond Tutu and Nelson Mandela, among others. Sanders exploits this link to stage the TRC as the scene of a Derridean exchange between host and foreigner.

trauma theory that believes not only in the narratability of trauma but also in the therapeutic benefit of such narration for the witness.

Sanders identifies the speaker and listener in testimony, the narrative exchange between 'I' and 'you', as the discursive dyad that enables not only testimony but also fiction:

> The ability to be repeated – which permits testimony to be reinscribed away from its origin, as in the Truth Commission's report; or to be translated with the aid of its simultaneous translation apparatus – is a function of an originary self-division. The commission's hearings encourage us to relate this ability to be repeated to the pragmatics of telling and questioning, and to a structure of address involving, as its possibility, at least two parties. A basic structure of alterity, such duality and partition is also a condition of iterability, and thus of the possibility of difference. And of fiction. (2007: 157)

Here Sanders' argument gestures towards the other pole of thought regarding trauma and narrative: that the witness to trauma, in the most agonizing of senses, cannot testify to the experience of trauma without depending upon an addressee, and thus without incurring the risk that that addressee may repeat the originary trauma by putting the testifier into question. The testifier poses herself or himself as a foreigner, putting the status quo into question. This aberrant questioning opens up the possibility, if not the probability, of deaf listening, in which her strangeness is dealt with once again by interrogation of the testifier, in an act of exemplary bad hosting.

To avoid bad hosting and deaf listening, one must respond affirmatively to the questions posed by the foreigner/survivor-narrator. Hence the importance of Lekotse's questioning of the conventions the TRC assumes, which are, in fact, irrelevant, even illogical, in the context of Lekotse's experience: 'How can you report policemen to policemen?' he asks, in a version of the question asked by the wives of policemen, whose own husbands have raped them (cited in Sanders 2000: 32). The 'fiction', then, that Lekotse resurrects before the ears of the (potentially deaf) commission, is not just the alterity of the world of trauma to which his experience belongs; it is also the alterity of a vision that sees the madness of the still extant world of torture and the dire need for a social language that would, through its very instantiation, render such violence unimaginable. This 'counterfactual', or, rather, 'inventive' imagined alterity is by definition 'unverifiable', as one cannot verify that which is a negative, an image of an Other world projected in recognition of what the extant worlds lacks.

Sanders' analysis represents the fundamental ambiguity of the instance of the TRC, and the instance of lyrical poetry, in terms of their shared conditions of possibility and of failure. '[...] Krog's own poems', he points out, 'are an exemplary case of how literary and quasi-literary works enable a process of identification and reciprocity, but often dramatize the difficulty, in spite of technics, the disruption, or the impossibility of discursive reciprocity, exchange and response' (2007: 159). The scenario of the testifying foreigner, illustrated by Lekotse, proposes that there is a possibility that the testifying foreigner's critique of the security of the host/Commission as proxy for an extant injustice is heard, perceived, understood. Nevertheless, the ambiguity of outcomes Sanders outlines for the discursive exchange that constitutes testimony is in no way abstract for testifiers: what happens when this possibility of hearing/ perceiving the radical alterity of the victim-survivor as witness is foreclosed?

### The Disembodiment of the Victim-Survivor in 'Deaf' Listening

Yazir Henri is eloquent on the question of how inadequate the time of testimony is to the 'durational' element of the victim-survivors' experience. Henri does not deny the importance of the process initiated by the TRC, but highlights how little the TRC seemed to understand victim-survivors' ongoing isolation and displacement, or foreignness:

> Even now I remember the energy leaving my body when the Archbishop said he has listened to my story with reverence and that he understood what I had been through. My head fell against the witness table and my knees would not carry me from his gaze. I felt the weight of his words tearing my heart from my body and my mind shouted, 'How can you say what you cannot know ... But I am not finished ... there is more!' The strength had left me then and I could no longer talk [...]. The Archbishop had completed my testimony for me. (Henri 2003: 270)

Here the Chairperson Desmond Tutu invokes closure that is ambiguous in its effects: the preposition 'for' proceeding the pronoun 'me' suggests that he helps Henri, as advocate; but the phrase 'for me' also suggests that the Archbishop acts for, usurps, Henri's place: by saying he 'understands' Henri's experiences, he assumes the position of the one who completes Henri's testimony for him.

In this respect, the site of institutionalized listening can exacerbate the displacement of the victim-survivor, placing her/him in a situation in which the expectation is for the survivor-narrator to tell her story, without the listener(s) understanding elements of the story that do *not* relate to what Sanders refers to as 'the world' that the commissioners' questions 'imply' – the *speakable* parts, to invoke the terms of Butler's *Excitable Speech* (1997) once again. Or to put the case from the perspective of the survivor-narrator, the listeners do not affirm her authoritative strangeness, but listen deafly, always only within the moment of originary trauma that constitutes the survivor-narrator exclusively as victim. When the recognition of the (traumatic) event completely overwrites our sense of narrative as an event in its own right, this denial contributes to the testifier's sense of her alienation. She is experiencing the narration of the trauma, not the originary trauma itself: deaf listening refuses this distinction and puts the testifier back into the time and world of the originary trauma. Deaf listening (re)visits trauma on the survivor-narrator in its inability to comprehend her violation, which is characterized as unspeakable not only for its foreignness, but also because her experience of narration is denied at the moment of its performance. This denial is reflected in Henri's observation that telling his story to the TRC 'was only the beginning. The challenge since has been to own this memory and history. I have had to avert the downward spiral of victimhood and the entrapment of the TRC's victim box to find my own humanity' (Henri 2003: 270).

The notion of listeners formulated by the TRC and described in theoretical terms by Sanders is one in which listeners conceive of themselves as assisting the victim-survivor to exercise, and thus exorcise, her anger, rage, fear and/or vengeance. This concept of advocacy is both valuable *and* potentially fraught with self-cancelling power in terms of its practice, if that practice fails to effect the affirmation of the narrator-survivor as 'foreign' (to use Sanders' term, following Derrida). That which haunts the survivor is not located within a single perpetrator, or even a regime alone ('the apartheid regime' or 'white rule'): this haunting involves the need, on the part of the survivor-narrator, for the contemporary society to do that for which it has little inclination and in which it has little experience: to affirm the underside of the survivor-narrator's tale, that which makes it unspeakable in 'sensible language' – language that is always censored, policed, limited by the social imaginary.

The haunting of the victim-survivor corresponds to what Charlotte Delbo calls 'deep memory' in her understanding of her experience as a Holocaust survivor – a concept that brings to the fore the relation of Judith Butler's censored or unspeakable discourse (1997) to her earlier work on the materiality of the body and the suffering of censored bodies (1993). Delbo's 'thinking memory' is that which, in the terms I am using, is speakable. Roberta Culbertson cites Delbo, who asks us not to confuse her descriptions of her Holocaust memories – rational, ordered, clear, within the realm of the thinkable – with what she calls 'deep memory', the persistence of the past in its own perpetual present:

> I feel it again through my whole body, which becomes a block of pain, and I feel death seizing me, I feel myself die [...]. The cry awakens me, and I emerge from the nightmare, exhausted. It takes days for everything to return to normal [...]. I become myself again, the one you know, who can speak to you of Auschwitz without showing any sign of distress of emotion. (Delbo cited in Culbertson 1995: 170)

Culbertson associates Delbo's distinction between 'thinking' or 'external' memory, and 'deep memory', with the inability of 'ordinary narrative' to articulate dreams on the one hand, and on the other, the body. Culbertson then goes on to explain how recovery consists of rendering body memories tellable, creating a self that undoes 'the grasp of the perpetrator and re-establish[es] the social sense of the self lost in the midst of violation' (1995: 170).

Culbertson's work, like Henri's, is exemplary in its description of the isolation of the victim-survivor and the necessity, despite the risk, of narration to the process of the victim-survivor's reclamation of agency. This agency depends upon affirmation of the survivor-narrator as a subject separate from both her perpetrator and the violation, as both a subject *and* one with a body, one who can speak of, exercise agency in relation to the violation without (always) being dissolved, attacked – hijacked – by the original traumatic experience and its re-presentations.

Culbertson hints that society imposes censorship on survivors through invoking what she at first calls 'narrative', but in subsequent iterations calls 'ordinary [,] notions of memory and narrative', or 'ordinary narrative' – what Butler calls the domain of the speakable: 'The demands of [this sort of] narrative for their part operate in fact as cultural silencers to this sort of memory, descending immediately upon an experience to shape notions of legitimate memory, and silencing the sort of proto-memory described' – that is, the memory of the body, the intrusion of fantastical or 'incredible' flashes of memory, unbidden, into the consciousness of the survivor (Culbertson 1995: 170).

The public setting of the TRC highlights the relevance of Culbertson's critique. Victim-survivors' stories have become virtual caricatures within a national economy in which the use-value of apartheid-era survivors' 'credentials' is highly rated, but the political will to deliver upon their actual demands for reparations and further knowledge of the conditions of their original violation is at an all-time low. The survivor who produces a narrative that is meaningful to the TRC in terms of its definitions of GHRVs and its formulation of the national subject puts herself in a position of vulnerability: her narrative easily becomes the stuff of the spectacular, the voyeuristic, of someone else's story, not her own. The task, then, of telling the underside of the story – including but not confined to 'bodily memory' – is hazardous, since it always risks the possibility, even the likelihood, that listeners will trap the victim-survivor within the confines of the sayable, thus initiating the survivor-witness's second betrayal.

Culbertson's argument, then, implies the need for, but does not iterate, an alternative vision to that which sees the isolation of the victim-survivor as entirely due to the extremity of her experience. Such an alternative vision would see the trauma survivor's isolation and suffering as at least partially due to the inability of a society to speak, and thus to hear of, those components of the narrator-survivor's experience that the society has stigmatized in the first place, including her body and the society's own role in the victimization of that body.

## 'Forgetting the Line' of the Speakable: Re-presenting Embodied Estrangement

The facility with which a culture produces rhetorical devices to domesticate what Sanders (following Derrida) identifies as the foreignness of the survivor-narrator's story is remarkable. Take, for example, the workshop production, *The Story I am about to Tell/Indaba Engziyixoxa* (Rampolokeng 1999). This production comprised three professional actors and three TRC testifiers, including the mother of Bheki Mlangeni, Catherine Mlangeni and Duma Khumalo, members of the Khulumani Support Group formed by witnesses to GHRVs. The performance

I attended was held in June 1999 to coincide with the 'Commissioning the Past' conference held at the University of the Witwatersrand to investigate the TRC and its associated processes. The play consisted of a simple set of six chairs, representing a mini-bus taxi. The dialogue involves a debate about the legitimacy and effectiveness of the TRC in the wake of apartheid.

Including victim-survivors as actors means that the work has not been vulnerable to accusations of appropriation of testimony; instead, it attempts to put those very subjects in command of the representation of their experiences. Nevertheless, by concentrating on the experience of victimization without taking into account the differential ontology of that event and the subsequent tellings of that event, the actors appear caught in the moment of victimization. As Shane Graham puts it,

> With each repetition of their stories, *The Story I am about to Tell* asserts the survivors' status as subjects capable of narrating their own stories, and simultaneously undermines that assertion by emphasizing their *loss* of subjectivity through trauma, and freezing their narratives into memorized formulas. The play is caught in an endlessly repeated cycle, with no way out [...]. The psychological truth of the event cannot be captured by the conventions of [this kind of] narrative, which reduce the traumatic events to language and present them in a linear sequence. (Graham 2003: 16)

This transformation of TRC testimony into a series of canonical narratives, even if these narratives are performed by the actual victim-survivor testifiers, produces a uniform replicability that con-fuses the moment of victimization with the moment of telling of that victimization.

This uniformity of representation spawns further misconceptions. It conveys the sense that the story, as told before the Commission, is 'the' story, the only way to tell the story, capable of communicating all elements of the experience of violation. To assume that the narrator-survivor testifying before the Commission has unmediated access to the original event in her relating of it, that she does not select the elements of the story to tell the TRC and that, by extension, her audience has the same unmediated access, is naive and once again erases the narrator-survivor's agency.

Indeed, the notion that the narrator-survivor may actually forget the trauma of her experience through the staged repetition of her narrative is introduced by the phenomenon in which the survivor-narrator-actor literally forgets his own story in the context of the play. William Kentridge explains that the most moving moment for him as a member of the audience of *The Story I am about to Tell/Indaba Engziyixoxa* 'was when one of the survivors (survivor of three years on death row) had a lapse of memory. How could he forget his own story – but of course, he was at that moment a performer at a loss for his place in the script' (Kentridge 1998: xiv). What moves Kentridge as an audience member here is, I propose, the foreignness, the lostness of the narrator-survivor-actor: a strangeness that has exceeded the best attempts to harness him within linear, 'external', speakable narrative. This is a moment in which the survivor-narrator resurrects his own strangeness by unwittingly performing his alienation from the set script to himself, and hence also to the audience. His 'forgetting' is actually *a re-membering of the dislocation of his victimized body*, performed both for himself and the commonality of the audience. The awkwardness of the silent body haunts the facility of the set script: the body resists deaf listening, which renders the speakable mute in the face of embodied suffering.

This moment has a correlative in the narrative of the survivor-narrator, Lekotse, in that both scenes of narrative witnessing – the 'forgetful' actor's and Lekotse's – played out within the public performance staged by the TRC, demonstrate the fact that the witness is not in control of the degree to which her listeners constitute her as foreign: her alienation from the realm of the speakable is not a distance over which she has command. Laughter at Lekotse's, the shepherd's, questions can be read as recognition of the absurdity of the TRC's questions – why would the TRC bother to ask Lekotse why he did not report his assault by the police to the state authorities who sanction the police in the first place? However, the laughter in the TRC audience's response to Lekotse's testimony can also be read, at one and the same time, as a TRC audience laughing at the absurdity of Lekotse's testimony, in which he refuses to subscribe, as much as is possible, to socially sanctioned narrative, describing himself in the very words of his assailants: as 'a *kaffer* and a dull donkey' (Krog 1998: 219).

Here Lekotse, as Sanders points out, registers his foreignness to his assailants, but also to his audience. He registers his strangeness to the listeners in two senses: in the sense of how strange he is to them; and in the sense that he registers to them the strangeness with which they perceive him. Importantly, Lekotse's performance of his strangeness does not protect him from his 'hosts', in that ridicule is an element of the audience's response to him, even if the 'hosts' may at the same time be embarrassed by the sense of Lekotse's ridiculousness they experience upon hearing his testimony. The embarrassment would not exist if the occasion for it, the audience's sense of how Lekotse could well be perceived as ridiculous, were not at some level comprehended by the audience.[21] Here the laughter of ridicule can be read as the body's simultaneous recognition and rejection of its own unspeakability.

21    Once, after Antjie Krog had read her version of Lekotse's testimony in Montreal in 2000, an audience member confided to me that she had never understood the narrative of Lekotse's testimony as it is laid out in *Country of My Skull* before that moment. This particular audience member was a South African born and bred, in Montreal on diplomatic service from South Africa. This non-comprehension of Krog's version of Lekotse's witnessing, without Antjie Krog's 'familiarization' of Lekotse's testimony to her audience in person, seems to me to have much to do with the puzzlement many feel in response to Lekotse's description of himself using the derogatory terms of apartheid.

Intimations from the Inanimate:
Estranging the Violence of the Human Animal

In this moment the survivor-narrator occupies a space in which she can be considered ridiculous, but can also cast light on the realm of the habitus as ridiculous and absurd, depending upon the response of her audience. The narration of the testimony as a performative event holds the potential for reassigning the survivor narrator to the category of the victim, that which is abject, and for audience members to constitute themselves as witness-listeners to the survivor-narrator's violation, in a process that has the potential to mark their complicity in rendering the victim-survivor ridiculous. The potential for absurdity to cut both ways, in a re-membering of the survivor-narrator-actor, and of Lekotse's performances, is invoked in Jane Taylor's and William Kentridge's *Ubu and the Truth Commission*.

This play is the result of collaboration between Jane Taylor, the author (see Taylor 1998), William Kentridge, artist and director (see Kentridge 1998), and Basil Jones and Adrian Kohler's Handspring Puppet Company. It has only two human actors, who play the roles of Pa and Ma Ubu. Alfred Jarry's Ubu is resurrected with a difference, since the burlesque tyrant of Jarry's play, whose actions have no consequences, is here transformed into the burlesque dirty tricks flunky Pa Ubu, whose actions *do* have consequences.[22] These consequences are registered in the puppets of the Handspring Theatre Company, who (re)enact actual testimony from the TRC transcripts during the course of the play.

A series of animal puppets rounds out the cast. Pa Ubu's companion is a three-headed dog, Brutus, whose composite form represents the foot soldier, the general and the politician. His body is a suitcase, into which Pa Ubu deposits incriminating evidence when he is in danger of being identified as an agent of apartheid. The crocodile puppet, which has a body made out of a canvas bag, serves as Ma Ubu's handbag and as a repository for the large objects the crocodile can swallow when they need to disappear from view; yet Ma Ubu finds clues to Pa's 'career' in the very same puppet – her handbag. The non-human animal puppets literally embody the economics of consumption, relating the perpetrator of gross human rights violations, Ubu, to the beneficiary, in Mahmood Mamdani's terms, of his actions, represented by Ma Ubu (Mamdani 1996a). In addition to these characters there is a vulture puppet, which is the source of many of the axioms projected on the screen behind the actors, as well as various photomontages and drawings by Kentridge and his team of animators that appear as commentary, dream sequences, and juxtapositions on the screen.

The puppets have manipulators who are visible on stage. In the 'human' category, there is, then, a clear distinction between Pa and Ma Ubu and the human witness-puppets, so to speak, whose handlers are clearly present on stage. This creates two different registers of action at the level of human

---

22 For a discussion of *Ubu and the Truth Commission* in relation to Alfred Jarry's *Ubu Roi*, see the introduction to Taylor 1998; and Kippen 2002.

figuration: that of Pa and Ma Ubu, and that of the witness-puppets; there is no contact or visual recognition between puppet handlers and the human actors.[23] The puppet-witnesses have two handlers each, in some ways replicating the physical cluster of witness, counsellor and/or family member, and translator, who are attendant upon the scene or were at the original witnessing before the TRC (Jones and Kohler 1998: xvii).

The puppets occupy the same time/space continuum as the actors; but the actors never see them. The puppets are beautifully crafted of wood; but they require the handlers to 'bring them to life':

> The manipulators, working in concert, split and somehow reduce their individual responsibility for the puppet's actions and the puppet's speech. This encourages us to enter into the illusion that the puppet has a life and responsibility of its own. But the fact that the manipulators are present also allows us to use the emotions visible in the puppeteers' faces to inform our understanding of the emotions of the puppet character, with its immobile features. (Jones and Kohler 1998: xvii)

The witness-puppet's movements are slower than those of the human actors, in order for the audience to register the tenor of their motion: that which is materially inarticulate requires co-operation in the act of communication to render its narrative speakable. This attention is required not only from the puppets' handlers but also from the audience, for, as Jones and Kohler, the puppeteers, note, 'puppets are brought to life by the conviction of the puppeteer and the willingness of the audience' (Jones and Kohler 1998: xvii).

The animate/inanimate juxtaposition produces an irony played out here, literally, between inanimate puppets and animate actors: those with truly human form are inhumane; and the wooden puppets, making their claim to be human, enact that which we conventionally think of as the human response within the drama. We may – and many do – laugh at Pa Ubu's crassness, absurd language, and pathetic attempts to keep his covert activities in the service of the state secret from Ma Ubu. She, too, increases the audience's sense of the absurd through her burlesque performance. She first attributes Pa Ubu's absences and suspicious behaviour to the realm of domestic infidelity; then expresses her pride at her husband's important work for the state; and finally takes possession of documents that incriminate him but that will, for that reason, provide her with an 'out', a future, if he is arrested and she needs to distance herself from him by outing his activities. Ma Ubu, then, is a beneficiary in more senses than one. Pa Ubu's language – foul, anachronistic, punning – and Ma Ubu's crass manipulations form a stark contrast to the stately, dignified movements of the witness-puppets.

The familiarity of Pa Ubu and his wife, despite the fact that Pa and Ma Ubu

---

23   Jane Taylor explains: 'Through the workshops we determined that Pa and Ma Ubu would be played by live actors with no puppet equivalents. These characters thus exist, as it were, on one scale. The witnesses, who are represented by the puppet figures, exist on another scale, and a great deal of their meaning arises out of this fact' (Taylor 1998: vii).

occupy the space of the (ordinarily) absurd, inheres precisely in the obscene violence they enact. The witness-puppets also occupy quotidian space, but with a difference. While Pa and Ma Ubu act as buffoons in a comedy of domestic betrayal that 'stands in for' Pa's nightly escapades in the service of the apartheid state, the witness-puppets make food, sell goods at informal street stands – *spaza* shops – and so on; and their testimony involves the genuinely intimate relations of the familiar: parents, in particular, relating the loss of their children and the discovery of their bodies, mutilated by the apartheid authorities.

The juxtaposition re-presents the possibility of what we may call reciprocal acknowledgement of absurdity to which we bear witness in listening to Lekotse's testimony. The puppet-witnesses occupy the realm of dignity at the same time that the audience responds to the spectacle of Ma and Pa Ubu with the laughter of recognition at absurdity. Pa Ubu is both an authentic and occasionally pathetic apartheid flunkey, and an inhumane monster. In this laughter, as in the embarrassed laughter of the audience at Lekotse's testimony, the plight of the witness-puppets is addressed. *Ubu and the Truth Commission* successfully negotiates the knife-edge contingency, the Janus-faced potential, of the reciprocal acknowledgement of absurdity between self and stranger, audience and witness, listener and narrator. The foundational 'discontinuity' of the play obtains in the puppet-witnesses' invisibility to the human actors, even when the puppet-witnesses register the extreme effects of the cruelty of the human actors' actions on their wooden bodies, with the assistance of the visible puppeteers. This is crucial to the play's registering the insane cruelty of the regime of Pa and Ma Ubu: the disjuncture registers the effects of tyranny. The potential continuity of the play – continuity between the human actors, the projected images, the animal puppets and the witness puppets – can only be constituted by the audience as witness.

While Pa and Ma Ubu do not recognize the witness-puppets as human, they recognize the materiality generated by the witness-puppets: effects to which they have no response other than consumption. If Niles the Crocodile and the dog(s) consume and conceal evidence of Pa Ubu's dirty tricks, Pa and Ma Ubu 'conceal' the witness-puppets from themselves through consumption of them and their goods. Pa Ubu kills witness puppets 'off-stage'; on stage he consumes whatever effects these material, non-material human dolls produce: in the opening scene, he absently, unwittingly and violently overthrows a bowl of soup being made by a witness-puppet; and in Act Two, Scene Five, the witness-puppet is an informal shopkeeper, owner of a small *spaza*, who sets out his wares on the table from which Ma and Pa Ubu eat their dinner, thus consuming – stealing – the puppet's goods and ruining his livelihood. The puppet is unaware of Ma and Pa Ubu's identity, but painfully aware of the disappearance of his meagre goods.

The scene, then, is rendered into one of witnessing only if the audience recognizes the being of both witness-puppet and the Ubus' theft as *material*: as a scene in which the Ubus' addiction to their creature comforts registers directly as a consumption of, a literal ignorance of, the witness-puppets' humanity. In this way, *Ubu and the Truth Commission* stages the translation of personal testimony *(parole)* into the consciousness *(langue)* of the body politic. It does so by underscoring the fact that the act of listening, of taking in stories, is constitutive, not merely reflective, of the role of community in welcoming the imaginative and material changes indicated in the reciprocal act of witnessing.

The particular plight of the puppet-witnesses, like that of the survivor-narrators of human rights violations, can be read as 'trying to become' human, to be acknowledged within the community of the human. However, the effect of experiencing Lekotse's gaze of absurdity on the extant 'community of the human' prompts us to reformulate this as not the appeal, but the generous offer, of the survivor-narrator. In the tradition of Moshe the Beadle, in the tradition of Lekotse, absurdly enough, the narrator-survivor offers to remake the category of the human, not despite of, but because of, the very inhumanity of her experience. Survivor-narrators relate experiences that may at first sound foreign, strange, absurd, mad, but our humanity depends upon our listening to them, always open to their sense of the absurdity of the habitus we have constructed for ourselves.

In this work I attempt to listen to specific sets of witnesses and their testimony in this way. The chapters that follow deal with narratives that sometimes constitute and sometimes confront non-human animals, racial others, children and adolescents, women, and those infected and/or affected by HIV, as marginal or non-subjects. In my commentary I attempt to take up the generous offer of the survivor-narrators – broadly construed as such, be they creators of life narratives, drama, fiction, non-fiction or official testimony – to use their testimony to reformulate the meaning of 'human being'.

# CHAPTER 1

# 'Going to the Dogs': 'Humanity' in J. M. Coetzee's *Disgrace*, *The Lives of Animals* and South Africa's Truth and Reconciliation Commission

### The Furor over Rape in *Disgrace*

With the transition from the apartheid rule to democratic government in 1994 came the hope, both within and outside South Africa, that 'the time when humanity will be restored across the face of society' had come (Coetzee 1986: 35). Yet Coetzee's first post-apartheid novel, *Disgrace* (1999), set in South Africa, is remarkably bleak. As Derek Attridge has remarked, *Disgrace*'s negative portrayal of the relations between communities, coming from an author widely read in South Africa and internationally, can be seen as a hindrance to, not a support of, the massive task of reconciliation and rebuilding that the country has undertaken. Touching on the central role of Coetzee's fiction in debates over the role of writers in contexts of extreme social injustice,[1] Attridge remarks that 'even readers whose view of the artist's responsibility is less tied to notions of instrumentalism and political efficacy than these questions imply – and I include myself among these – may find the bleak image of the "new South Africa" in this work hard to take, as I confess I do' (Attridge 2000: 99–100).

Within the ANC, *Disgrace* was rejected outright as racist. The ANC, in its 1999 submission to the Human Rights Commission's investigation into racism in the media names *Disgrace* as a novel that exploits racist stereotypes.[2]

In the novel, J M Coetzee represents as brutally as he can, the white people's perception of the post-apartheid black man. [...] It is suggested that in these circumstances, it might be better that our white compatriots should emigrate

1  For further discussion of the politics of Coetzee's reception see Attwell 1998 and Kossew 1998.
2  This caused a furor of debate in the press. For an analysis of the ANC"s response to the novel see Attwell 2002.

because to be in post-apartheid South Africa is to be in 'their territory', as a consequence of which the whites will lose their cards, their weapons, their property, their rights, their dignity. The white women will have to sleep with the barbaric black men.

Accordingly, the alleged white 'brain drain' must be reported regularly and given the necessary prominence. J M Coetzee makes the point that, five years after our liberation, white SA society continues to believe in a particular stereotype of the African [...]. (African National Congress 2001)

In this instance, I would *not* put Attridge and the ANC in the same camp. The ANC has been negligent in its refusal to confront the extent of women's abuse in South Africa; and the ANC's desire to see fictional production conforming to a positive image of the new(ish) South Africa cannot but be read with the basest of political motives in mind. Focusing on the supposed racism of the novel, the ANC is able to ignore the extent to which *Disgrace* explores the systemic aspect of the rape epidemic in South Africa.[3]

Coetzee, from *Dusklands* (1974) to *Disgrace* (1999), has consistently portrayed the role of discourses of engendered hegemony as key factors in a methodical brutality that is nonetheless sexualized for being racialized. Specifically, I wish to reflect upon *Disgrace* as a text that demonstrates Coetzee's commitment to the principle that, in order effectively to understand social violence, our most intimately held notions of what it means to be human need to be thoroughly scrutinized. *Disgrace* examines the extent to which the related concepts of 'humanity' and 'humanitarianism' on the one hand and patriarchal culture on the other are essentially constitutive of one another. The novel interrogates what to be humane might mean without recourse to the species boundary between human and non-human animals; what acting as a humanitarian might mean without invoking public testimony and the law as watchdogs; and how our sense of ourselves as human is radically undermined by our addiction to a cult of the 'rational' – what Coetzee's recent work identifies as an irrational fetishization of instrumentalism, a profoundly secular devotion to the god of 'efficiency'.

3  The statistics in South Africa concerning violence against women are extreme. For example, at least one woman in Gauteng is killed by her male partner every six days (see Vetten and Dladla 2000); in a study of 1,394 men working for 3 Cape Town municipalities, approximately 44 per cent admitted to abusing their female partners (Abrahams et al. 1999). Thirty-nine per cent of young women in South Africa between the ages of 12 and 17 state that they have been forced to have sex; 33 per cent said that they were afraid to say no to sex and 55 per cent agreed with the statement, 'there are times I don't want to have sex but I do because my boyfriend insists on having sex' (Africa Strategic Research Corporation 2001). For further material on violence against women in South Africa see CIETafrica; Human Rights Watch 1995; Kottler 1998; Leclerc-Madlala 1996; S. Stanton et al. 1997; and Vetten and Bhana 2001.

## Patriarchy, Colonialism and Racism in the Species Divide: Human/Animal

*Disgrace* acknowledges and interrogates a history of reading what is supposedly bestial about the human through reference to non-human animals. This is a history that Kate Soper, among others, has traced in the traditions of Western representation more generally.[4] In such traditions, that which is female, corporeal, black and/or otherwise anti-rational (and, therefore, anti-male) is allied with that which is animal.[5] Indeed, I read the somewhat uneasy reception of Coetzee's latest fiction in part as a response to our wariness of the proximity in which Coetzee places humans and other animals in this novel.[6] What, we may well wonder, is Coetzee trying to say about the relation between human violence towards other humans, and humans' inhumane treatment of dogs? Especially in the wake of the Tanner lectures,[7] we may well be tempted to speculate as to whether Coetzee, like Elizabeth Costello, the protagonist of *The Lives of Animals* (2001) and the subsequent *Elizabeth Costello* (2003), really believes that our treatment of animals as objects for consumption resembles the crime against humanity that is the Holocaust.[8] Further, are Pollux and Lucy's other, unnamed rapists, 'dogs' for raping Lucy, even in the post-apartheid South Africa of *Disgrace*, in which politics should dictate that as blacks they are no longer 'supposed to be dogs'? And if men – David Lurie, included, say – are 'dogs' who behave according to their 'nature' as non-neutered animals, is the rape, or, possibly, are the rapes of the novel explained, if not excused, on those terms?

I approach *The Lives of Animals* and *Disgrace* as enquiries in their different ways into our obsession with reading human behaviour against what we perceive to be non-human, animal behaviour. In his fiction Coetzee investigates the fact that our representation of animals is the locus of a language through which human beings measure their ethical worth as humans. The ironies of this are, of course, not lost on a writer such as Coetzee. Think of the scene in *Waiting for the Barbarians* when the magistrate is locked up. He reflects:

---

4   Soper (1995: 83) explains that animals, 'used as a means of naming or thinking [...] seem to offer themselves as a register or narrative of human self-projections', as 'a manifest text or displaced commentary that facilitates the evasion of 'a more direct confrontation' with devalued or disallowed human characteristics.
5   Judith Plant (1989: 2), for example, claims that 'there is no respect for the "other" in patriarchal society. The other, the object of patriarchal rationality, is considered only insofar as it can benefit the subject'. Edward Said (1994: 207) reflects that in this economy of the white, male subject, 'the Oriental was linked thus to elements in Western society (delinquents, the insane, women, the poor [and, Plant, Soper, Merchant and Plumwood would add, 'nature']) having in common an identity best described as lamentably alien'.
6   For an example of such dis-ease, see Fromm 2000.
7   Coetzee no doubt enjoyed the pun involved in giving a lecture series on animal rights with this title.
8   The Tanner lectures from *The Lives of Animals* are republished, along with Elizabeth Costello's further fictional academic exploits, in *Elizabeth Costello*, published in 2003.

39

> When warrant Officer Mandel and his man first brought me back here and lit the lamp and closed the door, I wondered how much pain a plump comfortable old man would be able to endure in the name of his eccentric notions of how the Empire should conduct itself. But my torturers were not interested in degrees of pain. They were interested only in demonstrating to me what it meant to live in a body, as a body, a body which can entertain notions of justice only as long as it is whole and well, which very soon forgets them when its head is gripped and a pipe is pushed down its gullet and pints of salt water are poured into it till it coughs and retches and flails and voids itself [...] They came to my cell to show me the meaning of humanity, and in the space of an hour they showed me a great deal. (Coetzee 1980: 115).

The obvious irony is that the animal supposed most capable of ethical thought, indeed, often considered as the only animal capable of ethical behaviour – the human – exhibits the most wanton cruelty.

Yet a less obvious irony presents itself. The object of the abuse, contrary to becoming more human in light of this treatment, becomes, in a sense, more of an animal. No longer concerned with 'throw[ing] high-sounding words in their [his torturers'] faces', the magistrate 'lie[s] in the reek of old vomit obsessed with the thought of water', not to wash himself, but because he has 'had nothing to drink for two days'. 'What I am made to undergo is subjection to the most rudimentary needs of my body: to drink, to relieve itself, to find a posture in which it is least sore' (1980: 115).

What I am calling the less obvious irony, then, is Coetzee's undermining of the notion that he who suffers unjust torture can be described as humane, 'civilized', within the conventions we have to describe those attributes. His struggle may well have ethical dimensions: but the victim's reduction to his bodily needs is more closely associated with a state we ascribe to non-human animals. His mind, his intellect, his 'human' attributes are sublimated to his effort to survive as a living body.[9] This explains why victims, even if their suffering is in the service of ethical resistance, can come to be described, or will describe themselves, as animals. The language of animalism is invoked to express the reduction of the victim to her or his body and its abuses. This creates a non-sense that we need to explore further: perpetrators are 'animals,' because of their infliction of HRVs on victims; but victims are also described as 'animals' because they are reduced to this status through their abjection.

---

9  In a rare comment on his own fiction, Coetzee remarks: 'If I look back over my own fiction, I see a simple (simple-minded?) standard erected. That standard is the body. Whatever else, the body is not "that which is not", and the proof is the pain it feels' (Coetzee and Atwell 1992: 248).

## The Body as Other

It is because of our need to live an embodied existence that we, as humans, have historically associated ourselves with beasts. Living with our bodies, at least from Descartes on, is a state we associate with the other. This other is both the Levinasian Other and more than that. For the other onto whom the non-thinking, non-moral body is projected is not a face per se, but a profoundly embodied other, whose corporeality exceeds the image of the face. To have a body in the Western tradition, both pre- and post-Enlightenment, is for the most part to acknowledge one's vulnerability. The body is predominantly the locus of desire, and thus sin, pre-Enlightenment;[10] post-Enlightenment, it signifies everything that is opposed to the rational. It is part of the pathology of the history of this tradition that the body is subconsciously read as the locus of vulnerability, and that this vulnerability is registered in the projection of the offending body onto the other.

This tradition is the one in which Coetzee is, by training and by conscious self-acknowledgement, deeply immersed;[11] it is also a tradition that he attempts – and this, to my mind, is the substance of Coetzee's ethics – both to inhabit and to envisage from the outside, from an-other perspective. In this respect, the language of *Disgrace* exceeds the language of Levinas in its commitment to specific, embodied, others. For in Levinas, what distinguishes the human is its distinction from the 'animal': the 'being of animals is a struggle for life. A struggle for life without ethics. It is a question of might [...]. However, with the appearance of the human – and this is my entire philosophy – there is something more important than my life, and that is the life of the other' (Wright et al. 1988: 172).

Mike Marais has pointed out that, following Levinas and Blanchot's description of how language brings death into the world, it is the very act of representing the other that obliterates that other. For Levinas, the very act of representation is an act of containment, of mastery: 'Intelligibility, characterized by clarity, is a total adequation of the thinker with what is thought, in the precise sense of a mastery exercised by the thinker upon what is thought in which the object's resistance as an exterior being vanishes' (*Totality and Infinity*, 124; cited in Marais 2000b: 59). Yet Coetzee's art – and this is one of Marais' key points – has consistently involved attempts to traverse competing ethical imperatives. There is the imperative to represent the other, in order to represent the other's violation; and then there is the imperative to represent the other so as to communicate to both the reader and the self – the writer –

10  For a reading of this tradition from Plato, through Christianity to the early modern period see Taylor 1989.
11  When questioned by Eleanor Wachtel about what he might consider the canon to be, Coetzee responds in the first instance by reminding her of the limitations of his own tradition, stating that he is 'someone of, finally, I think, Western culture, even though we're speaking in Africa' (2001: 40).

the unintelligibility of the other in the language of the self.[12] Thus if Levinas's concern is to confront, without objectifying, the other, Coetzee's task is possibly more specific: that of rendering the corporeality of the other in terms that do not fall back upon objectifying that corporeality through an identification of it with the traditionally objectifying discourse of the body as that which is animal, that which traditionally has no soul.

Coetzee's fiction has always existed in an uncomfortable space in the traditions of white South African writing because of the wariness of representing the other as intelligible. This is the source of the friction between Nadine Gordimer and Coetzee;[13] it can also be seen in the debates between Benita Parry and David Atwell over the nature of ethical responsibility in Coetzee's work.[14] Yet I take Coetzee's wariness of liberal gestures of inclusion as more than attempts to avoid patronization of the other. If Coetzee's fiction concerns itself with those figures whose otherness escapes us to the extent that we exercise violence upon them without compunction, Coetzee does not see the solution to this to bring those who have been considered outside the human – and thus outside the fold of ethical concern – into that fold. This would be the liberal gesture par excellence, involving nominal, but not ethically meaningful, recognition of the other within the extant confines of the language of the self.[15] Instead, what is interrogated is the status of the self as an ethical being. How does the language of the self stand up to ethical scrutiny? Specifically, how does the refusal of the self as having a body, and the subsequent projection of that corporeality onto the other – be it female/black/animal, or even dead bodies – render our subject, 'he/she who is humane', profoundly unintelligible *within* the parameters of our extant discourses of that which is 'human' as opposed to that which is 'animal'?

At the heart of the matter is a re-evaluation of our long-standing anxiety over who is considered to be within the parameters of the 'human'. Imperial anxiety over where to draw the line that defines the human as opposed to the animal pervades the sexualized and racialized discourses constructing black and female identity in the nineteenth century.[16] These discourses and their antecedents are

12  The language of the self here refers not just to the limits of various discourses, but to the actual limitations of a given language – in *Disgrace*, this is English. When Lucy gives Petrus and his wife a bedspread, Petrus thanks her, calling her his 'benefactor'. Lurie responds: 'A distasteful word, it seems to him, double-edged, souring the moment. Yet can Petrus be blamed? The language he draws on with such aplomb is, if he only knew it, tired, friable, eaten from the inside as if by termites. Only the monosyllables can still be relied on, and not even all of them' (Coetzee 1999: 129).

13  Gordimer's review of *Life & Times of Michael K.* (1984) is most telling in this regard.

14  See, for example, the debate between Attwell (1998) and Parry (1998).

15  We see this liberalism in its classic South African form in Alan Paton's *Cry, the Beloved Country*, the conservative lyricism of which can be traced to a tradition that includes Plomer; a tradition that insists on rendering 'black' and 'animal' as allied in the writers' culturing of what they perceive to be 'natural'. See Chapman 1996: 181–82.

16  See Gilman (1985) on the relationships between the female body, the body of the prostitute and the radicalized Other in nineteenth-century medical and scientific discourses.

not effectively contested, Coetzee proposes, by including women and blacks in an enlarged category of the 'human' in a sort of putative metaphysical search and rescue operation. The anxiety I speak of, which we would like to think of as an aspect of time past, still haunts the discursive space between marginalized 'humans' and non-human animals. This comprises the dis-ease with which the proximity between humans and animals in *Disgrace* is received; it also haunts our language when we attempt to think of the violence wreaked on humans by other humans. For if the human is opposed to the animal, how can the 'human' perpetrator – no matter how violent he is – become 'animal'? And how, as in the case of the magistrate in the passage discussed earlier, do we represent the violence inflicted upon victims without undermining the humanity of the victim, deprived as the victim is of human rights, by expressing the victim's corporeal vulnerability in the language we have been accustomed to use for this purpose, namely the imagery of the bestial? Finally, how can we name violent humans animal, while measuring humaneness in terms of how an individual treats non-human animals?

### The Non-sense of Animal Metaphors: Eliding the Difference between Perpetrators and Victims

The confusion of perpetrators and victims, in which both are described in the language of animalism, is no metaphysical matter. When we look at the transcripts of the TRC, we see precisely this confusion. The first usage of such imagery is one we might expect, in which perpetrators are described as treating their victims as animals. Thus Wendy Orr, one of the TRC Commissioners, says to Mrs Biko and her family, 'If we achieve anything in this process I do hope that we ensure that human beings are never again treated like animals and like non-people the way Stephen Biko was' (HRVTRANS 17–18 June 1997 HEALTH SECTOR).[17] Both Desmond Tutu, Chairperson of the TRC, and Dr Mgojo, a fellow Commissioner, refer to the perpetrators as those who have become animals because they are non-believers. Tutu responds to Ntati Moleke's testimony by telling him that those who tortured him are animals: 'It is only the beasts or wild animals, which don't have the image of God, could treat a person like that' (HRVTRANS 8–10 October 1996 WELKOM). Dr Mgojo repeats this conceit, praising a victim-survivor, Mrs Luthuli, saying that her faith has sustained her: 'a non-believer is just like an animal', he says; and he urges the public attending the hearing 'to recapture your humanity and stop behaving like animals' (HRVTRANS 4–6 November 1996 EMPANGENI).

On the other hand, there are many occasions on which victim-survivors describe themselves as being treated like animals; I shall enumerate just a

17  Note that this and all subsequent references to the TRC website are cited in the format that is most useful in terms of locating the precise location of website material quoted in this book. The reference is the precise name of the file containing the testimony.

few examples here. Mrs September describes a police attack: 'When they had finished shooting, some of them [the police] alighted from the Kaspir that was in front of the Matsolo house. I could see that they were pulling two people who I saw by the legs and they threw them into the Hippo [armoured vehicle] just like animals' (HRVTRANS 10 February 1997 CRADOCK). Mrs Gcina explains to Desmond Tutu that the most difficult time in her life was when her parents were taken into custody under Section 29, and she and her eleven-year-old brother were left alone in the house, isolated even by friends and family due to their participation in the struggle: 'We were treated like animals, my brother [...] and myself' (HRVTRANS 18 June 1997 – YOUTH HEARINGS PBURG). Mr Maluleke testifies that 'What hurts me most is I know that as black people we are like animals to policeman. Policemen, irrespective of colour, black or white treat us as objects like we are not human beings' (HRVTRANS 26–28 November 1996).

The next twist in tracing this discourse comes when both perpetrators and victim-survivors – the two opposing elements in the TRC – use the argument that because they, both victim-survivor and perpetrator, were as animals when the violation took place, another party should be held responsible. When Mr Mabaso and his companions were shot in the Durban area by a number of men who came from the Richard's Bay area, a court case was held to determine responsibility. The perpetrators' defence was that they were 'shooting at wild animals and actually killing wild animals' (AMTRANS 12–14 August 1996 DURBAN). At the amnesty hearing Judge Wilson asks the legal advisers for confirmation of this defence. Mr Purshotham confirms that in the original proceedings amnesty applicant Mr Marais stated that he 'believed black people were '*diere van die veld*' (animals of the field) and that they had no souls and as far as he was concerned it wasn't murder to shoot them' (AMTRANS 12–14 August 1996 DURBAN).[18] Here the victim-survivor argues for amnesty to be refused because he and his comrades were treated like wild animals; yet the amnesty applicant's original line of defence is that blacks are animals, therefore they can be shot. Here an element of racist discourse – blacks are animals – is used to explain, if not defend, the attack on the victims.

Note that the testimony from both sides – the TRC and the victim-survivors on the one hand, and the perpetrators on the other – form a series of tautologies. The perpetrators are animals because they have abused humans to such a degree that these victimized humans have been reduced to, or 'become', non-human animals; the perpetrators have 'become animals' in the process of victimizing humans; and the measure of a subject's humanity is reflected substantially in terms of that particular human's treatment of non-human animals. Hence non-human animals are made to stand both as a marker of humankind's barbarity and as a testament to humankind's innate humanity.

18  Mr Purshotham is referring to the original trial against the perpetrators, citing that this particular testimony comes from page 157 of the original trial transcripts.

Note also the specific tautology involved in these defences, which turns on questions of responsibility. If a man has acted 'like an animal' towards other men, he is either responsible for the violence because he acted violently, as if he were an animal; or he is not responsible, because he has always been an animal. Correspondingly, in the latter case, the victims are to blame for their victimization because they have always been latent, if not actual, animals.

What these tautologies betray is the way in which a cult of instrumentalism disguises questions of ethical responsibility. The base logic of 'getting the job done' is one in which perpetrators present themselves as agents in a larger discourse merely fulfilling the will of the church, nation or state. Yet when the state, in the example I shall give, is called upon to account for the violence committed in its name by the 'animals' it has, in some sense, created, it refuses to do so; suddenly the perpetrators can no longer be termed 'animals', because the state needs to attribute agency to the individual as a responsible citizen. In the case of the Caprivi Strip trainees, legal defendants of the apartheid state argue that, because individual personnel used their military training in ways that the state argues it did not sanction and had no knowledge of, the supposedly wayward soldiers are responsible for their own actions; the apartheid state is not culpable.

## Instrumentalizing Animals: TRC Victim-Survivors' Testimony

What this testimony highlights, in the context of Coetzee's work – besides the striking question of what one can or cannot tell from the manner in which humans incinerate dead dogs – is the similarity between the perverse uses of the primates to stand in for humans.[19] In *The Lives of Animals*, Coetzee (2001) has his narrator, Elizabeth Costello, relate the similarities between Kafka's Red Peter and actual events that took place on the island of Tenerife, where the Prussian Academy of the Sciences established a station devoted to 'experimentation into the mental capacities of apes, particularly chimpanzees' (2001: 27). Costello focuses on Wolfgang Kohler's record of these events, and especially on the fate of one Sultan, 'the best of his pupils' (28). Sultan is forced to jump through a series of supposedly intelligence-oriented mental hoops. For example, his bananas are placed in more and more difficult places to reach, and Sultan is given the instruments to reach them; in one case, three crates that have to be put one on top of another by Sultan for him to reach the bananas. Costello gives her reading of this episode as one in which Sultan is driven towards instrumental reasoning:

> At every turn Sultan is driven to think the less interesting thought. From purity of speculation (Why do men behave like this?) he is relentlessly propelled toward lower, practical, instrumental reason (How does one use this to get

19  I am thinking here of Lurie's mission in the latter part of *Disgrace*: to ensure the respectful treatment of the dead dogs whose bodies are incinerated in the hospital grounds.

that?) and thus toward acceptance of himself as primarily an organism with an appetite that needs to be satisfied. Although his entire history, from the time his mother was shot and he was captured, through his voyage in a cage to imprisonment on this island prison camp and the sadistic games that are played around food here, leads him to ask questions about justice and the place of this penal colony in it, a carefully plotted psychological regimen conducts him *away* from ethics and metaphysics toward the humbler reaches of practical reason. (Coetzee 2001: 28–29)

The assumption here, Costello emphasizes, is that instrumental reason marks the limits of ape intelligence; a second, more interesting assumption from our point of view is that this is imagined to be the point at which Sultan most approaches *human* intelligence. That this instrumental reason is highly prized by human animals is clear; that human animals prize instrumental reason as an ethical activity in and of itself, without recourse to ethical assessment of the goals to which it is put, is the condition Coetzee challenges. He does so by pointing out that this cult of instrumental reason is neither logical, nor ethical; and that its consequence is violence.

On the one hand, then, the primates can never aspire to be human; on the other, Red Peter – especially given Elizabeth Costello's reading of the Kafka tale – Sultan, and the baboons used in experiments sponsored by the apartheid state – are made to 'ape' human behaviour; and they are simultaneously evaluated as lesser beings because this 'aping' demonstrates their insufficiency as humans. In the case of Sultan, he is a slow learner because he has to learn how humans 'think' through a putative demonstration of instrumentalist behaviour; in the case of the Roodeplat baboons, humans kill the baboons because they are similar enough to humans to stand in for them; but this very capacity causes humans to kill the baboons. The other here is both like and not like that which is human. The other will be used in her capacity to mimic, be like, the human; but this use will be abuse to the extent that the other is not human.

Such moments suggest what we might have suspected all along, which is that what we say about animals says more about us than it does about the animals. Specifically, it says more about how we treat animals, human and non-human, than it does about the behaviour, subjectivity, agency or ethics of non-human animals. This does not mean, however, that we should discount the fact that victim-survivors do not just speak of themselves as being treated like animals; they occasionally refer to members of communities that were persecuted under apartheid as having *become* animals. What Elizabeth Costello makes evident in her explanation of Sultan's 'education' is that he is measured according to those standards that men hold themselves to, namely the standard of instrumental reason. It is not that Sultan can tell us what apes might think: it is that we are obsessed with replicating him in our own image. We turn him into an instrument, just as we teach him to view the world purely as an instrument for his own gratification. This is not about the education of the ape; it is about the training of Sultan to ape man. What I take Coetzee to be saying in this context is that any ethical sense of community – that is, one that would contest the profoundly human (but not humane) view of the human animal and its body as a potential object of use for instrumental self-gain in an economy of consumer versus consumed – has been eliminated. We have trained generations of South Africans, both black and white, to ape man, as Sultan has been trained to ape man.

## Instrumentalizing Women: A Culture of Systemic Rape

This training bears much in common with David Lurie's understanding of what drives so-called educational priorities in this day and age. It is also reflected in his attitude towards the sexual needs of his body and the ways in which he goes about gratifying them. Coetzee's fiction has always manifested a care to trace the relations between ideologies that themselves exploit the false, ends-driven 'work ethic' of instrumentalism. In many cases he investigates the complicity of colonialism and patriarchy in the construction of hyper-masculinities,[20] that is, masculinities that view the other as a threat to the self that can only be mastered through domination – a domination that is evidenced in both devastation of the land and the rape of women. Eugene Dawn, Jacobus Coetzee, the magistrate – even Magda in what we might call her fantastical, masculine determination – and, of course, David Lurie himself – all reveal elements of hyper-masculinity in their construction of land and women as properties to be interrogated, owned, exploited.

Of Lurie's job we learn that

> he earns his living at the Cape Technical University, formerly Cape Town University College. Once a professor of modern languages, he has been, since Classics and Modern languages were closed down as part of the great rationalization, adjunct professor of communications. Like all rationalized personnel, he is allowed to offer one special-field course a year, irrespective of enrolment, because that is good for morale. This year he is teaching the Romantic poets. For the rest he teaches Communications 101, 'Communications Skills' and Communications 201, 'Advanced Communications Skills'. (Coetzee 1999: 3).

David Lurie recognizes the dangers of a putative education system that values humans as objects that can be trained into instruments; but he is not so adept at realizing that, while he does recognize his body and its needs, his manner of satisfying those needs replicates the model of consumption he so avidly rejects as an intellectual in an education system that is, in actual fact, in the process of turning out instruments, not intellectuals. Indeed, it has been so successful at doing this that many of the students subjected to the training show signs of not

---

20 For examples of usage of the term 'hyper-masculinity' in international relations/development discourses see Ling 2002, Milojevic 2002 and Replogle 2001. For an understanding of the term specifically in the southern African context see Morrell 1998; 2001.

desiring to be treated as anything other than instruments. Soraya's training – since she is a consumable – is effortless: 'The first time Soraya received him she wore vermillion lipstick and heavy eyeshadow. Not liking the stickiness of the makeup, he asked her to wipe it off. She obeyed, and has never worn it since. A ready learner, compliant, pliant' (1999: 5).

David is not willing to be reminded that this relationship – if one can call it that – is one based on supply and demand. He appears genuinely surprised when Soraya objects to his stalking her and phoning her at home. 'You are harassing me in my own house. I demand you will never phone me here again, never', she responds. After a typical Lurie-like correction of her speech, addressed to himself ('Demand. She means command'), Lurie reflects: 'Her shrillness surprises him: there has been no intimation of it before' (10). Then he explains her rejection of him as attributable to the proximity between mothers and animals: 'But then, what should he expect when he intrudes into the vixen's nest, into the home of her cubs?' (10)

Melanie, the student who follows in the wake of Soraya from Lurie's point of view, is equally commodified. Her dark skin, 'Chinese cheekbones' and 'gold baubles on her belt [that] match the gold balls of her earrings' mark her as the exotic, desirable other. To his seduction of her she responds with a sense of her own commodification: if he gets sex from her, she should at least be released from her course requirements in return, especially since her malevolent boyfriend shows every sign of being able to retaliate for her perceived disloyalty to him by attacking not just Lurie, but Melanie herself. When Lurie takes her to task about absence from classes and missing a test, 'she stares back at him in puzzlement, even shock' (34).

Lurie has indeed exacted a great price from Melanie, if one thinks one can describe her violation in those terms: he has raped her. She tells him several times on the occasion that he turns up at her apartment that she does not want to have sex with him; but he, titillated by the image of her in high heels and a wig he remembers from the rehearsal of her play, grabs her anyway:

> "No, not now!" she says, struggling. "My cousin will be back."
> But nothing will stop him. He carries her to the bedroom, brushes off the absurd slippers, kisses her feet, astonished by the feeling she evokes. Something to do with the apparition on the stage: the wig, the wiggling bottom, the crude talk. Strange love! Yet from the quiver of Aphrodite, goddess of the foaming waves, no doubt about that.
> She does not resist. All she does is avert herself: avert her lips, avert her eyes. She lets him lay her out on the bed and undress her: she even helps him, raising her arms and then her hips. Little shivers of cold run through her as soon as she is bare, she slips under the quilted counterpane like a mole burrowing, and turns her back on him.
> Not rape, not quite that, but undesired nonetheless, undesired to the core. As though she had decided to go slack, die within herself for the duration, like a rabbit when the jaws of the fox close on its neck. So that everything done to her might be done, as it were, far away. (1999: 25)

Accepting the inevitable should hardly be rendered acquiescence. What we are dealing with here is an attempt by Lurie to associate a metaphysical ethic to what amounts to an attack on Melanie Isaacs, rationalized by her inability to force him away from her. If Wordsworth's view of the summit of Mont Blanc undermines his inner vision of what that moment 'should' have been like, Lurie's image of Melanie, the actress, Lurie suggests, is strong enough to override any sense of the actual view of Melanie's resistance for Lurie: the triumph of the metaphysical is evidenced in rape.

This tendency to overlook the corporeal being of Melanie is replicated in some of the secondary criticism of the novel. Take, for example, Michael Marais' reading of this encounter as one that mirrors Blanchot's myth of the creation of the art work as the descent of Orpheus into the Underworld to undertake the impossible task of repossessing Eurydice: 'Despite his observation that this invasion of [Melanie] Isaacs' privacy is "Not rape, not quite that", the Orphic terms in which the description is couched indicate that the scene must be read as Lurie's attempt to possess the Other, to assert control over her' (Marais 2000a: 175). So far, I am in agreement with Marais. But I cannot agree with what he says next:

> However, as the mythological allusions also suggest, she has always already escaped this attempted possession. This is the point of the references to death in the depiction of the scene. The Underworld in which Orpheus meets Eurydice and seeks to possess her is the realm of death in which power slips away and becomes impossible. Eurydice is dead and death is precisely that which cannot be controlled. It is not the *noema* of a *noesis*, an object of the will. In his encounter with Isaacs, then, Lurie is exposed to the radical ungraspability of death, its impossibility. (Marais 2000a: 175; Blanchot, 'Reading': 7–9)

I find this confusion of Eurydice and Melanie disturbing. It may be true that in the Underworld power becomes impossible; but in this world, Melanie is alive, and Lurie's power over her living body is all too evident. If she mimics death to communicate her loss of power in the face of Lurie's attack on her, this loss of power should not be attributed to Lurie by a metaphysical sleight of hand. He is the subject who has rendered her the object of his will. If she exceeds his grasp it is because she is alive as he rapes her and remains so afterwards; the rape has everything to do with his exercise of power, not his loss of it.

It is from this perspective that I disagree with those who view the rape of Lucy as Lucy's acceptance of punishment for the historical burden of apartheid. Admirably, Coetzee represents no alternatives that his female characters 'should' have taken to avoid rape. This is frequently read as a form of masochism evident in the victimized women he depicts; if not in Melanie, then most certainly in Lucy, whose discussion of the rape, meagre as it is, is taken to represent her acquiescence, rather than her acceptance, of the attitudes of those who have raped her. Of her rape she has only this to say to David:

"I think they have done it before," she resumes, her voice steadier now. "At least the two older ones have. I think they are rapists first and foremost. Stealing things is just incidental. A side-line. I think they *do* rape."

"You think they will come back?"

"I think I am their territory. They have marked me. They will come back for me."

"Then you can't possibly stay."

"Why not?"

"Because that would be an invitation to them to return."

She broods a long while before she answers. "But isn't there another way of looking at it, David? What if … what if that is the price one has to pay for staying on? Perhaps that is how they look at it; perhaps that is how I should look at it too. They see me as owing something. They see themselves as debt collectors, tax collectors. Why should I be allowed to live here without paying? Perhaps that is what they tell themselves." (Coetzee 1999: 158)

It is true that in this passage we reach the limits of the sympathetic imagination: our sense of decency is offended by the notion that Lucy, who is guilty of nothing, should have to pay for the sins of the fathers. But note that Lucy has never ascribed to metaphysical moral values; her forte is refusing her father's habit of seeing the world through metaphysical glasses. This is why she refuses his bid to call her plot a farm; she is aware of the many narrative lines, from 'modern girl' to sturdy *boerevrou* (literally, 'farmer's wife'), that he attempts to impose upon her. In this context, then, 'should' may well mean 'this is the way I should see it if I wish to understand how the rapists work; this is how I should think to figure out how to survive'.

The subsequent exchange between Lucy and David tells us that Lucy may well know more about the sins of the fathers than David could ever hope to know. David thinks that if Lucy felt only hatred in their hands, this must mean that Lucy hates them. But Lucy refuses to complete the tautology. Instead, she puts her energy in attempting to understand what makes a man a rapist:

"Hatred … When it comes to men and sex, David, nothing surprises me any more. Maybe, for men, hating the woman makes sex more exciting. You are a man, you ought to know. When you have sex with someone strange – when you trap her, hold her down, get her under you, put all your weight on her, isn't it a bit like killing? Pushing the knife in; exiting afterwards, leaving the body behind covered in blood – doesn't it feel like murder, like getting away with murder?"

*You are a man, you ought to know*: does one speak to one's father like that? Are she and he on the same side? (Coetzee 1999: 158–59)

Well may Lurie ask the question. For Lucy's description of a man, Lurie, say, having sex 'with someone strange', Melanie, say, does result in the obliteration of woman's – Melanie's – subjectivity for the duration of the rape. Even in the case of sex with 'Soraya', 'Soraya' turns out to 'live' only when the owner of the pseudonym is unknown, 'dead' to her sexual partner.

Yet Lurie has only inklings of his complicity in a sexual economy that preys on women. He views the rape purely as a consequence of racial difference, while Lucy sees it as an attempt to subjugate her as a woman living alone, easy prey for men who may seek to exact from her 'a price' for her aping of a man's independence. While Melanie attempts to exploit her status as a product for consumption within a masculinist economy, Lucy understands this to be her ontological status. Not surprisingly, she has difficulty in getting David to comprehend this aspect of gendered victimization. Lucy refers to the rapists as 'spur[ring] each other on':

> "That's probably why they do it together. Like dogs in a pack."
> "And the third one, the boy?"
> "He was there to learn."...
> "If they had been white you wouldn't talk about them in this way," he says.
> "If they had been white thugs from Despatch, for instance."
> "Wouldn't I?"
> "No, you wouldn't. I am not blaming you, that is not the point. But it is something new you are talking about. Slavery. They want you for their slave."
> "Not slavery. Subjection. Subjugation."
> He shakes his head. "It's too much, Lucy. Sell up. Sell up the farm to Petrus and come away."
> "No." (1999: 159)

Here Lurie cannot believe that Lucy 'chooses' to withstand the black predators. But Lucy is not talking about blacks, we find out. She is talking about men. Were she to leave the farm to Petrus, she would be giving up, as she puts it. She would merely be shifting from the protection of one man into the hands of another; her father's, say, or the patronage of unknown relatives of his in Holland.

Lucy is no masochist. Her response to David forecloses, as much as is possible, on the reader who believes in her masochism: 'You have not been listening to me. I am not the person you know. I am a dead person and I do not yet know what will bring me back to life. All I know is that I cannot go away' (161). We may be outraged at Lucy's situation; but we can accept it without acquiescing to the circumstances. Lucy acknowledges that her refusal to leave may result in her experiencing further violence. This is a clear-headed reading of the facts that results in her choosing to accept whatever protection Petrus may be able to offer her within their arranged marriage. Lucy's words make it clear that for her, leaving would be tantamount to 'giving up' – a spiritual death that would render her as inanimate as physical death, and no less corporeal.

After the rape she explains to an obdurate Lurie that what he proposes to her is not an option for self-preservation, but yet another form of subjugation: 'You do not see this, and I do not know what more I can do to make you see. It is as if you have chosen deliberately to sit in a corner where the rays of the sun do not shine. I think of you as one of the three chimpanzees, the one with the paws over his eyes' (161). Denial may be Lurie's initial course of defence, but we would not want to mimic him in this particular case; especially since Lurie's denial carries with it the taint of self-interested denial: Lurie does not want to see his own complicity with the rapists, as one who uses women.

Facing up – in Coetzee's fictional interpretation of Levinas – to the other has radical, and conceivably traumatic, consequences. Taking up the challenge of imagining the Other, and the ethical demands attendant upon this act, requires us to be vulnerable to Elizabeth Costello's insight: what we want to say about human society remains outside the realm of the sayable. In other words, the language of humanity can occupy the place of the chimpanzee with the paws over his eyes. We can only sustain our extant conception of what constitutes the humane by turning our faces away from an atrocity that remains largely unspoken.

The war on women in South Africa occupies the same discursive space as the war on animals in Elizabeth Costello's discourse, in that we have, to date, failed to grasp the quotidian consequences of gender-based violence for a vast majority of women in South Africa; and have thereby allied ourselves – through the complicity of silence – with the likes of Lurie. Note the description of Costello's alienation from the conventions that make a life of consumption without reflection possible; and her subsequent exhaustion at the prospect of alerting a largely uninterested populace as to the nature of their complicity in violence that they simply do not have either the will or the capacity to imagine. When her son, John, asks her what it is that will explain her interest in animal rights to him, she responds that what she wishes to say is not able to be spoken or heard in the language of everyday communality. This is the source of her alienation.

> "What is it you can't say?"
> "It's that I no longer know where I am. I seem to move about perfectly easily among people, to have perfectly normal relations with them. Is it possible, I ask myself, that all of them are participating in a crime of stupefying proportions? Am I fantasizing it all?" (69)

Just as Costello is tempted to believe that the wholesale slaughter of non-human animals for consumption may be a fantasy of her own making, we may be tempted to read Coetzee's depiction of the wholesale attack on women as a parallel fantasy. It is perhaps not surprising, then, that many readers have focused on the influence of assumed racial identifications to explain the violent interactions between characters,[21] much as Lurie focuses on race in order to ignore the factor of gender – indeed, his own masculinity.

*Disgrace* is easily consumed as a novel exclusively about racial identifications, as an (ungendered) report on violence in the 'new South Africa'. Yet if we ignore the challenge *Disgrace* poses to us – to envisage the epidemic of violence against women in South Africa in relation to international practices of patriarchy and ecological violence in the practice of redefining our humanity – we do so at our ethical peril. It may be tempting to allow ourselves to become Lurie, the one with his paws over his eyes. To do so, however, is to ignore the atrocities perpetuated by economies of instrumentalism and their inhuman and inhumane manifestations in definitions of the species divide; the category of the human; and who or what can be 'proved' to be victimized subjects before the law.

21    For an example, see Gorra and Fugard's notorious comments on *Disgrace*.

CHAPTER 2

# The State of/and Childhood: Engendering Adolescence in Contemporary South Africa

Coetzee's texts illustrate the instrumentalism with which the discourse of humanitarianism produces women and non-human animals as *necessarily* vulnerable. South Africa's TRC, I suggest in this chapter, is analogously complicit in producing children as instruments of post-apartheid nation-building. This instrumentalism is occluded in a spectacular narrativization of youth that produces them simultaneously as helpless and innocent victims of the apartheid state *and* as subjects all the more remarkable for the agency they express in their participation in the anti-apartheid struggle. The spectacular rendition of children as helpless victims, as we shall see, predates the TRC. Texts of the apartheid struggle render children and adolescents instrumental to adult visions, highlighting the fact that the spectacular conceptualization of youth as victims occludes the manipulation of the figure of the child as having no agency to suit adult ends. Further, it fails to account for youth themselves as perpetrators of violence. The trope of the always innocent child, then, prevents us from developing a sense of the intergenerational challenges faced by youth growing up under conditions of extreme pressure, fraught with violence.

Here I examine the discursive underpinnings of the language we use to explain the specific vulnerability of children; and how the linguistic conventions of these aetiologies may work against, rather than in the interests of, children, adolescents, and adults living with a history of childhoods that have been devastated by political violence, poverty, and abuse. I examine how childhood and adolescence were conceptualized during the struggle against apartheid; and how this history informs current ways of thinking about children's and adolescents' vulnerability, paying particular attention to the ways in which the conventional phrasings of childhood overlook the impact of gendered expectations on children's development through adolescence to adulthood.

The rhetoric that frames youthful subjects as victims or perpetrators, and concomitantly, either children or adults, in sets of mutually exclusive and related categories, overwrites adolescence and, in so doing, occludes the harsh engenderment of youthful subjects in South Africa. This culturing of adolescence as unspeakable produces child activists, who are now adult, as eternal children; and simultaneously as adults who have, it is acknowledged, 'lost' their childhood but have nevertheless somehow 'made it' successfully to adulthood. The child, it is assumed, has no agency, while the adult is accorded effective agency and full consciousness, despite the actual truncation of her agency by the constraints of post-apartheid conditions, and the impossibility of full consciousness of the processes of socialization that comprise the habitus from within it.

The responsibility of the state and society for its interactions with youth is effectively denied, as the impossible attributes of either no agency or absolute agency are assigned to the youthful subject. In this context children and adolescents become literally unimaginable as actual subjects of the state in their own right. This comprises the cultured violence to which youth are subject: they are made to perform as markers of the impossibly non-gendered, absolute authority of the individual adult who is the proper subject of the state. Consequently, the youthful subject is constituted by her vulnerability to adult (ab)use; or her 'unnatural' exercise of agency in her own interests. In either case, her potential agency is denied in terms of her very status as a youthful subject. Thus, adults perform a quintessential act of deaf listening to youth, as is evidenced in the TRC: youth are listened to precisely because they are youth; but their potential to be *heard* in all their resistance to their own unspeakability is foreclosed through the patronizing gesture that acknowledges them as at best quasi-subjects.

### Childhood Abuse: The Relations between Metaphorical and Actual Violence

In an article written in 1992 entitled 'Recovering Childhood', Njabulo Ndebele makes reference to a certain type of *bildungsroman*, one which follows the convention in which the innocent child is abused, and then turns on his abusers, as the defining act of his transition to adult independence. In this *bildungsroman*, a child protagonist, ill-treated from birth, grows to a position of power and then, instead of proceeding to ensure that he refuses to ill-treat others, wreaks vengeance upon the society that scorned him in the first place. Ndebele opens his comments with reference to the Basotho classic by Thomas Mofolo, *Shaka, King of the Zulus*. Shaka, the illegitimate child who flees the cruelty of his people as a youth, returns to build up the most powerful kingdom the Zulus have ever known. However, it is not long before the moral balance the narrative offers the reader is upset by the extreme tyranny of the avenging Shaka. Ndebele comments:

> [...] The travails of children are presented as reminders, probing the slumbering conscience of society, particularly in societies that may have experienced

extensive social disorder. Should the victims grow up to wreak vengeance upon us, we should understand that we should certainly be receiving our just rewards. The images of the travails of children become and remain powerful metaphors of indictment, calling for social redemption.

However, no matter how compelling the metaphors, there is a threshold that is seldom crossed. We are generally spared the ultimate horror: the sight of the blood of children. Seldom are we shown the dashing of little heads against the wall, or their splitting with pangas which are withdrawn dripping with the gore of blood and brains; seldom if ever are little children thrown into burning furnaces [...]. But should they appear they would most likely indicate the ultimate degeneration of society. They would indicate that there are few horrors left in society; for, horror that has become the norm, profoundly ceases to be horror. If such a point is ever reached, it would surely require much introspection for society to rediscover its conscience. (2007 [1992]: 35)

Ndebele goes on to discuss images of child brutality from a number of key South African texts from the *Drum* generation – Es'kia (Ezekiel) Mpahlele's 'The Suitcase'; Arthur Maimane's 'Just Another Tsotsi'; and Mtshali's 'An Abandoned Bundle'. He situates these in the context of the steady decline in the ages of youth entering the anti-apartheid movement, a phenomenon marked by 16 June 1976, now the internationally recognized date of the apex of the Soweto riots, in which the government proved itself capable of shooting children. 'If the targets of the government could be eight-year-olds, then the phenomenon of childhood in my country was dangerously at an end', Ndebele remarks (2007a [1992]). Ndebele – with his accustomed prescience – proceeds to discuss the implications of the 'near total devastation of the vast majority of the South African population' as being frighteningly evident in 'the current rampant violence in many parts of the country in which even children are not spared. The threshold of tolerable and metaphorical violence against children has been decisively passed', he concludes (39).

Rather than comment on the way in which such metaphoricity merely highlights certain images of child abuse as intolerable, it may be productive to explore how 'metaphorical violence' against children relates to the actual abuses of children which Ndebele properly labels intolerable. Central to the complex picture developed by fiction writers, TRC testimony and debates concerning child victims in South African society at large is the concern, fully acknowledged by Ndebele himself, that children who have themselves been victims of abuse can be, and often are, themselves perpetrators of violence. Ndebele phrases this turn from childhood victim to (assumed-to-be-adult) perpetrator as the 'effects *of* the invisible hand *of* an unjust and insensitive society' (2007a [1992]: 35). Yet what does it mean to attribute ownership of this disorder in a double genitive construction to 'society'? Is 'society' here an implied, if not grammatical, subject? If so, what kind of subject is it? If children are perceived as innocents on whom 'society' impresses its injustice, does this not promote a concept of children as subject to their own, assumed, 'innate' *object* status? And what happens to the notion of the responsibility of the subject, if the subject is on the one hand, an ill-defined 'society', and on the other, a child who is, in effect, not accorded the status of a subject due to 'its' presumed innocence?

In this case, 'innocence' appears to be an effect that adults attribute to children, not an element of any agency commanded by the children as subjects. In this respect, we should question the innocence of children, not because children are always already 'fallen'; but because the attribution of innocence to children by adults marks one of the ways in which adults can use the image of childhood – its metaphoricity – to fulfil their own desires. Such metaphoricity does have an effect on our actual treatment of children. It enables our perception of children as instrumental to the fulfilment of our world view.

A clear example of this exists in Deevia Bhania's work on young children, gender and schooling in South Africa. While interviewing teachers of primary school children in Durban, Bhania discovered a common view held by teachers that gender is an irrelevant topic in the teaching of young children as they are 'just kids' and 'still young'. Bhania highlights the fact that this attitude, a correlative of the belief that all children are innocent, allows adults to impress their power on children with impunity, and to refuse the necessity of thinking through the effect of gender constructs on young children. This comprises a practical example of how adults make children instrumental to adults' world view:

> The child is regarded as an incomplete version of the adult without the ability to make sense of the world. This conceptualisation of young children is deeply problematic. Children are assumed to lack knowledge, acquiring an identity that is observed and absorbed. The assumption is that they have a basic goodness. Absent in the 'just kids' teaching discourse are the gender dynamics of children and the play of power in children's cultures. It is also assumed that the children are passive recipients of gender messages. The discourse thus tries to make children unagentic and removes the significance of culture and race in gender interactions [...]. (Bhania 2003: 43)

Citing the work of G. S. Canella, Bhania concludes that 'this discourse is a means through which an attempt is made to anchor children's lives, confirm teachers' power and generate multiple sites of power for adults' (2003: 43). We shall cover up, rather than recover, childhood in South Africa if we do not find a way of perceiving childhood that renders children subjects in their own right, rather than instruments for the fulfilment of adult desires.

## The Culture of Child Abuse: A Communal Inheritance

Let us examine further Zeke Mpahlele's 'The Suitcase' (1989), one of the stories to which Ndebele refers. Mpahlele's story is telling in its tracing of the causes of the abused child to the specific deprivations that poverty visits upon township dwellers, specifically the way in which the lack of material objects to fulfil basic human needs creates the conditions for abuse. The protagonist, Timi, is out of work, and has been unsuccessful in his day's search for unemployment. He returns to his wife (who is ill, about to have their third child), boarding the bus on New Year's Eve for Sophiatown. Timi, who is clearly a law-abiding citizen, is driven to desperation. When the two women sitting next to Timi get off the bus, they leave their suitcase behind. Timi claims it is his, hoping that it will provide some benefit to him. He assumes that acquisition of property – the suitcase – will offer him a better future. He is accosted by the police, and argues that the suitcase is his, claiming that it is filled with his wife's clothing. However, what clothing is in the suitcase turns out to be torn and damaged:

> The constable, after taking the rags out, pointed to an object inside. *'And is this also your wife's?'* glaring at Timi with aggressive eyes.
> Timi stretched his neck to see.
> It was a ghastly sight. A dead baby that could not have been born more than twelve hours before. A naked, white, curly-haired image of death. (Mpahlele 1989: 77–78)

The story, published in February 1955, is poignant in its juxtaposition of the promise of new life and hope with the pathos of the dead baby. It is New Year, traditionally a time for celebration; but Timi finds himself destitute and in jail, his wife's pregnancy marked by some of the same socio-economic pressures, no doubt, that resulted in the death of the unknown baby.

While on the bus, before taking the suitcase, Timi does in fact notice the young women who leave the suitcase on the bus. Timi is aware of their connection and its unusual, apparent gravity:

> Two young women came to sit next to Timi. One of them was pale, and seemed sick. The other deposited a suitcase in front between her leg and Timi's. His attention was taken from the music by the presence of these two women. They seemed to have much unspoken between them. (1989: 74)

Here 'what remains unspoken' between the women cannot be spoken: the death of the baby, which speaks to an illegal abortion gone amiss, or an illegitimate child's death due to ignorance or willed action, and/or the killing of a child whose colour could be used as evidence in an accusation of miscegenation. In any case, Mpahlele refuses to demonize the women, as was frequently the case in the pages of *Drum*; the sick woman hardly presents an image of the violent perpetrator.[1]

---

1  For example, in January 1955 a photo of the illegitimate babies of the 'Good-Time Girls' of Cato Manor, Durban, appeared with the following commentary, which ignores the role of the male in producing illegitimate babies to the point of ludicrousness; and this in a magazine whose sales depended upon its pin-up girl photos and its image of the suave Mr. Drum (usually Henry Nxumalo), man-on-the-make: 'Some of the good-time girls of Cato Manor, Durban, have got a lot to learn. They gotta learn that if a baby is brought into this world it must be given a chance to stay. They also gotta learn that if they don't want to bring a baby into the world they must go to the chemist and buy some of the facts of life [...]. It's everybody's business when babies are abandoned by women who want sex without any of the side effects' (Schadeburg 1989: 84).

Further, Mpahlele seems at pains to suggest that the plight of the woman and her child is not one that remains a personal tragedy with no implications for the community – even the microcosmic community on the bus. Timi is challenged, when leaving the bus, by other passengers who saw the suitcase left by the women. As he alights from the bus, Mpahlele tells us, Timi does not hear a fellow passenger who cries out: 'That suitcase will yet tell whom it belongs to, God is my witness' (1989: 75). Of course, the reader is curious to know whom the suitcase belongs to and what is in it. In this respect, the irony of ownership – who owns, or who owns up to – the dead baby is staged for the reader, who only finds out what the contents of the suitcase are when Timi does. Timi then hides for a moment in an open back yard, and contemplates leaving the case there, to 'have his hands, no, more than that, his soul, freed of the burden':

> After all, it was not his.
> Not his. The thought reminded him that he had done all of this because it was not his. The incident in the bus was occasioned by the stark naked fact that the case was not his. He felt he must get home soon because it was not his. He was squatting here like an outlaw, because the case was not his. (76)

At this point, the reader is urging Timi to take the suitcase, both to alleviate his (unjustly proportioned) poverty, and because the reader is curious to know what could be in the suitcase. Timi does claim the case, hoping it will bring him new and better fortune.

Mpahlele has cleverly involved the reader in this process: we, too, are titillated by the thought of what treasures may lie in the abandoned suitcase. Yet this turns out to be no ordinary tale of a thief who gets caught according to his just desserts. Timi steals, but we do not know, at the time, that the case which is 'not his' will become not only his but the reader's as well. Our desire for the suitcase to contain some compelling treasure is revealed when the suitcase fails to deliver the instrument of our pleasure; instead, we are left with the dead baby. Indeed, Mpahlele's return to one of the conventional punchlines of a *Drum* tsotsi tale in the final sentence of the story emphasizes how Timi's personal plight *fails* to invoke satisfactory closure on the image of the baby presented to us:

> Timi gasped and felt sick and faint. They had to support him to the counter to make a statement. He told the truth. He knew he had gambled with chance; the chance that was to cost him eighteen months' hard labour. (1989: 78)

The plight of the living protagonist, the information about his arrest and sentence, provides the story with a conventional *Drum* ending. Yet the convention seems deliberately trite. The story exceeds the fate of its nominal protagonist, Timi: it leaves us instead with the image of the dead baby, who, in the course of the narration has become objectified by Timi and the reader alike, but is nevertheless the true *subject* of Mpahlele's tale.

What would it mean to take responsibility for this dead infant, not as a metaphor – which is a literary form of objectification in this context – but as metonym of an on-going social and ethical problem confronting contemporary South Africa?

The inheritance of the infant body – for whom no one appears to be directly responsible, and whose vulnerability is highlighted by the adult community whose members have rendered it an object for their own use – is one that makes its way firmly into the current era. The preying of adults on children takes many forms, not least of which is the sexual abuse of children in contemporary South Africa. In 2000, 21,438 cases of rape or attempted rape of were reported (Dempster 2002). In the same year, 65,000 infants and children were reported abused, raped and/or murdered (Waters 2001; this statistic relates to reported cases only). A number of infant rapes, many of them involving multiple abusers, have been reported.[2] Widely reported was the rape of 'Baby Tshepang', nine months old, raped in the Northern Cape town of Louisvale on 27 October 2001. The infant rapes also gave rise to a debate over the importance of infant rape in medical literature (Pitcher and Bowley 2002). BBC World reported a 400 per cent increase in sexual violence against children over the past decade, with many of the perpetrators themselves being children (Dempster 2002). Whether one believes there has been a dramatic increase in infant and child rape, or whether one sees this phenomenon as part of a broader picture of gender-based violence that has been brought to public attention through selective reporting of infant and child sexual abuse, the issue has remained prominent in the post-apartheid era.[3]

The apparently increasing selection of infants as victims may or may not represent a shift in victim selection, but, I argue, *not* in what we might legitimately call the habit of sexual abuse in South Africa, which involves children. Children's rights are guaranteed in Section 28 of South Africa's democratic Constitution; its passing into law was accompanied by South Africa's ratification of the United Nations Convention on the Rights of the Child and the Organization of African Unity Charter on the Rights and Welfare of the African Child. Yet, as Carol Bower, Executive Director of Resources Aimed at the Prevention of Child Abuse and Neglect (RAPCAN) points out,

> We have failed and continue to fail, at creating a South Africa fit for children at the level at which they are vulnerable – [we have failed at the level of] implementation. Despite many advances in policy and legislation, we are not fulfilling our national and international obligations to protect and promote the rights of children. (Bower 2003: 86)

Bower encapsulates the role that the joint legacies of the apartheid era and gender inequalities have had on levels of child abuse; she goes on to state that

2  For a sense of the ways in which writing on the subject tends to depend upon newspaper reporting, see as an example, Coetzer 2005.
3  For a sense of the debate on this issue see Jewkes et al. 2002, and Jewkes, Martin and Penn-Kekana 2002 in response to Pitcher and Bowley 2002. On the difficulty of measuring the incidence of child and infant sexual assault see van As et al. 2001.

the situation with regard to child abuse 'has not changed; if anything, it has worsened' (2003: 84). As with women's rights, the gap between the constitutional validation of children's rights and their actual implementation is vast. Child and infant rapes speak a certain truth about the value of life in conditions of abject poverty and hopelessness. This truth is that to the aggressors, the human being who is the child is not to be treated as a human being, but is to be rendered not only as an object but also as an object reduced to its use-value; an instrument for self-gratification.

Attempts have been made to rationalize the epidemic of child and infant rape in South Africa by reference to the 'virgin myth': the notion that an HIV/ AIDS-infected subject may be cured if he rapes a virgin. However, evidence suggests that this rather mechanical and singular explanation for such rapes may be a contributing factor, but it is not an adequate explanation of the phenomenon in its entirety, as Jewkes, Martin and Penn-Kekana have pointed out (2002). The victims of such rapes are often children and infants either abandoned by their mothers, or whose care-givers have been forced to leave them unattended or with inadequate care, due to extreme poverty. Poverty and its related socio-economic deprivations are part and parcel of a scenario that renders youth as object and vulnerable to extreme forms of abuse.[4]

The point is that the virgin-cure myth as an explanation for infant rape has the attraction of simplicity and objectification, in the sense of dislocating the aggressors, and victims, from the social context we share, the context that has contributed to the violent event. For being a poor child in South Africa, Bower reminds us, 'means being vulnerable to sexual abuse within a cultural mindset which both devalues you and sees you as an exploitable commodity' (2003: 86). Changing this cultural mindset is the task of an entire society; it requires 'a social revolution – the confrontation and addressing of both the basic values which are sacrosanct in our society, and the creation of a more equitable and just socio-economic dispensation are essential' (2003: 86).

## The Limits of Spectacular Narrative in Rendering Youth

South African literary and cultural history suggests most strongly that the use of extreme images of violence and abuse to attempt to shock a public into *owning* or *owning up to* violent social problems such as apartheid-era violence against blacks, or sexual abuse, or violent abuse of children, including sexual abuse, does not work. The *Drum* writers of the 1950s, the group with which Mpahlele is identified, studied this culture of violence intimately. Indeed, they documented the violence of the townships so graphically that their writings have been

---

4   On the context of the infant rapes, see M. E. Taylor 2002. Since 1997, Resources Aimed at the Prevention of Child Abuse and Neglect (RAPCAN) has argued that several forms of child abuse, including child labour and sexual exploitation, homelessness, neglect and child-on-child abuse, are directly related to poverty (Cassiem et al. 1997).

criticized, on the one hand for exhibiting too much journalism and too little fiction, and on the other for their spectacular representation of violence.[5]

In the 1980s, in a now well-rehearsed argument over the value of what he calls the ordinary, Ndebele criticized the lack of intellectual progression displayed by a literature of the oppressed that he viewed as performing no other function than identification of 'the oppressor' – the Boer, the policeman, the hypocritical liberal, or anyone of the numerous and dubious functionaries of apartheid life. Ndebele's key objection to such a literature is that it plays to

> a society of posturing and sloganeering; one that frowns upon subtlety of thought and feeling, and never permits the sobering power of contemplation, of close analysis, and mature acceptance of failure, weakness and limitations. It is totally heroic. Even the progressive side has been domesticated by the hegemony of spectacle. For example, it will lambast interiority in character portrayal as bourgeois subjectivity. (1991: 47)

I share Ndebele's concern that, once we know that there is an oppressor and that there is a victim, what we have accomplished is merely a drama of recognition, but not one of reflection. We need to be careful to read narratives of child abuse as narratives *other* than those of the spectacular; for, as Ndebele points out,

> the spectacular documents; it indicts implicitly; it is demonstrative, preferring exteriority to interiority; it [...] provokes identification through recognition and feeling rather than through observation and analytical thought; it calls for emotion rather than conviction; it establishes a vast sense of presence without offering intimate knowledge; it confirms without necessarily offering a challenge. It is the literature of the powerless identifying the key factor responsible for their powerlessness. Nothing beyond this can be expected of it. (1991: 46)

Here I employ Ndebele's critique of the spectacular not just to assess specifically fictional narratives engaging youthful subjects. Following the methodology outlined in the introduction, I extend his formulation of the spectacular to narratives we develop to account for actual events concerning such subjects, such as extreme forms of child abuse. What can we do to combat reading spectacular acts of violence involving youth spectacularly? Or, put another way, how do we make sure we move beyond identifying children as helpless victims and their abusers as aggressors, conceived of either in the rather impoverished term of a generalized 'society', or its equally impoverished counterpart, the pathological individual?

Before we can answer this question, we need to answer the prior question: how precisely do our current ways of conceptualizing childhood objectify both childhood victims and their aggressors, insensibly removing both from the social, political and cultural context described so aptly by Bower as 'the nursery of our high levels of abuse and neglect'? (2003: 84)

5   See Nkosi 1966 and Ndebele 1991.

## Narrative Acts: Denying Children Adolescence/Agency

Mpahlele's story presents us with a narrative line quite distinct from the traditional narrative of childhood innocence exemplified by Mofolo's *Shaka*. For the line of argument that suggests that abused children grow up to exhibit the violent behaviour with which they are treated not only naturalizes and to some large degree excuses the violent adult who was treated abusively as a child; *it also suggests that children are fixed in time, incapable of personal reflection and, in fact, remain objects of their childhood abuse far beyond the time at which the abuse took place*. In this respect such a narrative line may be said to spectacularize both child victims and abused-children-turned-aggressors, with the same cancellation of agency that Ndebele associates with spectacularized images of apartheid-era victims.

In this line of narrative our view of the child as an 'innocent' who merely receives the impressions of adults without the capacity to reflect upon them, reifies the child and leads to obscured thinking and inaction with regard to the cycle of violence that is often narrativized in terms of an appeal to an originary innocence 'gone bad'.

In the story Ndebele cites of Arthur Maimane, another *Drum* writer, entitled 'Just Another Tsotsi', two children, one white, one black, grow up on a farm and exchange blood wounds to cement their friendship. As adults, they meet again when the white man kills a suspected black criminal, noticing only after the fact that this criminal is indeed the black man with whom he performed the ritual of blood-brother bonding as a child.

This story contains the clichés of the apartheid narrative in which childhood is associated with a 'pre-apartheid' innocence – impossible in fact; the rural areas are represented as havens from city atrocity (but not, it is important to notice, by those blacks who actually live in rural areas); and the wholly 'innocent' child is inexorably corrupted by the evil of society as it grows older. This pairing of black and white friends, who would be bosom buddies throughout life were it not for apartheid, frequents South African literature, from Alan Paton (whose *Cry, the Beloved Country* may well have influenced Maimane) to the fantasies of racial mixing – accompanied by sexual overtones – that we see in the work of the early Brink; or in Mark Behr's *The Smell of Apples*, this time in the form of a set of opportunities for equitable inter-racial relationships that spear briefly on the horizon, only to be dismissed in view of the narrator-protagonist, Marnus's, deeply entrenched culture of racism: the context which Marnus uses to explain, if not explain away, his complicity with the apartheid's violence.

In fact, it is instructive to look at Behr's *The Smell of Apples* (1995) in the context of the image of the child who is able to do nothing but accept the imprint of the adults that surround him. It is tricky business to choose a child as narrator; such a narrator can encourage us simultaneously to overlook the fictionality, that is, the constructed-ness, of the childhood narrator, as well as the fictions that underlie our concepts of childhood. Behr is cited by Michiel Heyns, who argues that he chose a childhood narrator because the child's voice could, I felt, succeed in accusing the abusers while at the same time holding up mirrors. I hoped, and I doubted, that the text would show how one is born into, loved into, violated into discrimination and how none of us were, or are, free from it. But to do so I need a voice that would not seek to pardon or excuse, in a language different from the adult's which invariably contains in it whether it wants it or not, a corrupt and corrupting formula, always an attempt to justify or frequently to demand absolution. (Behr cited in Heyns 2000: 50)

There are a number of problems with this, however. For one, as Heyns has pointed out,

[...] the child's voice may have the advantage exactly in not needing to 'to demand absolution' in that it is granted absolution through the legal fiction that the child is not accountable, and the related fictional convention that children are 'innocent' in a generally unspecified sense. There is, in short, a kind of absolution of form in the rite of passage novel, in its characteristic presupposition of the myth of prelapsarian innocence. (2000: 50)

There is, in fact, an adult narrator in *The Smell of Apples*: the adult Marnus, who relates his experience from the border during the Angolan War in the italicized passages of the novel. Marnus, as childhood narrator, has an 'innocence' and tells a series of stories – the story, for example, of his father's pederastic rape of Marnus's best friend, Frikkie – that are seductive enough, so to speak, that the adult Marnus's narrative tends to be overlooked or barely discussed by the narrative's critics. The adult Marnus makes a statement at the conclusion of the novel that suggests that he was corrupted without any chance of being otherwise. It was, he suggests, his 'cultural' fate, just as perpetrators' advocates argue that it is the 'cultural fate' of their clients to have committed GHRVs: 'It is for the living that the dead should mourn, for in life there is no escape from history' are the last words of the adult narrator of the novel (2000: 198).

Of course, humans make history, just as Behr has constructed both Marnus the child narrator and Marnus the adult narrator. What the notion of the innocent, prelapsarian, pre-apartheid child allows for is a split narrative, in which the adult, complicit with apartheid, can argue two points that are complementary (and complimentary), from the perspective of the adult narrator. *The first is that the adult speaker's complicit involvement in violence is ethically unacceptable; the second is that such involvement was never his fault: it was fated to take place.* The latter refusal of responsibility utilizes the fact that the symbolic violence in which the adult is complicit is only recognizable *retroactively* as a justifiable defence for that violence.

In this respect, the glimmerings of light that we may see in the child Marnus's narrative in terms of opportunities for his 'conversion' to a non-racist life subsequently play an important role. These include the spectacle of Little-Neville, the coloured boy so brutally attacked purely on the basis of his colour; and Marnus's observations of the defection of his sister, Ilse, and Tannie Karla from the party/family line and the reasons for it. Such moments hold out the promise of change, crucial to the rite of passage novel, for a narrative in which change seems impossible is likely to provide a highly monotonous story. At the same time, Marnus's inability to develop the insubordination required for him to embark on an alternative career to his father's bears witness to the strength of the Afrikaner patriarchy. For surely, if the patriarchy were not so strong, the child could be deflected from his preordained 'history', in the course of his encounter with such moments.

Much has been made of Behr's 1996 confession that he spied on student activists at the University of Stellenbosch. Behr, who had received much acclaim for *The Smell of Apples* after its publication in 1995, made the confession at a 1996 conference held at Cape Castle, entitled 'Faultlines: an investigation into South Africans' culpability for violent acts committed during the Angolan War'. The confession was made, Behr stated, because he feared that he would be unwittingly 'outed' by those who knew of his past, especially in the context of the 1996 initiation of the TRC hearings. His apology fails to satisfy many, at least in part because Behr gave no details of what work he did, for whom, or when the betrayals specifically took place. He did acknowledge that he did not admit to his covert dealings, even once he became convinced of the violence of apartheid, because he feared that the members of the force who seconded him to spy for them in the first place would 'out' him as a homosexual, not merely as a rogue informant. More interestingly from our point of view, however, Behr stated that he had not given details of his covert activities because 'the truth', he said, 'was so big it could be described better and interrogated better through fiction' (Behr 1996).

If we take Behr at his word, the ethical problem this presents is the fact that *The Smell of Apples*, using the literary trope of the innocent child outlined by Heyns, re-entrenches the image of the child as one who is virtually an object; one who is only brought to life as a subject through 'being born into, loved into, and violated into discrimination'. This notion of the child as always already impossibly innocent or inevitably corrupted – the legacy of a prelapsarian imagination invoked with respect to children generally and apartheid children in particular (as in Paton, Maimane et al. discussed above) – is, as one might expect, mirrored in those giving testimony in the amnesty hearings of the TRC.

## Legal Fictions: the Innocent Child Abuser becomes the Remorseful Adult Subject

Nuttall and Coetzee have suggested that a typical mode of autobiographical writing in South Africa is one in which the author either proclaims her liberation from the past, or creates a split self, one that distances itself from an earlier self who committed crimes (Nuttall and Coetzee 1998: 6). Heyns has argued that many contemporary novels do this by splitting the self into a character, belonging to the past, who acted in an unethical way; and a remorseful contemporary character, one who knows better (1998: 54). Interestingly, however, very few of the amnesty applicants' testimonies appear to follow the pattern suggested by Nuttall and Coetzee as exemplary of post-apartheid written autobiographies. The applicants, for the most part, do not seem remorseful. Instead, they appear desperate from confusion and confused by their desperation. Rather than constituting confession or remorse, their narratives manifest difficulty in apprehending the change in values precipitated by the transition period.

Antjie Krog calls the perpetrators' amnesty 'confessions' (as opposed to the victim-survivors' statements) 'the second narrative' of the TRC: 'After six months or so, at last the second narrative breaks into relief from its background of silence – unfocused, splintered in intention and degrees of desperation. But it is there. And it is white. And male' (1998: 56). Heyns comments:

> As Krog implies, these confessions are more artless than her own [...]. Emanating for the most part not from a sense of remorse but from the need for 'full and honest disclosure' which was a condition for amnesty, these accounts are 'reinventions' also in the sense that they strive to cast the perpetrators of innumerable brutalities themselves as victims, misled into unthinking allegiance to a political system which they now recognize as evil. (Heyns 2000: 44–45)

Close reading of the testimony reveals that, while the applicants themselves appeared confused, their legal representatives in most cases attempted to give their clients a coherent narrative that would explain – and therefore, it was assumed, go some way towards excusing, explaining away – the actions of their clients. It is these *legally imposed* narratives that employ the form of the split self – the one who used to be informed by apartheid values – versus the present, supposedly remorseful self – the one who, supposedly, 'knows better'.

In most cases, tellingly enough, this process involves giving the amnesty applicant a coherent narrative of his childhood, one that closely mirrors that of Mark Behr's *The Smell of Apples*. We have already seen this at work in legal defences of how being raised as a 'traditional Zulu' would 'naturally' lead to 'animalistic' behaviour towards one's fellow man. The lawyers are appealing to what Heyns refers to above as the 'legal fiction that the child is not accountable, and the related fictional convention that children are "innocent" in a generally unspecified sense' (1998). Here, the problem of the transition from apartheid to post-apartheid values is explained through reference to the *unimaginable* transition from childhood to adulthood: *the impossibility of the political transition is spoken through the impossibility of adolescence,* in a culture that refuses the child the agency to break away from pre-established values. This creates the crisis: the child is to become an adult by establishing her own authority; but she is denied the agency to do so.

If we take a look at the amnesty applicants' testimony in the case of the death of Steve Biko, we find that Mr Booyens, their advocate, is anxious to establish how the applicants were, to use Behr's phrase, born (in)to discrimination. In the case of Harold Snyman and Daniel Petrus Siebert, Booyens' strategy is to manage his clients by having them read prepared statements, no small portion of which relate to their upbringing in conservative Afrikaner homes. This personal overview, or *persoonlike oorsig* (Afrikaans), is prompted by Booyens in each case:

> MR BOOYENS: Could you tell us the circumstances of your childhood.
> MR SNYMAN: I grew up in a conservative Afrikaans home.
> MR BOOYENS: Maybe you should read the first paragraph of this brief personal overview and we could expand on that.
> MR SNYMAN: I, Harold Snyman, is (sic) 68 years of age and was born at Uitenhage in the Eastern Cape. I grew up in Uitenhage where, (sic) in a strict, conservative and Afrikaans home. We were all members of the Dutch Reformed Church.
> [...] I joined the South African Police immediately after the completion of my schooling. During my formative years, I became unconsciously a member or took part in the apartheid era and was convinced at the end of my schooling that apartheid was necessary for the continuing survival of the Afrikaans speaking White person on the Southern extreme of Africa. (AMTRANS 8–11 September 1997 – PORT ELIZABETH)

Booyens then goes on to emphasize that his client's support for apartheid policy disabled Snyman from finding any 'error' in his beliefs 'against this background and the circumstances of [Snyman's] childhood' (AMTRANS 8–11 September 1997 – PORT ELIZABETH). Similarly, in the case of Siebert, Booyens prompts:

> MR BOOYENS: Let us pay attention, now, to the personal overview and personal circumstances. You mention, or rather, maybe, you can read from personal overview or *persoonlike oorsig*.
> MR SIEBERT: I am currently 51 years in age, I was born on the 20th of September in Bloemfontein [...]. I grew up in a conservative and Christian home. I am a member of the Dutch Reformed Church and have been actively involved in the Dutch Reformed Church since my childhood and have, for the past 26 years, served on the local Church Council.
> I grew up, during my formative years, in the apartheid era. The apartheid policy would, as a consequence, have been acceptable and justifiable to me since I was of the opinion, at that time, that this policy was necessary for the continued survival of the White and South African at the southern end of Africa.
> This point of view, in subsequent years, was additionally influenced and strengthened by the policy expressions or statements of political leaders as well as cultural and church leaders.
> As a result of these statements and rhetoric, I was convinced that the White Afrikaans-speaking person would have to fight for the right to survival and for the right to live as our ancestors did, with particular reference to our heritage, background, culture and political way of life. (AMTRANS 8–11 September 1997 – PORT ELIZABETH)

Note that the applicant uses the subjunctive mood in order to reflect, retrospectively, on why the apartheid policy 'would have been acceptable and justifiable' to him, only returning to the indicative mood to state the blunt fact that 'he was' of the opinion that apartheid was necessary to his and his community's survival. This grammatical inconsistency marks a tautological argument: the child/adolescent is unable to assess his culture because he helps to manifest that culture.

Booyens' next move is also a telling one. He emphasizes not only the concept of 'formative years' but also the importance of father-type figures in his applicant's supposed life narrative. He underlines Siebert's relationship with Colonel Goosen, who was the Commanding Officer of the branch at the time of Biko's death, and had been so for eight years. When Booyens asks Siebert about Goosen's character, Siebert replies:

> MR SIEBERT: Your honour, he was a very dedicated person with regard to his work circumstances. He believed in the politics of the day, with regard to the apartheid policy. At all times he would take the lead, even in very serious unrest and rioting situations. He would never stay back at the office and he was an example to us in that regard. In addition, he was a father figure for us, as younger people, particularly because we could see that he was willing to put himself in the firing line. (AMTRANS 8–11 September 1997 – PORT ELIZABETH)

Booyens also emphasizes the personal contact between Mr Vorster, Prime Minister, and State President Swart, during the course of Siebert's dealings as a VIP security organizer.

The reliance on the importance of the influence of fathers or father-like figures is underlined, just as it is in Behr's novel, by an emphasis on puberty. In the amnesty case of Cornelius Johannes van Wyk, his advocate, Mr Gimsbeek, makes the argument that the applicant, his client, was vulnerable to the negative influence of a far-right white supremacist group, the Church of the Creator, precisely because he and his natural father did not get along as the boy became a teenager. Gimsbeek asks van Wyk to 'start right at the beginning':

> R. C. J. VAN WYK: Yes. I think it will be suitable if I start during my puberty. I was about 12, 13 years old and at that stage – well I grew up in a very strict, conservative and rightwing home. I had very rightwing views right from the outset. I was never radically rightwing though until I met Mr du Plessis in standard 6 [roughly Grade 8] when I was in high school. I became good friends with him to such an extent that I visited him at his home quite often and had a lot of contact with his father, Mr du Plessis (Snr). And it was Mr du Plessis (Snr) who had this influence on me and which changed my views to a more radical direction, and he introduced me for the first time to the ultra rightwing thoughts.
>
> And I, at that stage, my father and I didn't have a very good relationship, we didn't talk very much, there was a bit of division between the two of us and I was therefore quite vulnerable and these new ideas had quite an effect on me.
>
> I was in standard 6 when I met Mr du Plessis and through Mr du Plessis (Snr) I was introduced to the very rightwing ideas and concepts such as the Church of the Creator. (AMTRANS 15–19 July 1996 – PRETORIA)

Mr du Plessis Snr initiates van Wyk into the tenets of the far-right belief in white supremacy and the need for militaristic intervention to sustain that supremacy. Mr van Wyk Snr, however, denies vehemently that he brought his son up to be racist. He cannot envisage how his son came to commit the atrocities he did against black people, ironically going so far as to swear upon the Bible that his son was not taught to be racist at home; this despite the fact that van Wyk Snr says that 'my son John grew up in a very conservative home. I am a member of the Reformed Church and the principles of this church were inculcated into them [the children] at a very early age' (AMTRANS 15–19 July 1996 – PRETORIA).

What the testimony of van Wyk Jnr and Snr have in common, however, is the notion that the child/adolescent is dictated to by adults, and has no legitimate subjectivity of his own. Van Wyk Jnr names Mr du Plessis Snr as the father-figure responsible for his (van Wyk's) subsequent acts; and van Wyk Snr emphasizes how he found his son an engineering position; 'forbade' him from getting involved in politics and 'let' him go to the army. Indeed, the more 'subject-less' the adolescent/applicant appears, the more easily responsibility for his actions can be laid at someone – or something – else's door. When Advocate Gcabashe questions General van der Merwe about his withholding of information from Minister Vlok regarding illegal acts committed 'for' the apartheid state, van der Merwe emphasizes that, while he comes from the now time-worn 'fairly conservative background', his actions are not those of an individual, but of a loyal servant of the state, involving 'no personal malice or ill will stemming from that background of conservativeness' (AMTRANS 1-9 June 1998 – PRETORIA). What this suggests, of course, like Behr's narrative, is the crucial authority of the father figure in the development of the child, in the child's successful negotiation of 'puberty'/adolescence. Yet the acceptance of the father figure's authority as key to the child's development is not only overly deterministic; it also judges the success of the transition to adolescence through the child's adherence to the father's rule, replicating the sort of emotional tautology with respect to adolescence I noted above, in which the child is to reject the father's protection to become 'a man', but is not granted the subjective agency to do so. This denial of the child's subjectivity is not only supposed to get the amnesty applicants off the hook in their present, adult, lives for acts they undertook as children but it also undermines the role of the predominantly black youth in overthrowing the apartheid regime because, they felt, their seniors were too complacent in the face of apartheid.

## Reifying the Child-Activist: Adolescence Denied

Much has been made of the heroism of the children who took up the anti-apartheid fight, an acknowledgement of the iconic status of these children in an increasingly entrenched understanding of how the post-apartheid 'nation' came about. Somewhat predictably, we find the TRC representatives concluding the testimony of the now adult victim-survivors speaking of their youth, with the conventional recognition of the child as having 'sacrificed' childhood:

> Mrs. Loliwe and Spongile, thank you. Spongile, we empathise with you especially because your childhood was taken from you. (Chairperson (presumably Desmond Tutu) to Spongile Manensa (HRVTRANS: 9–13 June 1997 – EAST LONDON)

> I want to honour you for that and hold you up as an example of how young people have been prepared to sacrifice their youth and their childhood for the struggle in this country. (Glenda Wildschut to Moegamat Qasim Williams (HRVTRANS: 22 May 1997 – YOUTH HEARINGS)

> But we've been in an incredible kind of country that has sought to chew up it's (sic) children. We said this morning that quite a few of our children didn't have the chance of enjoying their childhood. They became adults, [in] the twinkling of an eye. (Chairperson (presumably Desmond Tutu) to Ntombizanele Zingxondo (HRVTRANS: 12 August 1996 – BEAUFORT WEST)

> This has been a very painful story, but we take you as a hero. It is apparent that when you grew up, you lost your childhood, you never had a chance to be a child. You were thrown into the world of being an adult. And you lost your right to be educated. You also lost your right to humanity. (Unidentified Commissioner to Sylvia Nomhle Dlamini (HRVTRANS: 24–25 October 1996 – DURBAN)

This rhetoric suggests the extent to which the children of the apartheid era have come to occupy a specific place in the post-apartheid national imaginary, one that tends to entrench the image of the child who 'sacrificed' her childhood for the needs of 'the people', who subsequently – post 1994 – became 'the nation'. This image once again assumes a mythical 'normal' childhood as established, then disrupted: clearly a problematic narrative version of the move from innocence to experience in the context of South Africa, where the disruption of family life, even for those children not involved in the struggle, is legendary. Secondly, it tends to eradicate the differences between various different children's experience of the struggle, and denies the fact that many child activists, like their adult counterparts, were involved in illegal activities not always directly related to the anti-apartheid struggle. Finally, it tends to infantilize the victim who testifies as an adult about her childhood experiences. This element of patronization contributes to a context in which listeners, exemplified by the Commission, tend to focus on constructing a picture of the abused child – a powerful enough image to eradicate listeners' ability to hear the victim-survivors *as adults*.

This means that powerful and insightful testimony from such witnesses is lost to those thinking about the reconstruction of a new South African society that would be based on an understanding of what is required to integrate individuals into empowered communities at the local level, both geographically and in terms of family life (however variously that 'family' may be determined). In this respect the TRC as an institution of listening may well have contributed once again, however unwittingly, to the undermining of the subjectivity of victim-survivors testifying about their childhood experiences *in relation to* their adult lives. This is no small loss because, in many instances, the victim-survivors testify to the ways in which the communities for which they fought have *not* been actualized in the post-apartheid period, either in the form of the 'nation' (rainbow or otherwise), or at the most immediate level of the culture of communities. Here the absence of a successful transition from apartheid to post-apartheid society is spoken through the lack of recognition of the importance of adolescence in establishing non-violent, equitable gender relations and the consequence of this lack: the breakdown of community structures at the level of the family. The relation between adolescence and nation here is not metaphorical, a function of the retrospective gaze, as it is in Mark Behr's novel, or the way the TRC commissioners often read childhood-survivor testimony. Here the relation between adolescence and 'nation', defined as a collective of communities, is *actual*: denied adolescence reproduces the propensity for violent social relations in the present.

Let us take a look at the testimony of a few of those to whom the TRC responded with its acknowledgement of a childhood sacrificed, a response that became a convention as the TRC hearings proceeded. This approach seems to have caught the Commission in its own spectacular, not to say specular, glare, since it appears to have disabled the Commission from responding to the adult victim-survivors as subjects with the agency of narrative at their command.

For example, while Spongile Manensa is referred to as having lost her childhood, she was in fact eighteen or so years of age when she was shot in the head in Mdantsane, on the day of Mandela's release: 11 February 1990. She cannot give her own testimony due to the fact that a bullet, still lodged in her brain, has left her with a severe speech impediment. Her friend, Ms Nosipho Loliwe, delivers testimony on her behalf (her parents are both at work). We learn that after the shooting Ms Manensa went back to school, but was unable to cope. Her friend requests medical and educational assistance on her behalf. Ms Manensa is approximately 25 years of age at the time of her testimony. There is no particular evidence one way or the other to suggest that she participated actively in the resistance prior to her victimization.

The rendering of Spongile Manensa as a 'child' is somewhat problematic under these circumstances. She was clearly young at the time of the incident; but the TRC's response to her suggests an infantilization of the adult woman as a victim. This impression is further advanced by the circumstance of her inability to represent herself verbally. In addition, her interlocutor, Ms Loliwe, makes no requests on Ms Manensa's behalf directly: it is her 'parents' who ask for assistance in removing the bullet and getting her into 'some form of technikon'. Possibly some sense of unease with this form of representation *on behalf of* the adult testifier is apparent in Reverend Finca's question to the witness, the only question asked by any Commissioner in response to her testimony. 'Madam Chair', he says, 'how is Loliwe related to Spongile?[6] Are they related?' It transpires that Ms Loliwe is Ms Manensa's neighbour and a close friend: 'We are like sisters', Ms Loliwe says. 'We just take each other as siblings' (HRVTRANS: 9–13 June 1997 – EAST LONDON)

The pro forma response offered to Ms Manensa – thanks for having sacrificed her childhood – appears to have more relevance when it is utilized in the case of those who entered the struggle, consciously, at a very young age. Such is the case with Moegamat Qasim Williams, who joined the Bonteheuwel Military Wing (BMW)[7] at the age of eleven, and was forced to leave his mother's house due to being wanted 'by these people who called themselves the justice system, but we all know that they were the injustice system' (HRVTRANS: 22 May 1997 YOUTH HEARINGS: WILLIAMS.HTM). Mr Williams then goes on to testify that in 1987 the people who were looking for him named him as their informer to the other comrades in his group. He was then attacked by his 'brothers', set alight by them, nearly died, and was then arrested by the security branch and taken into custody. He was tortured in the Macassar police cells and attempted suicide. He was then transferred to Pollsmoor prison, charged, and released after four days at the age of fourteen.

### Imagining a Future Community: Even – or Especially – Now, the Child/Adolescent/Adult Refuses to Betray the Struggle

Moegamat Williams is very clear about his choice, as a child, to join the BMW. He is deeply offended at the treatment of his mother by the police who are searching for him when he is hiding in the house: 'You say your son is only 12 years old, you are worse than a prostitute, you do not even know where he is, how do you care for your children and it affected me a great lot', he testifies. Notice how the child – who is, in fact, an *adolescent* – is taking on a gendered, adult role in response to the police terming his mother 'worse than a prostitute', itself an attack on his mother's enactment of her gendered role. He also states that, as an eleven-year-old, 'I have sworn to myself that I will do it to the best of my capability to make the NP [National Party] Government ungovernable. I swore that to myself and I swore as well, irrespective I must lose my life in the struggle, I will do it, because I want my children and their children's children to live in a better society' (HRVTRANS: 22 May 1997 YOUTH HEARINGS: WILLIAMS. HTM) Here Mr Williams demonstrates an element of imagination that we like to think of exclusively as the prerogative of the 'adult': the ability to think as if he were a father/mother; the ability to think as a potential parent.

The fact that this drive to render the government ungovernable for the sake of a different future may have included illegal acts that undermine the

---

6   Reverend Finca refers to Ms Nosipho Loliwe by her surname here.
7   For more on the BMW, a youthful paramilitary organization formed to intensify the militant struggle against apartheid in Bonteheuwel, a coloured township north of Cape Town, see the appendix in the TRC Report on the BMW (TRC 1998; 2003: IV, 278–81).

TRC's production of childhood activists as heroes of the anti-apartheid era in an orthodox sense speaks to the TRC's manufacture of childhood activists in its own image of them. Obscured in the framing of youth activists as heroes is the fact that the category of politically motivated violence is hard to separate from a framework of entrenched violence more generally: making the state ungovernable, to use the well-rehearsed strategy cited by Moegamat Williams, entails acts of violence that may not fall easily within the framing of the armed struggle as one of pure heroism. The drive to forge community based on the sharing of violent experience along gendered lines, in the absence of alternatives, appears to speak to the plight of BMW comrades such as Moegamat Williams more accurately than the framing of his resistance as idealized childhood sacrifice.

The police use Mr Williams' dedication to his community precisely as the point of attack when they choose to name him as betrayer of that community. What the police cannot envisage is that it is precisely his sense of *refusing to betray a community that may not as yet appear extant* that sustains Mr Williams in his refusal to turn on the brothers who betrayed him. He understands that it is the police who rendered him 'turned around on', and not his comrades, members of the community for which he works. He also understands that they are attempting to bring him down by eroding the emotional bond that he is fighting to establish and maintain, that of a community whose brotherhood is unassailable:

> That was only where I could say my hell started, because I start having these nightmares, not knowing who to trust anymore, because of all these stories that I was told by them [the police]. I mean, I was told that my own brother informed me, I was told that my commander [in the BMW] informed me. They mentioned nearly all the names, because on the morning when they arrested me they knew exactly where to come. I did not sleep at home. They knew exactly where to come and they came to fetch me out there [...].

Yet, Mr Williams says,

> I was set alight by my own brothers who I believed in, but what this did inside of my heart, a build up, even a stronger grudge against the system, against the Boers and at that moment in time I forced myself, I told myself, this is my brothers that has done this to me. I am not going to leave them, I am going to stick like glue to their side, because I want to show them, I want to prove to them, I am not a traitor, I am still the same person who started out with them.
>
> I did exactly what I told myself to do. I kept on going out with my brothers, kept on doing things with them. I never pulled away from them once and today, still, when I hear a security branch officer's name being mentioned, I want to go out there and shoot to kill, because if it was not for that police on that particular Saturday night, I would not have been sitting here [as a victim] today. I would have died at the hands of my own brothers believing in what these security branch people, who was supposed to be part of the justice system, told them. I was nearly killed. I could not believe it. (HRVTRANS: 22 May 1997 YOUTH HEARINGS: WILLIAMS.HTM)

Clearly Mr Williams knows that the security branch is ultimately responsible for his torment; but his breakdown, significantly at the moment in which he rehearses the fact that his own comrades set him alight, is marked by a telling phrase: 'I could not believe it'. This obviously means that, at the most immediate level, he cannot believe what his comrades are doing to him. Taking the context of Mr Williams' own testimony into account, however, this refusal to believe not only indicates the horror of what his comrades are doing to him but also the larger, related horror: that the very community to which he has dedicated his life is being manipulated against him by the police. That Mr Williams never loses sight of this is demonstrated in his insistence, to those very comrades, that he is innocent and will maintain solidarity with them, even and most particularly when they – and the community for which he fights – are in danger; that is, when they are being duped by the police to think that Mr Williams is a traitor.

This tension between Mr Williams' immediate experience at his comrades' hands – that of being accused of betrayal to the police – and his staunch belief in the value of the community he envisages, constitutes the trauma. This trauma is both replicated and sustained in the tension he evinces in the present – that is, in the time of his testimony to the TRC – between what he and the comrades had envisaged the post-apartheid future to offer, and what it has, in actual fact, offered. The post-apartheid era has failed his generation. Mr Williams articulates clearly the effects of this failure on the well-being of his current family and community:

> If there is one thing that always gave me the strength and the courage to fight in the struggle, it was the points of the Freedom Charter and I would like to know, what I would like to know today is can anyone of the Commissioners explain to me what has happened to the Freedom Charter? The Freedom Charter was labelled the most precious document in the whole, wide world. I believe in the Freedom Charter, so did my brothers and sisters who fought together with me. We knew one day when we have power we are going to live according to the Freedom Charter. It has never happened. You do not ever hear about the Freedom Charter anymore. I would like to know was the Freedom Charter picked up, crumbled and thrown away. That is my pleas (sic) to you. I would like to know what has happened to the Freedom Charter. I believe in the document and I still believe in it.
>
> The ANC has taken over, they have got power, but all I can say, I have never once heard anyone of the Ministers nor the President mention the Freedom Charter or any particular points of the Freedom Charter and then I would also like to say today, as I am sitting here, I am a little bit cracked up. It might not look that way, but I am. I have brothers who were with me together in the BMW who operated for so many years with me. I am still seeing them today. I am still seeing them today. Now the only point is the places where I see them it hurts me most. There are a few of my brothers, their expectations was so high with the new Government take over. Obviously, they were so overlooked, forgotten, they decided to become vagrants walking around the streets of town. I found them in the docks, waterfront and Woodstock. (HRVTRANS: 22 May 1997 YOUTH HEARINGS: WILLIAMS.HTM)

The inability of the post-apartheid political and social world to incorporate Mr Williams' 'brothers' speaks to an ongoing alienation that has intergenerational consequences.

At one point, Ms Gobodo-Madikizela suggests that Mr Williams' trauma is all the more severe because he was a child at the time:

> As adults when we go through trauma we have some resources, we know how to defend against it, but somehow for you, as a child, being immature psychologically, but mature in your strength, you know, amazingly mature in your strength to be determined to do and engage what you chose to do is just most amazing and in a way that gave you strength, but at the same time there was a certain immaturity psychologically, just not having the strength developmentally at that time to know, to have the resources built for yourself for your adulthood, and I am wondering how that experience has affected you in your adulthood or how is it, how has it strengthened you? (HRVTRANS: 22 May 1997 YOUTH HEARINGS: WILLIAMS.HTM)

Ms Gobodo-Madikizela creates a version of the split narrative of Mr Williams' life narrative when she suggests he is too young to suffer trauma with mature defences, but is too mature to choose not to be 'strong'. More important for our purposes, however, is to note that she locates Mr Williams' development firmly within a narrative of the individual, isolated from community opinions, resources or deprivations.

In response to Ms Godobo-Madikizela's question, Mr Williams once again refuses to separate 'the struggle' from his personal struggle to develop proper relationships within his domestic setting. In speaking of courses he has taken, with the support of his former BMW commander, Faried Farels, to deal with his situation, he nevertheless ends his testimony with a record of his ongoing alienation. He stresses his discomfort as an unemployed man, 'unable to go home' in the most profound sense as a consequence of both his experience and his lack of paid employment, marked by the fact that he depends on his wife even for cigarettes. This is a reversal of traditional gender roles that stands in stark contrast to the 'brotherhood' ethos of the BMW:

> Yes, I will say in my adulthood, thanks to my commander of the former BMW, Faried Farels, who is also sitting in the audience, I would like this chance and opportunity to, like, thank him again for, like, meeting up with some people, American people and they are offering these kind of courses and these people, to some extent, they helped me forgot about what has happened in the past and I how to, like, try and cope with the future. I mean, there is still a lot of things ... I mean, okay, I am unemployed, I do not have any income. I am doing community work and doing it voluntarily and, I mean, it is kind of, like, hard sometimes *not being able to go back home*. I mean, I am married, got one child, got married in 1995, 30th of September. I mean, I, to me sometimes it is, like, hard especially on a Friday night, because my wife is working, I am not. Sometimes on a Friday night she ask me to you want a packet of cigarettes and then I feel so bad, my direct answer is, no, I do not want anything and I would walk out, just turn around and walk out, not saying

anything further. I mean, without explaining to her why my behaviour is like that and that type of thing. (HRVTRANS: 22 May 1997 YOUTH HEARINGS: WILLIAMS.HTM; emphasis added.)

Mr Williams' insistence on relating the ongoing struggle of his personal situation, in which alienation is marked by an inability to see himself enacting the gendered identity he sees as appropriate to his sense of self, is eloquent; and it is reflected in the testimony of other child-victim survivors.

While the TRC responds to the testimony by raising once again the spectre of a childhood that has been lost, the victim-survivors testify instead to the lack – not loss – of a community in which the proper relation between engendered subjectivity, and agency to achieve the subject's goals according to her or his proper human rights, can be attained. The lack of ability to communicate with one's spouse extends to one's children. It is telling that Moegamat Williams refers to his wife and child immediately before describing his un-familiar behaviour, for which he offers no explicit reason. But his narrative *does* offer us an explanation, precisely because Williams has the skills, imagination and sensitivity to testify to what the society lacks, what it needs to struggle for; and how this struggle is intimately connected to his own (lack of) culture of sociability. This sense of not being able to go back home is not simply geographical; the home for Moegamat Qasim Williams still needs to be made.

### Denying the Subject: The Unspeakability of Engendered Adolescence

The TRC's insistence on the testifiers' 'sacrifice' of childhood is apparent once again as a limitation to the understanding of the adolescent victim's suffering in a close reading of the testimony of women speaking about their adolescent lives. When Commissioners tell victim-testifiers that they 'never had a chance to be a child', as in the case of Ntombizanele Zingxondo and Sylvia Nomhle Dlamini, there is an assumption that the children's initiation into politically motivated violence somehow renders them, instantly, adults. This detracts from the painful imagining of the suffering of these victims having occurred when they were *adolescents*. Ms Dlamini joined the UDF when she was fifteen, and was subsequently detained for six months without charge. Her infant was separated from her for long periods of time; she was blindfolded and assaulted, and threatened with being thrown out of a window. Ms Dlamini was one of a cell of eight, of whom only two were women. Tellingly, she speaks of the same sorts of social alienation that Mr Williams does. Ms Dlamini's testimony also focuses on her perception of herself as inadequate in accordance with the gendered expectations of society. If Mr Williams doubts himself as a father, Ms Dhlamini expresses her misgivings about her role as mother: '[…] I am not sure whether I was a proper mother to my child, because I never had time to raise him up. So, I don't know whether I acted in the proper manner, I doubt myself as a mother' (HRVTRANS 24-25 October 1996 Durban).

What persists as a barrier to our imagining the distress of these victims is the insistence on a sudden, magical transformation that is assumed to take place between childhood and adulthood. The catalyst for this transformation is variously identified as engagement in the anti-apartheid struggle; becoming a mother oneself; or, perhaps most illogically, as in the case of Spongile Manensa, the very circumstance of having been physically wounded. Adolescence and its painful realities are not acknowledged in this rhetoric. When Ntombizanele Zingxondo is tortured, sexually, as a very young woman – her breast is forced into a desk drawer, which is then repeatedly jammed shut – she is told by the TRC that the experience of this, together with her false accusation of murder, in effect made her an adult. In this respect, to become involved with politics is associated with becoming an adult, which is, in turn, associated with a gendered identification as man or woman, potential or actual father or mother of one's own child.

The TRC rhetoric concerning childhood, then, entrenches a cyclical pattern of socialization that is profoundly gendered. *Such rhetoric is quite incapable of understanding child victims' subsequent testimony, given when they are adults, as productive of narratives that are deeply informed by the experience of the adolescent initiation into these entrenched, gendered roles as traumatic in and of itself.* This means that the cyclical patterns of violence attendant upon these gendered roles cannot be heard properly. Sheila Masote bears full witness to this nexus of problems in her testimony during the Women's Hearings.

Sheila Masote is the daughter of past PAC president, Zef Mathopeng, and wife of activist Mike Masote. Her narrative begins with her sense of alienation from her public persona, as daughter and mother in a high-profile political family:

> On the programme it says I'm here to speak about – on behalf of the family. No, that is not what I am here about. My mother has put in a submission as an individual and representing the family.
>
> I then felt, yes, I'm part of the family, but I refuse to be family and have no identity as Sheila. The problem that I have always suffered and I have always said to myself is that I don't seem to be having an identity like belonging to me. I'm always either Zef's daughter, Mathopeng's daughter or Mike Masote's wife. Or no, Masote's mother and Zef Masote's mother. But no, I feel I am me. And this is why I am here. (HRVTRANS: 28–29 July 1997 – WOMEN'S HEARINGS – JOHANNESBURG)

Ms Masote speaks movingly of her experience of being beaten by her mother, who sat next to her throughout her testimony. She explains that her mother was deserted, since Mr Mathopeng and his comrades were constantly away from home, working for the PAC or imprisoned because of their work. Mrs Mathopeng was unable to work, having been dismissed because she was the wife of an activist. She was, according to her daughter, lonely and unable to fulfil any role commensurate to that of her husband due to the society's expectations for one of her gender. Ms Masote gives this as the reason for her mother's abuse of her, explaining that the sons in the family were able to experience an 'outward-going' life, while she, as the girl, was trapped at home with a desperately unhappy mother:

> I have seen my mother break down. I have seen my mother when she did least expect it that I know, crying, sobbing. I had questions as a daughter. Mom, what's happening?
>
> Then PAC's policy was that women should stay at home, should not participate. [...] It was all by way of trying to say when we go out to jail, when we go out and be killed, you look after the children.
>
> So my mother was always there for myself and others. So I would always say, Mama, what is happening? And they were not told. The husbands wouldn't share much. And therefore this started to make me – because I didn't understand then – have an attitude towards my mother. Why, why doesn't she share with me? Why doesn't she understand? Why does she beat me up so much? Why?
>
> Because she was frustrated. And I was the only one close to home. (HRVTRANS: 28–29 July 1997 – WOMEN'S HEARINGS – JOHANNESBURG)

Ms Masote was eventually taken into custody, and experienced such a severe beating that she miscarried her child. She was then ordered to wash herself using an open drain in a compound in full view of men, who taunted her about her sex. Subsequently, Ms Masote's life repeated that of her mother; that of an isolated political widow, whom nobody in the community would support, because of her affiliations with supposed terrorists. Tragically, this extended to her own abuse of her son:

> I also bashed my son. I almost killed my son. Today he's in Switzerland. He is the finest journalist and the Lord dear hold the man in school. *I'm trying to show you how cultured we are.*
>
> But the sister at the age of about eight, saw him go up; he was about six, hanging himself, trying to hang himself in a tree when we were staying in Pefene. Because I used to bash my son. I would give him money at about four when I knew everybody has come back from school. Everybody is coming from work and Vugane's stores in Orlando West, was a busy shop. And I'd give him money just to go and buy a bread or go and buy things I don't have done.
>
> And when he goes, I know he's so short. The counter is up there, he will be asking for help. I would be calling him to pick up a fight. ([...] indistinct) As soon as this thing dries, you've had it, my son. My son would run. My boy would run.
>
> And as soon as he sees that saliva hit, spat, undressing, he doesn't even wait. That is now how he knew socialise by his mother. I would take a sjambock.
>
> That is what used to happened to me, my friend. I would beat him. I would beat him. I don't know what for. I would beat him until my neighbours jump over the fence. 'Shiela ([...] indistinct) Shiela'.
>
> That is what my son went through. I went through the same. I did it. (HRVTRANS: 28–29 July 1997 – WOMEN'S HEARINGS – JOHANNESBURG;

emphasis added)
Throughout Ms Masote's testimony she places an emphasis on the way in which the intrusion of apartheid forces into her life as a child, together with her deep socialization to be 'a good girl' – which entailed literally taking the place of her mother during her mother's absences due to illness and stress – forced her into an impossible situation. 'If I am not there', says Ms Masote, 'then my mother cannot survive'; and, 'I had to take over a mother role at an early age and I couldn't be me'. This inability to 'be me' begins and ends a testimony in which the culture of political responsibility entails a burden of personal agony that is profoundly gendered. In her penultimate question to Ms Masote, Ms Mkhize, the attendant Commissioner, asks, 'When you – before you were detained, here it says that you were detained because you were visiting your parents a lot, but were you at that time politically active yourself, in your own right?' Ms Masote replies:

> I shall put it this way. From my childhood I developed a block. I hated politics. I hated this gogga [poisonous insect] that took my father away from me. That destroyed my home. When I asked why is my father ([...] indistinct) I'm doing this to save my nation. I hated that nation. What is that nation that I can't touch? Where is that nation when we're going through all this anger. (HRVTRANS: 28–29 July 1997 – WOMEN'S HEARINGS – JOHANNESBURG)

Ms Masote's response suggests that, like Mr Williams, she is not just unable to have a home, she recognizes that her father's commitment to his political convictions has, in fact, resulted in her exclusion – as child, woman and person – not only from the culture of family but also from the culture of nationhood. Public discourse sees children and adults as mutually exclusive categories in which the latter are always seen as care-givers and social leaders; public discourse also separates the private from the public: hence Sheila Masote's plea that her abuse happened despite the fact that her family are 'very, very up', from 'the elite', and – a telling irony in the context of my argument – 'cultured'.

The 'culture' that emerges here is one in which these child-victim survivors have experiences that the culture itself cannot name. In Butler's terms, these experiences lie outside the realm of speakable discourse, and thus the culture can accommodate neither those experiences nor the adolescents/adults who survived them. Hence the adolescent/adult-victim survivors cannot, in effect, *be* themselves in this culture, which has become, in a profound way, irrelevant to them.

Sandra Adonis joined the BMW aged approximately fifteen and married another comrade, Jacques, when they were nineteen. Her narrative is different from Sheila Masote's in many ways, but a striking similarity lies in Sandra Adonis's and Sheila Masote's understanding of the lethal combination of apartheid patriarchy and domestic patriarchy in the obliteration of their ability to 'be' themselves. In fact, Sandra Adonis connects the apologies of her abusive husband to the apologies of the Boers in her rejection of both as irrelevant to her (in)ability to live according to her own prerogatives:

My husband was, like, quite, he would, like, sometimes go off his trolley. He would be like a mad person and because he knows that his anger, his frustrations that he felt at that time were supposed to be directed at the State, but because I was the nearest person to him, he lashed out. Well, I understood to a certain extent, but, I mean, how much can a person take and being involved since 15, not really having enjoyed a teenage life [...]. Those [my comrades] were the only people that I could trust at that point in time and sometimes you were not even sure if you could trust them and, as I said, like, my husband was just, got worse and worse and worse. I tried to get him to counsellors and things and he would not accept, like, being counselled. He would not accept being told by other people, because what he use to say to me is that, I had enough of people telling me, I have had enough of people trying to rule my life for me and I will do as I please and, like, he was never this kind of person before. I did not know him like that and always afterwards he would say he is sorry, but, I mean, as I said, how long can a person take somebody saying sorry to you.

Just like these very Boers who have been interrogating us and torturing us, is trying to say to us today, we are sorry, we did not mean that. We do not need their apologies. Well, I do not need them, because I think my life is messed up as it is, directionless. I mean, I have lost my education and I have lost my childhood although we have in return received our freedom and our democracy in this country, but to what extent did we, as the Comrades, members of BMW gain. I do not think we have gained anything, because we are still in the same position as we use to be, unemployed, homeless, abandoned and there is nobody that looks back and say, well, these are the people that has fought the struggle, that has been part and parcel of the struggle and has brought us to the point where we are now. (HRVTRANS: 22 May 1997 – YOUTH HEARINGS: ADONIS.HTM)

TRC evidence here, despite its intended use for other purposes, bears witness to the fact that the culture of negation of persons – children and adolescents and women – still exists in South Africa; and that the culture of reconciliation will only develop into a culture of affirmation when the structural conditions exist for the acknowledgement and subsequent erosion of the current abjection of children, adolescents and women. For it is an aspect of gendered notions of power that brings Moegamat Qasim Williams to devalue himself as unemployed while his wife works, despite his courage in the past; and it is this same aspect of power that brings Sandra Adonis to say that she is 'abandoned' or, to put it in Sheila Masote's words, the abuse she suffered at the hands of her mother 'was one of the things that have killed me'.

This is not to suggest that the disempowered are in any way excused from the abuse of women and children; it is, however, to claim that the child rapes we are now witnessing are at one end of a spectrum of gendered violence that can be related to an entrenched patriarchy that refuses children, adolescents and women both subjectivity and agency. In this respect, the 'death' of Sheila Masote *is* related to the physical rape and murder of women in South Africa. Similarly, the image of the dead child in Mpahlele's story represents what has happened to the subjectivity of children in the rendering of child victims as 'adults', thus denying them childhood and adolescence.

## Inscribing the Unspeakable: Narrating Choice into the Culture of Engendered Violence

How can we register, properly, the mutilation of adolescents, young children and infants at the hands of the actual rapists who live behind the spectacular-ized newspaper images of them as demons, offered as a gesture towards the moral (in)comprehension of South African society at large? How do we under-stand the victimization of youth, especially in the form of sexualized aggres-sion, in a culture that erases actual childhood in the name of a metaphysical childhood innocence? 'The privileging of children as non-gendered cloaks the construction of gender power relations, thus enabling unequal power relations to continue', observes Bhania (2003: 42). This move erases adolescence – the age of puberty, and of the entrenchment of gender roles.

This challenge is especially important as we tend to communities whose infants, children and adolescents it would be wilfully ignorant to conceive of as untouched by the often traumatic consequences of the engendered expecta-tions of puberty. For the culture of sexual violence, for the most part, does not lie outside conventional expectations for men and women in South Africa, but *within* them.

This entrenchment of violence as a key aspect of gendered maturation is conceived of as inevitable in narratives such as Mark Behr's, in which the acceptance of the father's role (in this case, as military defender of apartheid) is equated literally with Marnus's production of semen, as his father asks him obsessively whether there is 'froth' in the morning when he pees in the toilet. It is also rendered inevitable for Ms Masote, because the culture of political responsibility to which her family belongs has imposed a violently differential burden on men and women: men fight apartheid; women raise children in their absence; and if women do fight apartheid, they are policed by men who, as we shall see in the next chapter, may do this policing through rape of their own comrades.

This cult of masculinity, expressed as necessity, as inevitability, in narratives that naturalize gender, is expressed as a *choice* for men in the most acute of South African writing on the topic, not as predestined. In this sense, one can use imaginative narrative to confound gendered hierarchies. Take, for example, Njabulo Ndebele's short story, 'The Prophetess' (1992), written in 1983, which has since been edited and published as an illustrated children's story. Here a young boy, whose family consists of himself and his mother, is dispatched to the prophetess to get holy water for his mother. On his return, he runs into a group of older boys, one of whom is exhibiting his penis, supposedly shortly after having had sex with Sonto, a 'hard girl to get' (Ndebele 1992 [1983]: 28). The boy is threatened by Biza, who asks him what he has seen, intimating that he will attack the boy for saying that he has actually seen Biza's penis. The boy runs from the scene, only to crash into a man on a bicycle, who curses the boy for his clumsiness. The boy, having lost the holy water when the bottle containing it breaks in the crash, decides to fill another bottle with water, which he them takes home to his mother. He is apprehensive that it is not the original holy water, but feels that his decision is justified when his mother pronounces the water soothing.

In this story there is no attempt to edit out the way in which the high school boys gather around Biza to view the apparent evidence of his 'masculinity': the conquest of the girl Sonto. Yet in no way does Ndebele suggest that the boy sees Biza and his colleagues as role models. Instead, the boy apprehends the foolishness of the exhibition in Biza's aggression towards him after his has seen Biza's 'cigar'; he is aware that, to those outside Biza's circle, the display is, in fact, the opposite of what it is intended to be: he, the boy, sees the display of the adolescent as childish.

The child's own move towards adulthood, interestingly enough, is not evinced in the judgementalism with which he views Biza and his mates. In fact, the bicycle accident takes place precisely when the boy is revelling in his feeling of superiority over Biza and the other high school boys. Instead, Ndebele suggests the child protagonist's maturity lies in his rejection of conventional morality: his movement away from seeing himself as 'lying' to his mother by giving her the holy water, and towards his understanding that the important element of his experience is the fact that he *did* go on his mother's behalf to get water blessed by the prophetess. His replacement of the water becomes not a deception, but a sign of his love for his ailing mother. The story is written from the perspective of the nameless boy; and the narrative, while expressing his childhood fears, nevertheless demonstrates his ability to assess his own and other's behaviour creatively.

In this way Ndebele accords his protagonist and his childhood readers the agency denied most of South Africa's child protagonists, fictional and actual. Here Ndebele's writing both exhibits and enacts the fact that successful transition through adolescence is not about the *imposition* of gendered roles that are often violent in their origins and/or effects. Successful adolescence is about educating children that growing up means choosing from a broad range of options of how to be themselves and how to assess that be-ing; *and* it entails providing them with the requisite material and social space to do this, as my last two chapters will illustrate in relation to women and men respectively. Bhania calls for just such a re-imagining in her proposal that both teacher-training institutions and those who plan school curriculums need to 'rethink the readings of the young child' (2003: 44). Such an approach would enable coming home, in Moegamat Qasim Williams' imaginative sense – not his lived experience – of what it would mean to be able to come home.

# CHAPTER 3

# Spectral Presences: Women, Stigma, and the Performance of Alienation

So far, I have investigated what is marked as human and inhuman behaviour through the (shifting) discourses used to demarcate the difference between human and non-human animals. I have also explored the ways in which the imposition of gender roles, overwritten in the convention of acknowledging adolescent activists as having 'given up' their childhood, or identifying adolescents who have had traumatic experiences and/or little care as having had 'no' childhood, can have traumatic effects in and of itself. These effects, I have argued, are disguised, rather than made visible, in the division of subjects into categories of perpetrator or victim, 'innocent' child or conscious adult. The quasi-legal arguments depicting human behaviour as either able to be explained *or* condemned with reference to (the shifting metaphors of) non-human animal behaviour, expose the arbitrariness and thus the inadequacy of the human/animal binary in constructing human rights even within a space constitutionally defined precisely in order to restore human dignity. The association of childhood with innocence, specifically innocence from both political and gendered impositions, and adulthood with precisely the inverse – namely, simultaneous full cognition of one's political and gendered rights and ethical responsibilities – marks the occlusion of adolescence, the traumatic silencing around the assumed but never explicitly acknowledged engendering of the child/adolescent, who is transformed by political activism, as if by magic, from 'child' into 'adult'.

The refusal to name, to own up to, the social construction of gender roles marks both 'child' and 'woman' in deference to the assumed and unexamined category of 'man' as the ideal subject of the state, both pre- and post-apartheid. Whereas prior to 1994 women, and black women in particular, were not regarded as subjects in their own right legally, post 1994 the Constitution attributes rights to both women and children.[1] Here I investigate what it means to be

1    For the text of the Constitution and its relevance to the rights of women and children see

assigned a subject status with rights in law that is unsupported in practice; what the experience of living in this 'no woman's land', so to speak, is. This challenge is often attributed to the gap between practices on the ground and the ideal of women's and children's rights expressed in the post-apartheid Constitution. This gap is constructed, in part, by the very same discourse used to accord rights to those previously marginalized under apartheid, because the language used to express and construct those rights more often than not renders the engenderment of the subject *unimaginable*. I shall trace this failure of discourse to 'speak' gender through an analysis of narratives that illustrate the unintelligibility of 'woman'.[2] The failure consists in the ways in which women exceed their nominally assigned subject position within the discourse of human rights as those rights were conceived of during and in the wake of the TRC.

Fiona Ross's excellent work on women and the TRC, *Bearing Witness* (2003), describes the various ways in which the TRC as an institution exhibited a structural inability to hear many aspects of what women's testimony conveyed – a classic case of what I call 'deaf listening'. Ross concentrates on the ways in which the female subjects demonstrate how women's silence can be seen as a marker of agency, despite the TRC's reading of silence as 'unhealthy' and/or purely a symptom of oppression; and how women's quotidian lives exceeded the constitutive parameters the TRC 'set' for them. I attempt to expand this argument by focusing on continuities between pre- and post-1994 valuations of 'woman' in terms of the ways in which this discursive categorization is stigmatized by physical sexuality and its link to shame, particularly through comparing society's view of rape and women's actual experience of sexual assault; and the impact of this discursive categorization on women's actual experiences of (attempting to be) subjects in contemporary South Africa. Undertaking this analysis entails a brief rehearsal of how the Commission came to recognize 'woman' as a subject within its discourse.[3]

Initially, the Commission appeared 'deaf' to the centrality of women's narratives, according key importance instead to men's experiences as 'frontline'. Women were more often than not perceived as secondary players in a story whose focus was seen to be the interaction between male perpetrators and their overwhelmingly male 'primary' victims. This language of primary and secondary victimization was utilized by the Commission during its initial proceedings: primary victims were understood to be direct victims of organized, political violence or torture; and secondary victims were those family members or others who witnessed the violence directly.[4] As Commissioners listened again

---

the website of the Constitutional Court of South Africa, http://www.constitutionalcourt.org.za

2   In this chapter I often use the singular, 'woman', to refer to the categorical subject position to which and by which actual women are confined.

3   Elements of this story appear in the work of Goldblatt and Meintjies 1996; Truth and Reconciliation Commission of South Africa Report (2003a [1998]: vol. IV, Chapter 10); Graybill, 2002, Chapter 7; comprehensively in Ross 2003; and in Sanders 2007, Chapter 3.

4   Yasmin Sooka, one of the Commissioners, subsequently raised questions about the

and again to women telling the stories of the gross human rights violations suffered by their partners, husbands, children and grandchildren, the absurdity of ignoring women as victim-survivors, authors and subjects of their own narratives emerged. Joyce Seroke pointed out that the categorizations of primary and secondary victimization meant that 'the voices of women were not being heard; that their real stories were not being told. Women were being cast as secondary victims of apartheid – as the mothers, the wives, the sisters and the aunts of the primary victims who were almost all men' (Seroke 1999).

As early as June 1996, Commissioner Mapule Ramashala expressed concern over the fact that women who testified to their own experiences of violation, rather than those of their family and community, were in the vast minority. Ramashala noted this fact, remarked on 'the male-dominated structure of the Truth Commission', and then went on to ask a question:

> Women are articulate about describing their men's experiences but are hesitant about themselves [...]. The pain expressed has been the pain of others, not of themselves. Are we colluding by not providing space for women to talk? [...] If women do not talk then the story we produce will not be complete [...]. Culturally, we think we understand. For example, people may not have told their spouses. We should have special in camera hearings, but then do men learn from these? (cited in Ross 2003: 22–23)

By June 1996, in response to this phenomenon, which was highlighted by the Gender submission written by Beth Goldblatt and Sheila Meintjies in May 1996, the Commission had decided to institute Special Hearings on Women; these were held in Cape Town (8 August 1996), Durban (24 October 1996), and Johannesburg (29 July 1997). By April 1997 the form used by the Commission to record statements had been modified to include the following caution: 'IMPORTANT: Some women testify about violations of human rights that happened to family members or friends, but they have also suffered abuses. Don't forget to tell us what happened to you yourself if you were the victim of a gross human rights abuse' (TRC 2003a [1998]: 4: 283).

As Fiona Ross points out, this rendered the Commission's approach to the subject – 'woman' – supplementary (2003: 25). In this regard, Ross cites Joan Scott's work on the danger of adding women's experiences to an extant body of historical knowledge: this strategy can exclude critical analysis of the conditions which produced the discourses that excluded women in the first instance. In such cases, the attempt to incorporate 'woman' as a subject replicates what I earlier described as the putative search and rescue mission entailed in attempts to incorporate 'black' and 'woman' into the category of the 'human' (as opposed to the non-human 'animal'). Ross's response to the challenge of extending the category of the subject to include women beyond the confines of the Commission's officially sanctioned discourse is twofold. First, she examines the limitations imposed on women as testifiers within the Commission. She then

primary/secondary distinction, suggesting that it may have obscured as much, if not more, than it illuminated (Sooka 1999).

follows the lives and stories of women from Zwelethemba, deftly describing and analysing the interplay of discursive and ethnographic features to demonstrate the ways in which women's stories and everyday practices exceed the disciplinary constraints placed upon them by the TRC, the media, and other public forms of relating – and relaying – what is accepted, or socially recognized, as 'women's experience'.

I examine further what, precisely, constructs the contestation, often marked by violence, between women's range of possibilities of conceiving of themselves, and their constitution as subjects within the fields of social, cultural and political life. This, in turn, allows me to explore the precise connections between women's subjection in the apartheid era and the scandalous post-apartheid gap: the gap between women's rights as they are upheld by the post-1994 Constitution, and subsequent constitutional challenges, and the actual impossibility of the majority of South African women enacting those rights in the context of their quotidian experience. Understanding this impossibility enables us to conceive, properly, of what is at stake for the development of democracy in South Africa should this gap continue to be institutionalized, given the evidence we do have of women conceiving of themselves very differently from the way in which they have been and are categorized by patriarchal cultural practices.

The first part of this chapter, then, describes women's subjection and their performance of their acknowledgement of this subjection; the second describes their performance of their resistance to that subjection.


## Performing Women's Alienation

### 'Woman': An Unaccustomed Subject

Numerous examples provide marked and noted instances of the inability of the TRC to hear women's stories in terms of the significance the women attribute to their own narratives. In the Zondo case, the police refused to return the body of an activist named Andrew Zondo who was sentenced to death for terrorism. As Lalu and Harris point out, the fact that the mother's custom demands appearance of the body to confirm death and carry out the appropriate rituals is ignored completely by the police in this situation. In this sense, Ms Lephino Zondo experiences disrespect both for her person and her tradition through the withholding of her son's body (Lalu and Harris 1996: 35–36). This case is also the focus of Sanders' work on the intersections between 'custom', 'tradition' and law with respect to the recognition of women's rights, including both constitutional law and the South African classification of 'traditional' law recognized by the Constitution (2007: 77–98).

Sanders points out that the specific impossibility of Mrs Zondo *being heard* when she requests her son's body 'because it's our custom', does not only relate to the dismissive authorities who refused the family the right to see the body after Andrew Zondo's hanging. This 'deafness' also extends into the era of the TRC. The specific legacy of apartheid and, before it, the British colonial legal system, was to codify two sets of laws: 'modern law', administered by magistrates to whites; and 'customary law', administered to 'natives' by Commissioners and traditional chiefs.[5] In both cases – and especially in the colonial codification of native law – women were positioned at the confluence of patriarchal power wielded by the colonizers and offered by them to the local chiefs as an attraction within the codified traditional legal economy. Post-apartheid, the Constitution made certain concessions to 'traditional law', which was demanded most notably by the traditional chiefs.[6] Hence, Sanders claims, when Lephino Zondo claims her son's body in the name of 'custom', this custom is inexorably entwined with the construct of 'traditional law', which places Lephino Zondo – and her claim – within the context of an (atavistic) colonial construct of the 'atavistic' native (woman):

> To reclaim 'custom' in sub-Saharan Africa today is thus not to counter the universal calculus of law and rights in the name of cultural difference but rather to negotiate a split within the customary – between customary and 'customary law' – which precludes any pure opposition between law and custom, because law itself generates the customary in the form of a system of customary law that contaminates any reclamatory invocation of custom. (2007: 79)

Since the initial publication of Sanders' essay there have been constitutional challenges to the rights of customary law, as customary law is trumped by women's equal rights within the letter of the Constitution.[7] However, this is not a solution per se: the Constitution cannot legislate custom as it relates to the status of women. The proclamation of women as equal subjects with men before the law does not enact 'woman', as a subject who commands the agency attributed to her in law, in practice. Just as 'custom' in contemporary South Africa cannot simply and immediately be divorced from the incapacitating aspects of 'customary law', constituting 'woman' as a customary subject – as one to whom it is customary to ascribe autonomy – is not simply effected by virtue of constitutional decree. In this respect, women perceive the experience of being a subject in law as spectral, not actual. I shall use Sepati Mlangeni's testimony before the TRC as an example of women's perception of their own experience of being a subject as spectral.

### Enunciating Spectrality: Sepati Mlangeni

Bheki Mlangeni was a legal activist who was killed by a tape bomb sent by the Vlakplaas operators (secret security police), which he started to play on his car audio system. It exploded and he was killed. The testimony of his mother,

5 Here Sanders cites the work of Mamdani on the 'bifurcated state' (1996b: 16–23).
6 For an overview of the issue see Mokgoro 1996–1997.
7 See the woman's rights section of the Constitutional Court of South Africa web page (Consitutional Court of South Africa n.d.) for a list of key cases affecting the relations between customary law and women's rights. See also Himonga and Bosch 2000.

Catherine Mlangeni, describing how she found Bheki in the garage, has received significant attention. Such testimony is detailed and devastating, and carries its own immediate authority. On the other hand, Mlangeni's widow, Sepati Mlangeni, was unable to testify as coherently as her mother-in-law, and her testimony has received less repetition for that reason.[8] Her extreme distress was expressed in a cry enunciating the fact that, since her husband was killed, she is not a person any more: she has no status, describing herself as an 'outcast' within her society. While the senior Mrs Mlangeni's testimony enables, even demands, a reasonable response from its audience, his widow's cry is less obvious in its implications; yet it demands attention for the knowledge it offers of the status of the widow as she experiences it *in the present*.

This attention was not offered to Sepati Mlangeni at the hearing in 1996, which I attended. There was much sympathy from the Commissioners for the loss of her husband. However, no response was made that indicated that Sepati Mlangeni was testifying to the traumatic loss of *Sepati*, not exclusively Bheki, Mlangeni. It is important to state that the transcript of the hearing could not and does not record incoherent words spoken in extreme emotion; the fact that certain statements were cried out in agony; and the body language of the speaker. This means that the transcribed record of the testimony can suggest an emotional coherence was present at the time the testimony was given, in contradiction to the actual performance of the testimony.[9] In the case of Sepati Mlangeni's testimony I have, as Ross puts it, 'rendered into words what was implicit in the performance' (2003: 35). 'Implicit', but, therefore, not necessarily subtle or occluded: Sepati's presentation conveyed pain in no uncertain terms through her verbal incoherence and her bodily 'failure' to assume the status of the composed witness.

The fact that her testimony was often incoherent, in the sense of being hard to hear or grasp due to the witness's bodily expression of emotions, is to the point. In this respect, I see the fact that the TRC and the public overlooked Sepati Mlangeni's relative 'incoherence' in order to concentrate on her mother-in-law's chronological narrative concerning Bheki Mlangeni's death as a key moment marking the spectacular failure of the Commission to recognize women in their own right. Meaning is ascribed to her narrative through the mediation – or disciplinary conformity – of Catherine Mlangeni's narrative, in which there is close correspondence between chronological event and narrative: a correspondence

8  Catherine Mlangeni's testimony has been widely reported because of the dramatic nature of the case and its connection to Vlakplaas agents; it is also dramatized through her participation as a witness-actor in the context of the play, *The Story I am About to Tell/ Indaba Engziyixoxa*, discussed in the introduction.

9  Ross comments: 'Gaps in information, poetic language, emphases, diversions, fluctuations in narrative's time flow create a rhythm in what Coplan describes as "aural" processes that may seem peculiar or limited when subjected to writing's linear rigour' (2003: 35). She then goes on to point out that written testimony may appear, for this reason, nonsensical. In the case of Sepati Mlangeni's testimony, I suggest the converse: that familiarity with written narrative can encourage us to see coherence in the transcribed narrative where that coherence did not exist in oral performance.

that careful attention to Sepati Mlangeni's testimony actually disrupts. When we make sense of – or construe as a subject, 'Sepati Mlangeni' – through reference to Catherine Mlangeni's chronological and relatively coherent narrative of her son's death, we are, in fact, granting Sepati Mlangeni subject status by recourse to what Mamphela Ramphele has described as the socially sanctioned role of the political widow as bearer of public suffering on behalf of the community. Ramphele points out that there is no space for the widow's private grief within this model of recognition of her subjectivity, nor is there any space for her as a full citizen: '[…] as long as women have to resort to "widowhood" to be able to make claims on a society that does not recognize the wounds it inflicts, the dream of full citizenship for women will remain unattainable' (Ramphele 1997: 114–15).

The Commissioners and the public had sympathy for Sepati Mlangeni in the instance in which her collapse was/is read as a sign of the widow's grief for Bheki Mlangeni, her husband and partner. However, this moment can be read differently: as a marker of Sepati Mlangeni's (quasi)subjectivity, demonstrated in the only way it can be demonstrated in a society that places women under censorship. Here Sepati Mlangeni performs the inability of the patriarchal society to hear anything she has to say in a status that (would be) neither that of Bheki Mlangeni's widow, nor that of the daughter-in-law. Her cry is a cry for the never-having-been-able to be recognized Sepati Mlangeni. When Sepati Mlangeni does speak, she does not speak of the manner of Bheki's death, but the non-quality, so to speak, of her life, as a consequence of the fact that the death of her husband renders her a non-wife, at best a 'loose' woman, unable to act in her own right, but more than available to be acted upon:

> Today I'm a widow, I'm an outcast in our society because I'm a widow. In our community and our society you are associated with all sorts of things when you are a widow because of a person who didn't think through when they were doing this, so that when this person comes to you to ask for amnesty, how do you forgive such a person? (HRVTRANS 2 May 1996 – JOHANNESBURG)

There is a considerable amount of information on the status of the widow in the sub-Saharan African context and elsewhere, which, as Ramphele points out, marks the widow both as contaminated by the death of her husband and potentially contaminating. While this ritual danger is associated with dirt and any number of other threatening attributes, 'it is the sexuality of the widow that is singled out as the ultimate reservoir of extreme danger to herself, any partner she may encounter, and the community she lives in' (Ramphele 1997: 100). The widow, for this reason, is literally stigmatized: she may have her head shaved, smear a mixture of ground herbs and charcoal on her body, have to wear black clothing, including a veil, and so on. Ramphele and, following her, Ross, point to the status of the widow as dangerously liminal until it is harnessed by ritual in a form of public mourning that once again renders the widow a subject exclusively through reference to her (dead) husband.

One can see how this aspect of widowhood merely makes visible the wife's dependence on her husband and/or father for her identity *even when he is not dead*. Miriam Tlali has made famous the fact that the contract for her first novel, *Muriel at Metropolitan/Between Two Worlds* remained unsigned because she refused to have her closest male relative sign on her behalf. Note, too, how Sheila Masote, daughter and wife of two famous anti-apartheid activists, whose testimony I introduced in Chapter 2, represents herself, in Ramphele's terms, as suffering the political 'widow's' inability to grieve, even when her husband and father were alive and not necessarily physically absent from the home:

> [...] yes, I'm part of the family, but I refuse to be family and have no identity as Sheila. The problem that I have always suffered and I have always said to myself is that I don't seem to be having an identity like belonging to me. I'm always either Zef's daughter, Mathopeng's daughter or Mike Masote's wife. Or no, Masote's mother and Zef Masote's mother. (sic) But no, I feel I am me. (HRVTRANS 28–29 July 1997 – JOHANNESBURG)

There is no language, then, in Ramphele's words, for the widow, or 'widow' during her husband's life, to obtain acknowledgement from society for the harm it has inflicted on what Sheila Masote calls 'me': the woman as subject without her authorization as such by father/spouse. This 'me' is, to all intents and purposes, at best a quasi-person within the realm of what can be socially recognized.

What does it mean, then, for Sepati Mlangeni, in the TRC's terms, 'refuse' to grant her husband's killers forgiveness? Perhaps it is that she does not see how she can grant them forgiveness for what to them, and to the Commission, is a *non*-event: the failure to imagine that the consequences of their actions precipitate her from being a woman who receives recognition by virtue of her status as married to Bheki Mlangeni, to that of a quasi-person. For a widow – in the context that Sepati Mlangeni describes – is someone who is supposed to gain identity through an alliance to a person who is no longer a man, but a spectre. His status 'grants' – and has always granted her – subjectivity by virtue of the patriarchy. His death, then, renders her a doubled spectre-in-life, a trace of a spectre. She has always been not Sepati Mlangeni, but Bheki Mlangeni's wife, and in this sense, a spectre. Yet now her spectrality, her immateriality to society, is highlighted by Bheki Mlangeni's death: his death throws even her spectral identity as wife into the crisis of widowhood. Sepati Mlangeni – her person, body, actions, feelings – is censored all the more: 'In our community you are associated with all sorts of things when you are a widow' (HRVTRANS 2 May 1996 – JOHANNESBURG). She comes under scrutiny by society – and, in this instance, specifically by the Commission – who will grant her subjectivity only to the extent that she performs the role of the political widow, 'symbolically removing transgressives from the liminal unknown to the liminal known, where social tools [the role of political widow] exist to deal with them' (Ramphele 1997: 111).

The crisis of widowhood is by no means confined to the narrow definition of political widows. The implications of this for women widowed by HIV/AIDS and other premature deaths are highlighted by this woman's comments on how the death of her husband encourages other men within her rural KwaZulu/Natal community to a) treat her as a child because she has no husband to protect her, assuming her incapacity; and b) assume her availability to them as a sexual partner. In female focus groups structured to shed light on the ways in which relations between the sexes are perceived by the community in the context of what are termed South Africa's dual epidemics, HIV/AIDS and gender-based violence, we asked women what they considered the ideal man to be like.[10] In many cases, this resulted, somewhat predictably, in answers detailing what he should not be like. A woman in the female focus group age range 25–35 reflected upon her widowhood in this context:

> The reason I don't respect men is that, since my husband passed away, men will come and say whatever they want to me, and I disagree with them, not interested in what they have to say, then I lose respect [for the men]. Men have their own nonsense; they always have 'dirty thoughts'. Since they know that I am a widow, they feel they should come to me. My husband's absence/death doesn't make me a girl. I am a mother with children. In this area [a rural KZN community] they have that habit of wanting to take over once your husband is dead (*ukungenwa*). I completely lose respect [for them] when they do this to me. (Boyce, Jolly et al. 2003–2006).

This woman comes from a community in which HIV/AIDS prevalence is said to be, conservatively, 31 per cent (Province of KwaZulu-Natal, Office of the Premier 2006). The implications of what she says are real for the increasing number of relatively young women finding themselves widowed through HIV/AIDS. The rendering of women, especially widows, as 'girls' who are available for sex without their consent, primarily because they have 'lost' the male with whom they were identified, sexually and otherwise, reveals the construct of women as free and equal subjects within the society to be unreal(ized), even unrealizable,

10 The full programme of research from which the interview material on HIV/AIDS and gender-based violence and coercion is drawn was funded by the Canadian Institutes of Health Research and entitled 'Transforming Violent Gender Relations to Reduce Risk of HIV/AIDS Infection among Young Women and Girls'. The investigators, other than me, were Will Boyce, Alan Jeeves and Nomusa Mngoma, Queen's University; Sarita Verma, University of Toronto; Steve Reid, Centre for Rural Health, University of KwaZulu-Natal (critical review of the proposal, instruments, procedures and data collection); Eleanor Preston Whyte, HIVAN, University of KwaZulu-Natal; Tracy Vienings, Centre for the Study of Violence and Reconciliation, Johannesburg, and Claudia Mitchell, McGill University (critical review of the proposal and procedures); Belinda Dodson, University of Western Ontario (critical review of the proposal and data collection). The following gave valuable support to the project as research assistants: Diane Davies, Ncedile Mankahle, Vuyelwa Mkhize, Tobias Mngadi, S'thembile Ngidi, Cyril Nkabinde, Hana Saab, Sid Sahay and Siduduziwe Zulu. The interviews that were gathered as a result of this joint collaboration are all referenced as Boyce, Jolly et al. 2003–2006, to distinguish them from material gathered by me alone. Where I refer to colleagues' interpretations of this collabora-tively gathered evidence, I name the colleague, as in my joint writing with Alan Jeeves. Otherwise, all interpretations of this material are solely my responsibility and are not the product of joint collaboration.

within such a context. The convention also has obvious negative implications for prevention strategies that depend upon knowledge and/or behaviour change to reduce HIV/AIDS infection rates. The implications for reducing practices of gender-based violence and coercion are, correlatively, equally negative.

In the next section I trace the relationships between the threat of women's sexuality being dangerous unless it is demarcated within a masculine economy; her stigmatization through reference to that sexuality; and the telling element of 'shame' as a discourse that, by definition, positions 'woman' as a subject who is, in effect, a quasi-subject – one who lives under censorship, one who cannot speak on her own terms and is unspeakable within the discursive constraints allotted to her.

## Dishonouring Victims

In *Disgrace* (1999), J. M. Coetzee presents us with Lucy, a female character who is gang-raped by three men. Against her father's wishes, she refuses to report her rape to the police. Whatever the specifics of her reasons for refusing to lay charges, Lucy's decision appears to be based on her judgement that nothing positive will ensue for her if she reports her rape to the authorities. As if to underscore this silence as an act of agency, Coetzee presents us with yet another instance of a character who refuses to report sexual assault. This time it is the author-character, Elizabeth Costello. She tells us something, she says, she has never told anybody; a contradictory gesture, of course, telling us the secret that is to be kept her own forever. She tells us of abuse she experienced when she was nineteen, in Melbourne. She allowed herself to be picked up, went to the man's flat, and then apologized, saying she could not go through with the act of sex. The man thought it was a game, and then began to abuse her seriously, so that she ended up with multiple injuries and a wired jaw:

> It was her first brush with evil. She had realized it was nothing less than that, evil, when the man's affront subsided and a steady glee in hurting her took its place. He liked hurting her, she could see it; probably liked it more than he would have liked sex [...]. By fighting him off she had created an opening for the evil in him to emerge, and it emerged in the form of glee, first at her pain ('You like that, do you?' he whispered as he twisted her nipples. 'You like that?'), then the childish, malicious destruction of her clothes. (Coetzee 2003: 166)

Elizabeth Costello reflects that what is important about this episode is the fact that

> she has never revealed it to anyone, never made use of it. In none of her stories is there a physical assault on a woman by a man in revenge for being refused [...] what happened in the rooming house belongs to her and to her alone. For half a century the memory has rested inside her like an egg, an egg of stone, one that will never crack open, never give birth. She finds it good, it pleases her, this silence of hers, a silence she hopes to preserve to the grave. (2003: 166)

In his other works, there are clues to what Coetzee may be up to in his representations of the relations between the telling of violent acts and the contamination that may be incurred in doing so. In *Giving Offense* (1996), he appears to support a rape victim-survivor who refuses to risk re-victimizing herself by telling her testimony for the purposes of prosecution because, he argues, the courts may hold to a discipline of the guilty versus the innocent, but the court of public opinion has not relinquished a contradictory 'moral': that of honour versus shame (80).

Coetzee is remarkably prescient of South Africa's TRC in this respect, when one looks at the narratives of women who refused to testify to abuse, particularly sexual abuse, for the reason Coetzee outlines here. In some measure it is due to the fact that shame trumps the innocence of the victim-survivor that Lucy, after her rape in *Disgrace*, refuses to take her assailants to court. To the extent that the representation of sexual assault, of Elizabeth Costello or Lucy, would raise the spectre or the reality of re-victimizing both of them as shamed – would, in fact, contaminate them despite the fact that they are victims and not the perpetrators of the evil inflicted upon them – silence would seem valuable in their cases; a cost not to be given up lightly.

In Coetzee's recent work, *Diary of a Bad Year* (2007), we are presented with yet another character who suffers sexual abuse at the hands of three men. This time it is Anya, the writer-narrator's muse of sorts, who tells the story of her and a friend being invited aboard the men's yacht in Cancún, refusing to sleep with them, and then being raped by them. Anya and her friend report the rape to the police, but only after being warned of the consequences by the police captain. Anya relates the story to the writer-narrator:

> You are sure you want to do this (meaning, are you sure you want this story to get out) [the captain asks], because, you know, dishonour, *infamia*, is like bubble gum, wherever it touches it sticks.
>     You know what I said? I said, 'This is the twentieth century, capitano' (it was still the twentieth century then). 'In the twentieth century, when a man rapes a woman it is the man's dishonour.' (Coetzee 2007: 100–101)

The men's yacht is impounded, and news of their dealings reaches their family and friends back home. Anya is making the point that the dishonour that the writer-narrator, whose name is in fact Coetzee, appears to experience, in the era in which states sanction torture, should not properly be his. 'Dishonour' should not 'descend upon one's shoulders', she argues, if one is the victim and not the perpetrator of the deed:

> When you [Coetzee] tell me you walk around bent under your load of dishonour, I think of those girls from the old days who had the bad luck to get raped and then had to wear black for the rest of their lives – wear black and sit in a corner and never go to parties and never get married. You have got it wrong, Mister C. Old thinking. Wrong analysis [...]. Abuse, rape, torture, it doesn't matter what: the news is, as long as it is not your fault, as long as

you are not responsible, the dishonour doesn't stick to you. So you have been making yourself miserable over nothing. (2007: 103–105)

Coetzee replies that he feels the dishonour that should accrue to the three men who raped Anya and her friend; further, he alienates Anya in the extreme by claiming that she, too, continues to be dishonoured by their abuse of her. 'No man is an island', Coetzee tells us he replies to Anya:

She looked blank. We are all part of the main, I said. Things haven't changed, Mistress Anya. Dishonour won't be washed away, won't be wished away. Still has its old power to stick. Your three American boys – I have never laid eyes on them, but they dishonour me nevertheless. (2007: 107–109)

I shall return to the question of the dishonour Coetzee feels later in this chapter, and once again in my conclusion to this book. First, I wish to explore the mechanism by which dishonour falls upon the victim, rather than the perpetrator of the crime, even in the twentieth and twenty-first centuries, despite laws that are intended to demonstrate otherwise.

### 'Woman': Stigmatizing the Subject who Speaks

Fiona Ross emphasizes that the category women had to inhabit to testify before the Commission was that of 'victim'; and that many women refused to identify themselves in this way, deliberately choosing not to testify. 'Given the Commission's equation of voice with self', Ross points out, 'it is important to consider what the experience of inhabiting a subject position that carries negative social and cultural worth may be' (2003: 163). Women's testimony before the TRC, and their decision *not* to testify, are witness to and revealing of the fact that many women, much of the time in their quotidian lives during apartheid, at the time of the TRC, and now, do not have a choice about whether they inhabit a subject position of negative social and cultural worth. This is because the category of 'worth' is affective; it is socially, culturally and politically constituted through an interplay between 'woman' as a category, the culture that generates that category, and individual women attempting to 'bear' (in Ross's sense of 'bearing witness') the burden of their categorization.

This categorization is 'woman' as the quasi-subject for whom the putative search and rescue mission outlined in Chapter 1, the mission to bring women/blacks into the domain of the human, needs to be accomplished. The actualization of this search and rescue mission is rendered visible in the call to women to see themselves as victims. The rhetorical form that this call took is highlighted by Ross:

Sexual violence was represented in the hearings and in public discourse as a defining feature of women's experiences of gross violations of human rights. It was identified as an experience about which women *could* and *should* testify, and about which they *would* testify under certain conditions. It was considered incumbent upon women to describe in public the kinds of sexual harms to which they were subjected. (2003: 24)

'It is disturbing', Ross concludes, 'that men were not called to testify about sexual violation' (2003: 24). The making of woman, not man, as subordinate through the marking or stigmatization of her body as the locus of sexual difference, made visible in sexual forms of bodily torture, has a rationale: it conforms to the domain of the speakable as it pertains to 'woman', manifesting the inability of the discursive construction of human rights within the post-apartheid era to accord women their legally sanctioned place.

The TRC Report (2003a [1998]) recognizes its inability to address women's experience and in so doing demonstrates the fact that it is 'haunted', to use Butler's term (1997: 133), by lacunae surrounding what it calls 'women's experiences'. It quotes Ms Ilse Olckers, a lawyer who described the requests of women working on gender issues to selected Commissioners to gender their approach this way: 'It was as if they were asking them to convince the other members of the Commission to see the Earth as round. We added a third dimension to a task already wearisome. A task which they felt they could hardly cope with in its current two dimensional state' (TRC 2003a [1998]: IV, 287).[11]

The Report states that 'to integrate gender fully, however, would have required the Commission to amend its mandate and how it defined gross HRVs' (IV, 287). It goes on to explain that apartheid itself has been considered a gross HRV in the full legal sense of the term; yet the Commission's mandate did not include the daily violence inflicted upon women, abuse that was far more common and has longer-reaching consequences than the narrowly defined political abuse on which the Commission concentrated. The Report quotes Fiona Ross's observation that the Commission's focus, despite its comprehensive definition of gross HRVs, has been 'on bodies and on the visible embodiment of suffering', excluding the quotidian from its purview (IV, 303).

The Commission's inability to conceive of women's quotidian experiences, underscored by Ross, bears witness not simply to an omission, but further, to the discursive unreality of women within the Commission's domain of the speakable. The search and rescue mission that brings 'woman' into the category of the human here works though her association with the body and its vulnerability in the spectacle of her sexuality. To radically redefine the 'human' in a way that would render this patronizing mission unnecessary would be to attempt to constitute 'woman' as a subject in terms that the norms governing what is able to be spoken render fundamentally unimaginable.

The discursive form that the search and rescue mission for 'woman' takes in the TRC discourse is through the association of women with that which is (as with the animal, as with the black) associated with the body. In the case of 'woman', however, the body is what Ross terms 'naturally gendered' in the radical reduction of women's testimony – however unwitting – to an emphasis on women's bodies and the traditional symbolism associated with those bodies. This is manifest in the TRC Report's focus on women's plight in terms of stories

11    Ross spells Ms Olckers' name 'Olkers'. The journal index of the article cited by both Ross and the Report reads 'Ilze Olckers, "Gender-neutral Truth: A reality Shamefully Distorted", *Agenda* 31 (1996), 61–67'.

of women whose pregnancies were harmed and whose babies were used as threats against the women; the torture of women involving their reproductive organs specifically; and women's vulnerability in terms of their menstrual needs in prison, or the opportunity they represent both to male comrades and apartheid enforcers for rape.

Focusing on women's reproductive organs and capacity, the Report refrains from commenting on the overwhelming evidence that speaks to the sexual element of *men's* torture of men in the Report. While it acknowledges in the gender chapter that the abuse of women was used, at least in part, to indicate to the men on the opposite side their inability to protect their own women, the sexual nature of many of the torture methods used by men against men is not recognized in the language of the report. The implication is that the sexual abuse of women is *the* key aspect of their victimization; and conversely, that the (sexual) abuse of men cannot be demarcated, in discursive terms, as in any way different from the range of abuses suffered by male subjects testifying as victims. Antjie Krog (1998: 181–82) points out that in these terms, only women can be raped.

In this respect, the Report replicates what Goldblatt and Meintjies, citing Agger, discuss as a trope in which male identity is seen to be under attack through their rape, whereas, in the case of women, rape is seen to accentuate a 'core' female sexuality of passivity and shame:

> Although women and men are tortured equally, it is clear from South African accounts and parallel international experience that the differing constructions of gender shape their experience and treatment. Although studies of political violence do not highlight men's gendered experience of their torture, studies of ordinary prisoners reveal systematic attacks on their masculinity. An interesting hypothesis, posed by Inger Agger suggests that sexual torture of men aims to induce sexual passivity and to abolish political power and potency, whereas, behind the sexual torture of women is the activation of sexuality to induce shame and guilt. (Goldblatt and Meintjies 1996)

Here we arrive at a remarkable vantage point: we can trace the ways in which female sexuality is presented as *stigma* to enable her occupation of the subject position, 'victim'.

The origin of the word 'stigma' in fact reflects bodily violence. Its range of archaic meanings include predominantly the scar left by a branding iron; its plural, stigmata, commonly refers to the wounds of Christ. Its contemporary meanings are telling: a mark of shame or discredit; a stain; an identifying or characteristic mark, specifically used in terms of the diagnostic sign of a disease. In the testimony of women speaking at the TRC of their sexual violation, and in those who refused to speak of their experiences of sexual assault, we can trace the narrators' awareness of the shame attributed to them, not the perpetrators, as a consequence of sexual violation.

Thenjiwe Mtintso's testimony bears out Agger's point – that the sexual torture of women is aimed to produce shame and guilt – while describing how the torture of a woman may produce marks that stigmatize her as the one who exceeds the category of 'woman' by refusing to be cowed. A man who withstands torture is seen as a hero, she says; but a woman who does the same is viewed as having betrayed some 'essential female virtue' of modesty and submission:

> [...] when men were tortured and suffered in the hands of the police and they stood ground against the physical abuse, there was a sense of respect – where the torturers would even say '*hy is 'n man*' [Afrikaans: 'he is a man']. There was that respect for that man. But when a woman dared, when a woman dared refused [sic] to cow down, to be cowed down; then that unleashed the wrath of the torturers, because in their own discourse a woman, a black '*meid*' [Afrikaans: derogatory diminutive, a 'girl'] '*kaffermeid*' [added racial deroga-tion, 'kaffir girl'] had no right to have the strength to withstand their torture.
>
> They could understand a man, but not a 'kaffermeid'. So the torture in that way began to be even more than it would have been had you been probably a White male or even a Black male. (HRVTRANS 28–29 July 1997 – WOMEN'S HEARINGS – JOHANNESBURG)

Jessie Duarte has pointed out that in cases where women were raped by state functionaries, the rape survivors were perceived by women and men of their own communities as having been weak, as having sold out:

> [...] women could not say they were raped in the eighties because from the position of the people they worked with that was considered a weakness. If women said that they were raped they were regarded as having sold out to the system in one way or another [...]. The consequences of these rapes were the same for these women as criminal rapes. A political rape has no different consequences. It has exactly the same reason behind it – a violent act against a woman [...]. In fact women were being punished as women. (Duarte cited in Goldblatt and Meintjies 1996)

As Duarte's observations suggest, whether a woman experienced sexual violation as a consequence of torture sanctioned by the apartheid state, or at the hands of her comrades, the effect is the same: testifying to the viola-tion brings censorship and shame down upon the woman, not the perpetrator. Lyn Graybill tells the story of Nita Nombango Mazibuko, who was accused by her MK comrades of being a spy. She was subsequently detained, raped and tortured by her comrades in exile. In her testimony she claimed that two weeks after she had given a written submission to the Commission, ANC premier of Mpumalanga, Matthew Phosa, phoned her and tried to persuade her not to testify. After she testified that a comrade had 'cut through my genitals and ... he ... also pour[ed] Dettol over my genitals', Phosa threatened to sue her and she recanted her testimony (Graybill, 104).

Women's hesitation or refusal to testify demonstrates their understanding of the stigma testifying would revisit upon them. Their statements suggest that they are aware that the composure they may have struggled to regain after rape would be obliterated by being registered forever in the public mind as rape victims. Hence Thenjiwe Mtinso, chairperson of the Gender Commission at the time of the Women's Hearing held in Johannesburg on 28 July 1997, and previously an MK commander, introduced the hearings by commenting on her own refusal to speak. She expressed support for those women who were prepared to speak out – and gratitude – because, she said, they speak on behalf of many women who are 'not yet ready': 'I speak as one of those [...] I could not speak last night, because I sat with myself. I sat with my conscience. I sat with the refusal to pen those wounds. I have built armour around this pain ...' (HRVTRANS 28–29 July 1997 – WOMEN'S HEARINGS – JOHANNESBURG). Many potential testifiers occupied (and continue to occupy) senior positions in the post-apartheid regime and fear the diminishment of their effective authority in the wake of an 'admission' of rape. Nomfundo Walaza, a clinical psychologist present at the gender hearings in Cape Town, questioned the wisdom of assuming that revealing 'weaknesses' publicly would subsequently strengthen the witness; she also speculated about what an observer might think of a female Minister of State whom that observer now knew had been sexually tortured in prison: 'what would go through your mind when you saw her on television?' The risk of speaking out also entails curtailment of professional opportunity: 'Another deterrent is that some of the rapists hold high political positions today – so if you spoke out you would not only undermine the new Government you fought for, but destroy your own possibilities of a future' (Graybill, 104).

*Transforming the Meaning of Shame*

In the coalescence of 'woman', victim, sexuality in stigma and the shame it entails, we can begin to gender the irony, posed by Primo Levi and others in the context of the Holocaust, in which the victim, not the aggressor, suffers shame; the 'dishonour' that Coetzee's character, Anya, refuses to acknowledge. Of the women who spoke about their sexual violation in public, many stated that this was the first time that they had told anyone of their experiences. Thandi Shezi, one of these women, was gang-raped by four policemen when she refused to give them information they attempted to extract from her through torture. She testified that 'I thought I had done something that I deserved to be treated like that' (HRVTRANS 28–29 July 1997 – WOMEN'S HEARINGS – JOHANNESBURG). An anonymous testifier at the Durban gender hearing stated that she had never told anyone of the rape she experienced by IFP members: 'Sometimes I feel like I invited trouble myself' (cited in Graybill 2002: 105).

Of course, we all know that the victim-survivor 'should not' attribute responsibility for her violation to her own actions, a response that once again places responsibility on the shoulders of the survivor. However, there is an alternative response. Here I draw on Judith Butler's sense of how implicit censorship works, Kelly Oliver's suggestion that witnesses to atrocity are seeking a hearing for horrors beyond recognition, and Giorgio Agamben's reflections on survivors' shame in the context of his work on the Holocaust. I do so to dislodge rape survivors' testimony of experiencing shame from being read as an 'improper' response, instead reading the testimony as witness to the implicit *non*-recognition of 'woman' as properly commanding human rights; as witness to the profound betrayal of 'woman' within the domain of the speakable as women experience it at the time of witnessing.

In *Witnessing: Beyond Recognition* (2001) and subsequent works, Kelly Oliver argues that testimonies of those speaking to victimization as a consequence of regimes of oppression – slavery, racism, the Nazi death camps – are not only seeking recognition of what can be seen as their wronging; they are also seeking to bear witness to atrocity so dire that it cannot be recognized. Her point is not, as I understand it, akin to its most obvious counterpart (at least superficially speaking) in Holocaust studies, namely the notion that the Holocaust is radically unrepresentable, because rendering it speakable would diminish its horror. Instead, she suggests, the atrocity is unable to be recognized precisely because the terms of recognition are structured by hierarchy, rather than by the dialogic of address and response constituted within social relations. In other words, Oliver rejects witnessing being reduced to the call for recognition precisely because it replicates the patronizing search-and-rescue approach to human rights we have already encountered:

> If recognition is conceived of as being conferred on others by the dominant group, then it merely repeats the dynamic of hierarchies, privilege and domination. Even if oppressed people are making demands for recognition, insofar as those who are dominant are empowered to confer it, we are thrown back into the hierarchy of domination. (Oliver 2004: 78)

This hierarchy of domination can be seen as that which structures any marginalized subject's attempt to communicate her marginalization – or quasi-subjectivity – as an appeal, not a right.

Instead of understanding witnessing through the structures of recognition, Oliver poses the structure of address and response as the constitutive element of witnessing: a definition of witnessing characterized by its inter-subjectivity. Oliver cites Dori Laub in this regard:

> [...] Dori Laub concludes that psychic survival depends on an addressable other, what he calls an 'inner witness'. The inner witness is produced and sustained by dialogic (and I would add nonlinguistic forms of communicative) interaction with other people. In order to talk, think, act as an agent, the inner witness must be in place. This is to say that we learn to talk to ourselves – to think – by talking to others. Our experience is meaningful for us only if we can imagine that it is meaningful to others. Creating or finding meaning for oneself is possible only through the internalization of meaning for others. (Oliver 2001: 83)

We can supplement Oliver's comments on the severe limitations on recognition as driving social change, specifically in relation to gender-based violence, with Agamben's reflections on shame. Agamben, drawing heavily on the writings of Primo Levi and others in relation to survivors of the death camps, argues that the shame experienced by the survivors is not that of 'survivor guilt', because it has nothing to do with the culpable states of either guilt or innocence.

Instead, this shame derives from 'being assigned to something [let us say, using Kelly's vocabulary, a subject position] from which we cannot in any way distance ourselves' (2001: 105). Here shame is specifically *not* an assertion of responsibility on the part of victim-survivor for her violation; it is, instead, her registering the impossibility of distancing herself from the subject position to which she has been consigned by a publicly constituted visibility that sees her exclusively as (the raped) woman. She sees herself being seen as that which is not coincident with her sense of herself.

Following Agamben, when the anonymous rape survivor from Durban states that 'Sometimes I feel like I invited trouble myself', the grammatical reflexivity of this statement reflects the notion of shame as a quintessential moment of self-consciousness. This moment is characterized by the double movement in which, simultaneously, the subject, by instantiating herself as a subject within what Butler calls the domain of the speakable, is at that very moment witness to her own desubjectification:

> Here the 'I' is thus overcome by its own passivity, its ownmost sensibility; yet this expropriation and desubjectification is also an extreme and irreducible presence of the 'I' to itself. It is as if our consciousness collapsed and, seeking to flee in all directions, were simultaneously summoned by an irrefutable order to be present at its own defacement, at the expropriation of what is most its own. In shame the subject thus has no other content than its own desubjectification; it becomes witness to its own disorder, its own oblivion as a subject. This double movement, which is both subjectification and desubjectification, is shame. (Agamben 1999: 105–106)

The framework constructed through a theoretical triangulation of Butler, Oliver and Agamben allows us to read shame such as the victim-survivor's as recognition of her own irrelevance to the social order in which she finds herself. This irrelevance is thrown in her face when her violation cannot be registered because she is, at best, a quasi-subject, whose violation is therefore a quasi-violation – itself, tellingly, an impossibility. As we have seen, the victim-survivor's awareness of her impropriety as a subject in the order in which she finds herself is registered by her, in narrative form, in the tropes of shame in terms of the public view of her. The tropes that appear when she reflects upon her own position of being an impossible subject are those of insanity.

### Being Unspeakable: Social Meaninglessness and Insanity

In this context the risk taken by women testifying to their subjectivity, that is, the risk taken by women who speak *as* subjects in public, becomes apparent. If there are, as the TRC Report put it, no 'ready listeners', then testimony becomes a denial of self in public; and, by valid extension, so do other public acts in which women risk acting as subjects where the absence of listeners (in the Commission's sense of listeners who are willing to hear) is omnipresent. This is the precise opposite of the recognition it was hoped the TRC would offer and the new Constitution would ensure. There is no reciprocity, in Oliver's terms.

The performance before the TRC becomes a demonstration of the fact that there is no witness to the subject herself and, therefore, to the violation of that subject. Therefore there is, to use Dori Laub's vocabulary, no 'inner witness' – the factor that results in extreme isolation and alienation for the quasi-subject from the social fabric of the community, and the experience of 'feeling insane'. Utilizing the language of speech act theory, we can describe this process of alienation as having the systemic aspect of social ignorance of the subject.

Judith Butler provides an entry point in her discussion of the relations between censorship and subject formation. She describes the relations between what we may call censorship of the subject – her delimitation as a subject by social, political and linguistic convention – and her potential agency: the capacity of the subject to participate in radically new ways of thinking. Furthermore, she does this by underlining the relationships between the social and the political in the formation of the subject:

> Censorship seeks to produce subjects according to implicit and explicit norms, and [...] the production of the subject has everything to do with the regulation of speech. The subject's production takes place not only through the regulation of that subject's speech, but through the regulation of the social domain of speakable discourse. The question is not what it is I will be able to say, but what will constitute the domain of the sayable within which I begin to speak at all [...]. (1997: 133)

Butler (1997) addresses the constraints on the subject through her references to theorists J. L. Austin and Pierre Bourdieu on performative speech acts. Consummate examples of speech acts are those in which what the speaker pronounces is thereby effected: a judge pronouncing a sentence, for example. Austin points out that performative speech works because it derives its forcefulness, and thus its efficacy, through recourse to established conventions. Bourdieu builds on this argument to account for what Butler calls the 'thinness' (1997: 146) of Austin's theory in terms of the social context of performative language. For performative speech acts do not rest on a series of static conventions that Austin assumes (according to Bourdieu) to be inherent to language. 'Authority comes to language from outside', says Bourdieu (1991: 109): it is the conventional power of certain institutions that is lent, as it were, to language in the instance of effective performativity.

The strength of Bourdieu's theory is that it underlines the way in which social conventions underwrite speech to produce the *embodied* subject. In so doing, Bourdieu supplements Austin's approach, which constructs speech alone as the key to performative acts. Bourdieu explains that our social understanding of the rules of convention is enacted in a bodily understanding, or habitus. This habitus is, importantly, not limited to the self-conscious adherence to social dictates. A performative act that works depends upon the person enacting it having been authorized to do so by social convention. It depends, in TRC terms, on 'ready listeners' who have been made so though the specific deployment of authority within a given social, political and cultural context.

To the extent that women are literally considered *immaterial* – in the sense of not being able to command an audience to bear witness to (the violation of) their (proposed) status as subjects – women are relegated to the domain of the unspeakable, and thus become, in turn, literally those who *cannot* speak. The cruelty of this can be at least acknowledged, if not fully recognized, when we revisit Butler's work on what constitutes the domain of the unspeakable:

> *To move outside the domain of speakability is to risk one's status as a subject* [...]. 'Impossible speech' would be precisely the ramblings of the asocial, the rantings of the 'psychotic' that the rules that govern the domain of speakability produce, and by which they are continually haunted. (1997: 133)

In discursive terms, the 'rantings' of the 'psychotic' can certainly be seen to haunt the rules that constitute the domain of the speakable. However, *in material terms, the converse is true*: it is these rules (those that constitute the domain of the speakable) that render women immaterial – spectral – within the South African contexts we have been investigating. My point here to Butler would be that this reflexive 'haunting' of (unable-to-be spoken) women by the rules that determine what is speakable and what is not, is crucial, because it is this inversion of Butler's formulation that renders the women unable to speak; literally, ghosts of themselves. This being immaterial to the society one inhabits, if one recognizes it, causes the subject to *feel* insane.

The isolation of insanity ensues when there is an absence of – to use Kelly Oliver's term – the essential 'addressable other'. We see this in retrospective narratives of women who detail the events of the apartheid era. Here is a woman in her seventies, 'Tauhali', speaking of her life during this time:

> To me looking back at my marriage as a married woman and a mother, born and bred within the system of apartheid, reflecting on that period, evokes only sadness and mixed feelings [...].
> As a young bride I stepped into marriage with all the typical expectations, looking forward to a life of fulfilment and peace. But that was not to be [...]. The marital laws of apartheid, the apartheid teachings, ruined my life almost completely. They made me lose all the high regard I had for the institution [of marriage] which seeks to remind a woman and a man into a permanent living relationship of respect.
> The marital laws reduced my husband from being the affectionate, considerate young man I married into the domineering, dishonest and morose bully he became. It is not that [...] we are trying to put all the evil deeds of individuals and their creators and witnesses at the doorstep of apartheid, I realize that. It is true that the system deeply ingrained the foundation for those perhaps human shortcomings to germinate and corrupt even the most harmless of us. That this is true cannot be denied. The so-called marital power, the blatant evil of one human being holding absolute, intangible authority over another purely on the basis of sex was in fact the power of life and death on us African women that apartheid bestowed on our men [...].
> *Institutionally, I felt like a mere creature without a mind of my own.* If official police had been different, democratic and accommodating, allowing me the

right to determine my destiny, I might have opted to leave him or rather bolted out of the virtual prison I was in. I could, for instance, sue for divorce and be on my own. But that too I realized would be no solution to my problems. Where would I go to? Who'd take me into his room with my children? As an African woman I was a perpetual minor. My right to be in Johannesburg where I was born and raised was not recognized. I could remain and perhaps find employment if I was under the control of a man as either a wife, a daughter, or even a sister. If I was a widow I'd also be under my son. The pass laws curtailed my movement. If divorced I would have to be out on the street because then I would have to leave our house as my right to be there was only because I was his wife. I had personally seen how women, some of them my only friends and alas even relatives who had been divorced who were forced to virtually roam the streets with children because they could not remain in their houses. This piece of legislation [the marriage laws] in many cases was used by some men to force women to tolerate whatever misconduct or cruelty, even unfaithfulness, which they could feel like committing toward their wives. *I was extremely emotional, I was under emotional and extreme torture.* ('Tauhali' 1996)

'Tauhali' realizes implicitly that when apartheid established what it considered the domain of the speakable, in its own interests, she, as a woman, was rendered meaningless: 'I wonder whether [...] it was necessary for the architects and exponents of the system of apartheid to render our lives, the lives of South African women, hazardous and meaningless, to denigrate us so that the grand plan of apartheid should succeed'. Further, 'Tauhali' states

that I did not end up in the insane asylum was what I consider as one of the greatest miracles that ever happened to me. I had kept the emotional abuse, the lack of honesty we [her husband and herself] had in our life together a close secret. Although I was often moved to shedding tears in my bed at night I kept everything to myself. *I did not want everyone to guess that I was always [in fear] and worried* [...]. ('Tauhali' 1996)

Deborah Matshoba says, 'When I look around, I marvel at how we battle to be normal – and no one knows how shattered we are inside' (Krog 1998: 185). The element of isolation is mirrored in Thandi Shezi's testimony:

MS SHEZI: I was very deeply hurt. As result, there's nobody I've been able to relate the story to. My mom is hearing this for the first time. Other people might have only known this through counselling, because I've been going through counselling at Wits, because I wasn't able to speak about this. I just kept it in myself. I thought it was going to be my secret. I thought I'd done something that I deserved to be treated like that. (HRVTRANS 28–29 July 1997 – WOMEN'S HEARINGS – JOHANNESBURG)

The understanding these female victim-survivors demonstrate on their own behalf is that they should protect themselves from disclosure of their 'psychotic' state, because of the public humiliation, rejection and abjection that will result if they let themselves *be*.

The stigma-shame-insanity nexus in the context of rape has not disappeared in the wake of the TRC. The Women's Hearings took place in 1996–1997, and I conducted the interview with 'Tauhali' in 1996. Almost a decade later, the Canadian Institutes of Health Research team on the relations between gender-based violence and the spread of HIV/AIDS in KwaZulu/Natal of which I am co-Principal Investigator interviewed a focus group of women aged 35–45 about how a woman who has been raped by someone other than her husband is perceived. Note how 'the community' is figured as visiting responsibility for the act, in the form of stigma and shame upon the victim-survivor:

D: …The people in the community do not believe you have been raped, they think you agreed to sleeping with that man (the rapist), whereas you are hurt because someone has forced sex on you.

C: Yes, that's how it is

E: Yes. You do tell your husband about this, although it is hard, but he does not reject you; the community will assume you were lovers with the rapist […].

F: Yes, you do tell your husband, because he knows you personally and your behaviour, when you tell him that you've been raped, he will understand, but community people will think that you are just playing around, they will say the person who raped you is your lover, why else would he choose to rape you and not others.

B: It is as they say, some tell their husbands about this unexpected occurrence, others are afraid to share this with their husbands, saying Wee! (*exclamation*) because no-one saw me, I will not tell anyone […]. (Boyce, Jolly et al. 2003–2006)

In this community, as in many others in rural KwaZulu-Natal where workshops on women's constitutional rights have not yet been held, the word 'rape' is not associated with unwanted sex imposed upon a woman by a member of her own community. The implication is that a member of her own community would not force her to have sex with him unless such an act was in some way justified: that the victim had acted in some way as to bring the sexual aggression down upon herself. Thus interview subject B continues:

B: Knowing that in the community this is your issue, they will say how different you are from the others [other women in the community] that you got raped, the community will think that the people who raped you are your people, you know them and then it becomes hard to tell your husband. It is also hard for your husband; he loses trust in you, thinking it was your people. (Boyce, Jolly et al. 2003–2006)

The level of alienation of a raped woman in this context of community is extreme. Since rape by someone entirely unknown to the community is extremely rare, the implication is always that the woman has 'misbehaved' in some way to bring such an act upon herself.

Of course this is to some degree the case in many societies globally, where issues of sobriety, dress and the like are brought to bear in discussions of the victim's reliability as a witness. Here, however, the victim's assertion of her rape is seen as her own betrayal of her community, in a structure analogous to the one enunciated by Jessie Duarte, in which to assert one's rape by a comrade is to be viewed as a betrayer of the struggle. That, following Agamben, this position of concomitant 'subjectification and desubjectification' in shame, or 'unspeakability' in Butler's terms, results in the loss of reciprocity so vital for successful witnessing outlined by Kelly Oliver, and ensuing feelings of insanity, is recognized by the women of the community, if an appropriate context is offered in which they can enunciate this phenomenon. Immediately following the discussion reported above demonstrating the interpretation of rape as betrayal of the community by the victim, when asked about what a woman might do if she had been raped, if there is somewhere she might go for help, a respondent replied that the woman would need to go to the hospital for counselling: 'She will have to go, because I believe you get disturbed mentally if you've been through this' (Boyce, Jolly et al. 2003–2006).

Women's narratives – be they the Sowetan inhabitant or TRC victim-survivors – link the failure of society to produce an addressable other, or reciprocity in the face of the victim-survivor, to a devastating lack of faith in intimacy as reciprocal within the private sphere, and to her objectification within social exchange. The effect is that of profound alienation, expressed in abjection, in the abject body. Notice how Thandi Shezi juxtaposes the notion of her body as a strong body with her feeling towards that body as one that is radically unstable, one that cannot risk intimacy. She explains that, as a comrade, her strength was trusted:

> MS MKHIZE: You said you were working underground. Could you actually explain to us, that as a woman, what the role did you play, what role did you play to actually make you trusted in that male dominated area and their activities underground?
> MS SHEZI: I think the comrades I was working with in a Umdane, (sic) this unit, they trusted me. Maybe they saw bravery in me. I used to be able to withstand difficulty. They were not even too alarmed when they heard that I'd been arrested and detained, because they knew I was a strong person, I could withstand difficulties.

Note how the strength Ms Shezi registers above is turned literally inside out in the wake of her rape:_

> MS SEROKE: The whole time you were quiet and not sharing this with anybody and you say even your mom is hearing this for the first time that you were gang-raped. How did you feel about this?
> MS SHEZI: Within myself it was very painful. It was very painful. Even now I'm suffering from a womb. It's as if there's something jumping inside my womb and I still have those physical pains. Even other people tell you you're just cold. Even if I get involved with relationships, they say to me I'm frigid and I'm just cold. Because if I get involved with a man I get very scared. I can't allow myself to be involved and love the person. (HRVTRANS 28–29 July 1997 – JOHANNESBURG; emphasis added)

This is a common symptom of rape victim survivors. But if what if we were to read this response not only as 'symptom' – not even primarily, for the purposes of this exploration, as symptom – but rather as that to which we might respond with reciprocity? We would need to find a way to respond that does not entail further objectification of the victim-survivor. We would need to disassociate the narrator's status as victim from the social construct of shame, since – as the victim herself points out – it is this very status as victim within the public sphere that results in the risk of her further objectification:

> MS MKHIZE: That is why you say you don't need any pity. You don't see yourself as a person who needs any pity. You see yourself as a hero.
> MS SHEZI: I do want people to empathise with me and share the pain with me, *but I do not want them to reduce me to an object and see me as just nothing.* (HRVTRANS 28–29 July 1997 – JOHANNESBURG; emphasis added)

While acknowledging their subjection, women also perform their resistance to that subjection. Just as Thandi Shezi wants to share her pain without being victimized – a desire that cannot be fulfilled within the law of the speakable that constructs women as victims within the stigma-shame-insanity nexus – women can and do speak against their subjection: but, as we shall see, they put themselves at risk in doing so.

## Risking Performing Resistance

### The Potential of the Performative

In order to understand the structure and risk of performing one's rejection of the position of negative moral and social worth to which one is assigned, I shall rehearse Judith Butler's theory of implicit censorship in some detail. Butler enacts a debate in her work between Austin and Bourdieu on the one hand, and Derrida and Shoshana Felman on the other. Austin points out that performative speech works because it derives its forcefulness, and thus its efficacy, through recourse to established conventions. Bourdieu builds on this argument to account for what Butler calls the 'thinness' of Austin's theory in terms of the social context of performative language. For, as I noted earlier, performatives do not rest on a static series of conventions that Austin assumes (according to Bourdieu) to be inherent to language; to cite Bourdieu once again: 'Authority comes to language from outside' (Bourdieu 1980: 109). As I have outlined above, instances of effective performativity mark the conventional power of certain institutions being assigned to language in those instances. A performative that works depends upon the person speaking it having been authorized to do so by social convention.

The strength of Bourdieu's theory is that it underlines the way in which social conventions underwrite speech to produce the embodied subject. As I outlined earlier, in the context of my discussion of what constitutes the speakable in Butler's terms, our social understanding of the rules of convention is embodied in a bodily understanding, or habitus. Bourdieu's habitus, I highlighted, is not limited to the self-conscious adherence to social dictates. Yet Bourdieu's under-standing can be seen to be as static as Austin's in that neither account for the fact that conventions change. Despite his critique of Austin's formalism, Bourdieu's description of the practice of the habitus does not account for change, let alone breaks in, social conventions.

This is where Felman and Derrida come in. Felman (cited in Butler 1997: 141) points out that the body, so crucial to Bourdieu's conception of the speech act as possessing – or being possessed by – a social, embodied context, can under-take actions that are in contradiction with the ostensible meaning of the words which that body speaks. In this way, gesture can betray the ostensible adher-ence of the speaker to social convention, or the rules of censorship, broadly defined. In addition, Derrida contributes to the sense of ways in which language may break with its conventional context to create new meaning. For if conven-tion resides in (re)iterability, Derrida (cited in Butler 1997: 147–50) argues that every sign marks a break from its semantic context structurally: the force of the performative, then, resides not in its adherence to (in Derrida's case, semantic) conventions, but in the very impossibility of the performative, as sign, to be commensurate with its 'putative [site of] production or origin' (Cassiem et al. 1997; Butler 1997: 148).

The arguments of Bourdieu and Derrida each exhibit, according to Butler, a weakness; and these weaknesses can be revised to understand the mutuality of the social and the linguistic in the constitution of a performative: what I call its culture. Bourdieu's insistence on the prior authorization of the speaker as an essential condition for the success of the performative is profoundly conserva-tive, in the sense that it rules out those cases in which, without prior authoriza-tion, a performative gains authority: Butler mentions Rosa Parks as a case in point. On the other hand, Derrida configures the radical break all signs make from their previous iterations as a structural force of separation inherent in performatives as signs used in a context in which the semantic and the structural are always at war with one another. This excludes the question of the social contingency of performatives altogether, dehistoricizing the linguistic act.

At this stage I want to foreground once again the Austinian notion of ritual as the form of all performatives. Here ritual does not refer merely to the conservative aspect of social convention that delimits the effect of performatives beforehand, as Bourdieu would have it. Nor would (or could) it refer to the Derridean concep-tion of the structural 'subversion' inherent in all performatives as signs, since this is a linguistic formulation that excludes social context. Instead,

> [...] the performative is not a singular act used by an already established subject, but one of the powerful and insidious ways in which subjects are called into social being from diffuse social quarters, inaugurated into sociality by a variety of diffuse and powerful interpellations. In this sense the social performative is a crucial part not only of subject formation, but of the ongoing political contestation and reformulation of the subject as well. The performative is not only a ritual practice: it is one of the influential rituals by which subjects are formed and reformulated. (1997: 160)

The ritual of the performative, then – what we may call its culture – can be exercised both in the subjection and instantiation of othered (quasi)subjects. How do women's narratives reflect the latter capacity of the culture of the performative, that is, its potential to 'reformulate' the subject?

In Butler's scheme, the subject is not seen as sovereign. She cannot be 'free' of her socialization in any simple way. It is true that her socialization within the habitus will create certain dispositions which 'incline' the subject to 'act in relative conformity with the ostensibly objective demands of the field' (1997: 155). However, the subject is not a slave to such demands; the subject cannot and should not be thought of exclusively as a victim. For to conceive of the subject in such a way is not only to acknowledge the force of the conventional performative: it is to mythologize the origins of the conventional performative, as though such origins lay outside the realm of human speech and bodies. Such mythologizing would replicate the myth of apartheid itself in terms of its structure of totalitarianism.

What we need to do, then, is acknowledge the complexity of the performative as a ritual 'by which subjects are formed and reformulated'. Butler points out that there is a tacit performativity to power that has effects which are both injurious and productive. This complex concept of performativity allows us to understand how conventional performatives can be appropriated, not necessarily consciously, in contexts, moments and bodily actions that defy the traditional, conservative power of the conventional performative. Butler uses the example of hate speech here. Hate speech subjects those it censures to harm. Yet we know from Rosa Parks, Nelson Mandela, not to mention the shepherd Lekotse, and numerous others that the very terms of that speech – both explicit, as in 'black', 'nigger', 'kaffir', and implicit, as in s/he is not a person, not a subject – can be reappropriated by the margins precisely in order to enact a critique of their dominant, or conventional, terms of reference.

In the final section of her argument, Butler points to the challenges involved in undertaking such a critique. Anyone who moves outside the range of conventional meaning – who speaks without the prior authorization Bourdieu highlights as necessary for the effective performative – whether it be with the aim of critiquing that meaning or not, jeopardizes her status as a subject. Performing within the limited zone between conservatism and stasis on the one hand, and what is all too easily perceived as the mutterings of the insane on the other, is a risky business. Yet it is also true that those most inclined to take such risks are subjects already put in jeopardy by the status quo. Put bluntly, the subjectivity of the black, the woman, the homosexual has already been put at risk: and not by the subjects in question. *How do the black South African women-narrators I discuss here take the risk of speaking as subjects that are implicitly censored?* In a play between appearing to meet certain conventions, yet appropriating those conventions to exercise their own subjectivity – despite the high risk of being disregarded, unheard, unrecognized as persons – these subjects become adept at taking the risk of acting *as if they were* persons, in order to create opportunities for eliciting a commensurate response to their performance, a response that recognizes their authority as subjects.

*So What's New? – Imagining Women as Subjects*

The narratives I address here are deliberately drawn from a set of contexts that range between the public and the private: a play set consciously within the realm of the domestic – Fatima Dike's *So What's New*; narratives generated by women in the physical space of their own homes in Soweto in the 1990s; and some extracts from narratives gathered in the context of focus group discussions held in 2006 to generate information about the relationship between gender-based violence and coercion, and the spread of HIV/AIDS in rural KwaZulu-Natal (Boyce, Jolly et al. 2003–2006). I do this in order to indicate the tension that these contexts raise between the need for a protected space for the perform-ance of women's identities on the one hand, and the need for public recognition of women's subjectivity on the other. While women *may* find protection in the sanctuary of their homes – it would be unwise in Soweto as elsewhere to assume the home in general as a sanctuary for women – this intimate communication cannot be both protected *and* the site of a public performance of women's subject status. A further tension obtains in the juxtaposition of women's ideals of independence, agency and reciprocal acknowledgement, and their experi-ences of abuse, deprivation and denial.

The desire to see 'the rediscovery of the ordinary' performed in the wake of – and in resistance to – what Ndebele in the mid-1980s phrased as a debili-tating culture of the spectacular geared towards the opposition of apartheid, motivates Loren Kruger's 1995 review entitled '*So What's New?*: Women and Theater in the "New South Africa"':

> The political force of anti-apartheid theater depended on exploding the boundaries between public and private spaces, between the political and the domestic spheres. Intimacy became impossible or dangerous in a state that had outlawed normal daily life for most of the population. In the last few years, however, writers and performers, many of them women, have returned to the representation of domestic space, inner life and fantasy. In the South African context, this return does not signify a retreat into the confines of the naturalist box. Rather, it heralds an attempt to rediscover the intimate spaces buried by the turmoil of the last several decades, and to explore the possibili-ties of genres and modes of performance – melodrama, fantasy, even soap opera – previously ignored or dismissed as escapist, irrelevant, or, worse, emasculating. (Kruger 1995: 51)

While I agree with Kruger's reading of the discourse of private and public space under apartheid, I have questions about the conceptualization of her critique.

Firstly, I would argue that it is impossible for a majority of women to have 'returned' to the representation of the domestic, since the history of published and performed black women's creative work in South Africa is short, and notably dominated by a profound reluctance to discuss private or domestic space. Miriam Tlali, the first black woman to have published a novel in South Africa, pointedly excluded the domestic life of her protagonist, Muriel, in *Between Two Worlds*, arguing that it is only in post-apartheid South Africa that women have been able to write about the violence of black patriarchy that underscores any revelation of the domestic (Tlali 1998: 146–47). Any attempt to do this prior to 1991 was read as black women selling out the struggle. Similarly, when Kathy Perkins interviews Fatima Dike about the situation of black women in theatre in the new South Africa, asking if it has improved, Dike responds:

> Yes. There is a lot more freedom. If one wants to do something, you don't have that fear of what are the brothers going to say. You just go on and do what you want to do. You see, what governed us before was the struggle. I couldn't have written *So, What's New?* in the 1970s, as much as I would have loved to. The whole idea was that we had to harness our power together to fight the struggle through theatre. (1998a: 25)

Secondly, while I appreciate Kruger's call to see the 'the representation of domestic space, inner life and fantasy' (1995) in women's cultural productions, she makes this call without seeming, in the rest of her review, to understand the risks taken by women attempting to perform in public the parameters of intimate, domestic space. For this task may be nominally 'permitted' by the demise of apartheid, but it is certainly not enabled by the still extant patriarchal structures of society at large.

Kruger's review of theatre in the 'new South Africa' calls for a validation of genres conventionally ascribed to women – 'melodrama, fantasy, even soap opera' – and speaks of the 1994 Grahamstown Festival as revaluing these 'allegedly effeminate genres'; yet she goes on to give a somewhat less than glowing review of Fatima Dike's *So What's New?* 'Like the soap opera the women watch, *So What's New?* has a meandering, gossipy plot that revolves around its characters rather than developing them; it also relies too often on emotion at the expense of complex feeling' (54). While earlier in the review Kruger points to the difficult heritage of black women in terms of large, commercial South African productions in which women's bodies are used as exotic spectacles, her comments nevertheless suggest that roles for black women should now be able to accommodate the intimate, or what she terms 'complex feeling'. Yet the fact that these roles offer women, both actors and those in the audience, the opportunity to act as legitimate subjects in an arena in which the stakes are not as high as those involved in TRC testimony, or even drama of a more confessional cast, is in itself significant. I would *not* call Dike's drama unsubtle or simple; but it may well lack the kind of 'complexity' desired by viewers seeking representations of 'true South African women' in the transitional era (Dike's play was first performed in 1991 at the Market Theatre, Johannesburg). Dike offers no such apparently high-minded fare, resulting, perhaps, in Kruger's criticism for the play's melodrama, but praise for the 'resilience' of the characters, who watch *The Bold and the Beautiful* for entertainment, yet must contend with an extremely violent existence outside the confines of the set, which comprises the house of the key character – Big Dee – in Soweto. While Kruger refers to the soap opera element of the play as 'necessary escapism', this would seem to undermine the fact that the three protagonists – Dee, who runs a shebeen (an illicit bar or club), Thandi, who runs drugs, and Pat, who is a housing sales agent in Soweto – cannot watch the soap opera without playing with the idea of themselves as appropriate actors and subjects worthy of representation.[12] The three have a shared history of performing in a popular but ill-paid singing trio, the Chattanooga Sisters, and fantasize, together with Dee's daughter, Mercedes, about returning to the performing life. They decide, at one point, that the South African Broadcasting Association (SABC) should do a soap opera about them:

> THANDI  We're not rich enough.
> DEE  We're not beautiful enough.
> PAT  Between you and Big Dee we're rich enough, and I'm beautiful enough for all of us.
> DEE  Raaaaa!
> THANDI  Speak for yourself.
> PAT  Alright then, it can happen in the future, in the new South Africa. I'll be Patricia Mahambezuza of the Mahambehlala Estate agency and I'll sell houses only to the rich and the famous. I'll run advertisements in all the Sunday papers in the country.
> DEE  Dream on. I love this. And me – what will I be in the soap?
> THANDI  You'll be the shebeen queen of course.
> DEE  What?
> PAT  Oh ja, you'll run a high class shebeen. Remember that Italian's house in Saxonwold? I'll sell it to you. Everyone will want it, even Ridge [the hero of the soap opera]. (Dike 1998b: 33)

Pat goes on to fantasize about taunting Ridge with the prospect of the house, and finally betraying him, after he has made love to her in Sun City on the Wild Coast, by selling it to Big Dee.

In fact, there are many indications of the women's desire to have men see how they treat women as objects by treating men as objects in their turn, using them as they feel they have been used as women. This works not only at the level of fantasy but also in terms of form. While Percy Mtwa, Mbongeni Ngema and Barney Simon in *Woza Albert!* (1990) include a scene in which the apartheid authorities attempt to seduce Morena (God) away from espousing the black cause by giving him the key to Sun City and the girls to go with it, Dike includes the Sun City element in an ironic turn that highlights the men's use of women as mere sex objects. The emphasis on identity as performed, rather than pre-given, enables the women character's sense of themselves as subjects throughout, in contradiction to this patriarchal commodification of their bodies. At one point, lines spoken by Pat and Dee highlight the role of wife as precisely that: a role, no more, no less. The discussion takes place, inevitably, in relation to the characters of *The Bold and the Beautiful*:

---

12  I am deeply indebted to Lori Dawn Pollock, whose discussion of the play in her PhD thesis informs my reading of it (Pollock 2000: 282–97).

PAT   Why does Clark always mess his relationships up?
DEE   Because he is arrogant and he thinks he is God's gift to women. He is
not afraid to stand in church and promise to love and cherish any woman till
death parts them in front of a minister before God.
PAT   'Till death do us part'. I think that *line* is stupid. (1998b: 43; emphasis
added)

Dee's syntax suggests that the marriage itself erases communication between
husband and wife at the moment of the union, a sort of death; and Pat's diction
proposes that the marriage promise is merely a 'line', both in the sense of a role
that can be rejected, and a set of expectations sold to an unwitting prospective
bride. Finally, should we believe that the women are unaware of the dangers
of 'lines' sold to others for financial gain, all three women at various points
express their dismay at the fact that their livelihood depends on taking advantage of others, through alcohol, drug abuse and, in the case of Thandi, the
selling of houses to couples whom she knows will default on their mortgage
because their incomes are insufficient to make the purchase. Should there
be any doubt that these characters are savvy as to the 'line' being sold them
by North American television, Pat's comment reflects the double edge of the
capitalist/consumption conundrum: 'Hey I love ads'. she announces in the first
scene of the play. 'They give me a chance to grab another beer' (28). The play as
a whole, then, is not so easily dismissed, even as *necessary* escapism.

### Women's Life Narratives: Resilience in Performing the Gap between the Actual and the Desired

I came across this same sense of contradiction between lived and desired lives,
specifically with regard to marriage, when I visited three women I was interviewing in Moroka (a district in Soweto) in December 1998. I did this in connection with a project Miriam Tlali and I were pursuing, exploring gender violence
and its effects on women's lives during the apartheid era. These women are in
their seventies or older and have worked all their lives. They are not middle
class, but would have been under circumstances that did not entail apartheid
and its concomitant marriage laws, specifically as they related to black women.
One is a retired teacher, one a retired nurse, and the host was my colleague,
Miriam Tlali.

We met at Miriam's house in Moroka, Soweto; but before we did so, the
teacher insisted on showing me her house, where we had tea. She had done
much to improve her house over the years. This turned out to be a goal and
point of pride for a number of the women I have worked with: those who
have managed to keep their houses despite profligate and alcoholic husbands,
who have threatened their status as homeowners over the years. When we got
to Miriam's house, the same ritual of beverages and conversation took place,
focusing on a photo album that one of the women had brought with her. I knew
that our interviewees, Miriam's guests, had been abused by their husbands; yet
the photo album focused on wedding pictures. When I hinted, after a couple of

hours, that we might get down to business soon, the women stopped me. We were to eat a lunch of Soweto chicken first. Then we would 'go in the back' to talk.

After lunch we made our way to the garage, where Miriam has a couch, a desk, her books and a computer under a sheet. This was a clear demarcation of space. Miriam's house consists of two tiny bedrooms, a kitchen, a small living-dining area, and a small bathroom, none of which showed signs of her profession as a researcher and writer. Here, in the back on the cement floor, Miriam's most treasured possessions – her manuscripts and the like – are kept. And it was here that the women broke out of a mould of polite conversation and started ordering me to tell people 'outside' what their lives are like on the 'inside', in strident and unambiguous terms.

It took me a long time to make sense of the juxtaposition represented by these two spaces. To borrow Kruger's terms and use them in a different context, it seemed to me as if the photos of the proud family unit and all they stood for comprised a 'necessary escapism'. Yet I came to realize that this was not the case. The conversation and photos stood for a promise of what might have been. It was crucial for me to understand this promise, in order to understand the dimensions of the betrayal of these women in their lives subsequent to their marriages. Their bitterness is matched only by their resilience, as the following excerpts from their narratives demonstrate. These testimonies give plenty of evidence of the mixed response these women have had towards the transition. On the one hand, they are happy about the apparent independence granted to women, and are genuinely pleased that their material possessions cannot be plundered from them by their estranged husbands, who, nevertheless, still live with the women, who have been the primary breadwinners and are therefore the primary recipients of pensions now ('Thandi' 1996).[13]

The women's narratives demonstrate the fact that the new regime also has the potential to make promises that will be betrayed, just as these women experience the betrayal of their marriage vows. This woman's rejection of marriage is couched in the tensive space between welcoming the new legal rights of women and a profound skepticism about the ability of these rights to change the actual attitudes of men at the grass roots level:

> I am very thankful that we now have this government where we even have women in parliament to speak for us. We can now do our own thinking and not be dependent on what someone else thinks 'for us' [...]. These menfolk, even if things change, their arrogance and conceit does not stop – say what you like [...] when things are now different.
>
> If someone were to say I must get married again, I would never make that mistake, never. ('Palesa' 1996)

Notice how this subject's expression of her fear, that the law will not deliver what it promises for women, can appear as Butler's illogical rambling to 'listeners' who are not disposed to hear what she is saying.

13  In fact, nurses in particular were termed 'jackpots' by men in terms of the potential marriage market, because of their earning power and related benefits.

How can she rejoice at the new dispensation, the notion that she will not have to have a man 'think for' her, this argument would go, yet at the same time say that men will continue to be arrogant and conceited, leading her to refuse the state of marriage, even under the new dispensation? Such a reading would deny this woman's key recognition of the fact that her subjectivity within the new dispensation is suspended between the promise of recognition (as in her marriage) and the possibility (if not probability) of the violation (as in the institution of marriage as she experienced it in the apartheid era).

This failure is experienced, in fact, by the second subject, who explains how the new government, just like the old, enables the situation in which her husband has the right to consume her property entirely:

> Looking at my retiring years, I started packing my bags and putting money in the bank and improving my house which was now a little bigger [...]. He [her husband] retired in 1992. He was given R5000 which he spent so fast and was left with nothing. I joined him [in retirement] in March 1994 and received my benefits from Old Mutual and from Home Trust known as Metropolitan. The Department [of Education] delayed in paying me but eventually I got a good sum and channelled it properly. So my husband applied for old age pension and made a mistake by handing over my bank book which carried deep secrets. The answer he received was go home and enjoy your wife's money. It is too much. What is all that? This is apartheid continued even by the new government of the day [...]. What a sad ending. ('Thandi' 1996)

Key to the current South African government's stated policy of enabling women at the grass roots level is a considerable demonstration of will and the commitment of adequate resources, financial and otherwise, to ensure that women are not once again betrayed, this time not only through marriage but also by the state's actual reneging on its promise that women and men are equal subjects before the law, and that their 'treatment' by the law should reflect this equality. What the narrative over pension rights tells us is that many women are still not perceived as worthy of owning property; they (and their goods) *are* property, still owned by men, the new Constitution notwithstanding. If ownership of property equates to the extent to which a subject can exercise democratic rights – not just voting, but, for example, the legal contestation of the pension official's ruling in the case outlined above – this bodes ill for the quotidian reality of the vast majority of women in South Africa's new democracy.

Women, as we shall see in Chapter 4, are often puzzlingly 'complicit' with the structures that position them as subject to patriarchal interests. In the context of increasing commodification, women themselves may come to see themselves as 'proper(tied)' subjects in relation to how much they own. This is evidenced by the work of Mark Hunter and others on the role of transactional sex in constructing women's desire: here women become involved in sexual relationships not only for subsistence, but to fulfil their desires for the 'three C's' – cash, car and cellphone – and other commodities. One response to this phenomenon invokes a moralistic tone to censure such behavior, positioning women as ignorant and/or 'sellouts' (Hunter 2002). However, the proto-capitalists of Dike's play suggest an alternative: women may exercise their desire for material goods *with* an awareness of the risks involved in the social performance of their desire and its fulfilment, doing so in hope of a different future, however imperfect

Women negotiate the gap between the actual and the desired, and the burden it places upon them, by placing worth on the future in terms of their children's lives. The character of Mercedes, Big Dee's daughter, figures this potential in terms of both risk and possibility in *So What's New?* Her name reflects the risk of becoming the commodity, as does her desire for her boyfriend; the fact that the fantasy of women's independence ends with a gunfight outside that concludes the play with the women taking shelter in fear of their lives under-lines this risk. Nevertheless, there are also signs that Mercedes imagines her relationship with her boyfriend and their prospects for the future differently from Big Dee's generation. This moment is poignantly enunciated by an inter-viewee from among the women in our focus group aged 25–35, presumably of an age with Big Dee, Pat and Thandi (Boyce, Jolly et al. 2003–2006). I end with the resonances one can find in her testimony, as I frame it, with Dike's play, in that both perform risk and resilience, where resilience is properly interpreted as resistance in terms of the immense burden the limitations of the speakable imposed upon this speaking subject:

> What is problematic nowadays is that we as women are enlightened, when there is a problem and you realize that you are being abused, you want to find the solution for that problem, whilst trying to find the solution, there is that pressure coming from men, they oppress you at that point and that makes it difficult. Maybe it will be easy for the next generation of women because as it is whatever we are doing, we do it for the sake of our children, so that they will live better in their times. (Boyce, Jolly et al. 2006)

## Postscript: A Dedication to 'The Ladies' of Soweto

Out of gratitude and respect for Miriam Tlali and 'the ladies', as she calls her friends, I wish to mark their generosity and their achievement. When I first attempted to interview 'the ladies', they refused to meet with me in person until I had explained to them in detail, using Miriam as an intermediary, precisely why I was interested in their lives. Once again, this indicates the need to protect the self from abuse, in this case the abuse of story-stealing and/or voyeuristic spectatorship: the turning of the self into an object.

The statement I wrote for them did not take the form of telling them why their stories were important to the oral, historical record. They told Miriam that they knew why that was the case, and had had enough of white people coming into Soweto 'from the university' and getting information from them without giving anything back. They demanded that I write a life narrative of my own, which they used to judge whether they would enter into a relationship with me or not. They responded sympathetically to parts of my narrative, parts that they saw as testimony to a somewhat difficult life: I was amazed, for I had never thought I had the right to see my life in that way. The women were quite willing to afford me the subject status that has eluded them, almost all their lives, in the society in which they live.

This community initially responded to my approach with astute scepticism: they knew little of me and feared exploitation. Yet in the process of protecting themselves from me, they got together to discuss strategy, developing a social fabric that has, in fact, nothing to do with me: tea, shopping days, even the option of spending nights in one another's houses when they have been, or are in danger of being, abused. This, then, is the space in which they become, albeit provisionally, subjects in their own right.

Here, the women are effectively – but of necessity, informally, without the assistance of professional counsellors – creating the space which Thandi Shezi calls for in her TRC testimony, when asked by Commissioner Mkhize what she, Thandi Shezi, would suggest to assist survivors of sexual assault such as herself:

MS SHEZI: I think what could help them, is that our Government must make a women centre where women can go and *voice their innermost feelings* and concern, because it would seem in most cases our Government looks after male needs and I think we played a very important role in the struggle and the history.

And some of our guys, the males who were beaten up, but then they didn't have to go through that sore that we went through, but if there could be like centres, counselling centres and give women something to do, give them an opportunity to express themselves.

As I have spoken here, I'll go home with this trauma, but fortunately I have been receiving this counselling, but what about somebody else who have (sic) experienced similar situations and they just go back with the wound having been opened and thereafter they don't get any assistance in the form of counselling and support.

So if there could be some kind of centres where that could support women who have gone through similar experiences. (HRVTRANS 28–29 July 1997 – JOHANNESBURG; emphasis added)

While the institutionalized space Thandi Shezi recommends has not materialized in any significant way for the vast majority of South African women, the Sowetan 'ladies' have demonstrated their resourcefulness in developing a limited context in which, at the very least, making the category of the unspeakable the subject of conversation becomes possible. This always-vulnerable-to-rupture social cohesion is a strategy for survival. Sadly, it is a social space whose very constitution involves the protection of the women from their spectral status in the society at large. As such, it cannot impinge upon the very institutions that appear unable to imagine women's status as subjects, let alone their acts of agency.

The opportunities for institutional listening to women in a context in which they command full status as subjects in their own right remain few and far between in post-apartheid South Africa. Yet women's dramatic performance of themselves as persons who (should) enact their full rights under the new Constitution will continue to play a crucial role in marking the need for translation of women's rights to subject status into actuality. The Sowetan 'ladies' see their gift to me not as a gift but as the reciprocal acknowledgement of one's person that is the right of all women. It is to Miriam Tlali and her 'ladies', then, that this chapter properly belongs.

## CHAPTER 4

# Men 'Not Feeling Good': The Dilemmas of Hyper-masculinity in the Era of HIV/AIDS

I have addressed the roles that concepts of non-human animals, children, women and, specifically, abused women, play in determining the actual living conditions of these subjects in terms of their relationships with their immediate families, their communities, the state, the public, and their negotiation of their own identities within these complex networks. Now I wish to turn to the question of male agency in the current post-apartheid era. If I had concluded with the last chapter, my project would risk implying that masculine agency in South Africa is not only essentially violent, but overwhelmingly powerful. In this chapter I would like to demonstrate that *fear* of the shame instantiated by entry into the domain of the speakable and the subject's simultaneous bearing witness to her desubjectification, constitute a crucial element in understanding *men*'s specific, complex vulnerability within the post-apartheid landscape: this vulnerability can translate on the one hand into violence, but on the other into a positive resilience.

Men, open to alternative ways of thinking and being, do renegotiate relationships with the women and men in their lives to redistribute gendered power. As always, this re-imagining and enacting of private space cannot be viewed as a triumph over prevailing political, social and discursive practices. Just as the women of Soweto with whom I worked were able to form a private network of support that was limited in its scope; just as the final scene of So What's New? frames the women's sanctuary of play within a space increasingly threatened by external violence as the drama concludes; so are individual men's desires and actions to improve gender relations circumscribed by the public, national, communal and legal contexts within which they undertake change. In this respect, the resilience I refer to above designates men's ability not only to make changes in terms of gender relations within their personal relations but also to negotiate, simultaneously, the constraints that spheres beyond the home, beyond the personal, bring to their crucial, alternative performances of masculinity. In a chapter that reflects upon the narratives of rural men attempting to renegotiate power relations within their personal relationships, Tina Sideris acknowledges the hopefulness that such narratives represent in terms of their 'openness to new ways of thinking and a commitment to trying to find ways to relate that are not oppressive'. However, she cautions,

> In [the kind of work that] focuses on the details of personal relationships between men and women, there is a danger of celebrating the creative force of human agency, whilst ignoring the power of deeper psychological anxieties and wider social structures that sustain relations of domination and subordination. For men who experience the contradictions between received interpretations of gender and lived relations the challenge lies in shifting the discussion from the private to making links between personal and relational struggles and wider structures of privilege. (2005: 135)

This chapter looks at the power of deeper psychological anxieties and wider social structures that sustain relations of domination and subordination in contemporary South Africa, by tracing narratives of masculine vulnerability through a series of overlapping lenses: the constitutional declaration of women's rights; the challenges presented by the phenomenon of the HIV/AIDS epidemic, especially in terms of the linked discourses it has generated between HIV/AIDS stigma and the call for men to change their attitudes and behaviour in relation to sexual behaviour; the politics of the distinctive mix of liberal economic policy, the African Renaissance and the AIDS denialism of Thabo Mbeki; and the juxtaposition of this politics with the entirely different attractions that Zuma, as a populist and as an explicit performer of a particularly highly profiled image of Zulu masculinity, holds for his ardent supporters. To address the challenge Sideris proposes, that of linking private and public worlds, I draw, once again, from a range of narrative sources: personal, political, analytical and fictional.

I begin with what constitutional change, in terms of the legal provisions intended to ensure gender equality, means on the ground in the post-apartheid state. It is, of course, impossible to address how constitutional change has comprehensively affected the variety of individual men from a vast range of gendered, racial, ethnic and culturally diverse contexts. The point I want to start from here is, however, one made by several observers of masculinity in the post-apartheid period: that at the very moment the Constitution appears to a variety of men to imply, through its provisions on gender, that heterosexual men have been and are in privileged positions of power, many men who identify as heterosexual experience their current reality as one in which their power is being increasingly diminished, rather than one in which women have acquired rights that men have always and are currently enjoying (Jolly and Jeeves forthcoming).

The Pressure of the Dual Panopticon: The Gaze of the Law and the Gaze of Social Sanction on African Masculinity

The Zulu men in the area of rural Sisonke, KwaZulu-Natal, in which we have been working since 2003, describe rights as a zero-sum game[1]: if women are achieving constitutional rights, men must be losing them (Boyce, Jolly et al. 2003–2006). Both men and women report that when women are challenged on their behaviour by men, they respond '*Savota 50/50*', meaning 'we voted for equal rights'. The numerical expression of the gender equality provisions manifests the notion that rights belong to a closed set that can only be divided among 'recipients', not extended beyond the set. This concept of the allotment of rights, combined with a sense that the post-apartheid era has increased, not decreased, poverty in the rural areas, means that many of the men (and some women) we interviewed construct the constitutional provisions on gender equality as a kind of malevolent third party that destroys 'proper' or idealized relations between men and women. Men view South Africa's human rights legislation as yet another aspect of post-apartheid modernity that threatens their traditional role and sources of authority: 'What has happened now, is that roles have been reversed. Men are now oppressed. Because of Human Rights (women's rights), women are now able to take men to court if they fail to support them and their children financially' (2003–2006). As one woman put it, 'I would say human rights laws really affect men's relations with women because men don't even want to hear that [...] men and women have equal rights, they hate it so much, it doesn't make them feel good' (2003–2006).

This 'not feeling good' is borne out by the men's interviews. One informant explicitly links the emotional vulnerability of 'not feeling good' as a consequence of women's constitutional rights to increased violence against female partners. The legally expressed rights empower women nominally, but not in actual fact; and the insecurity they (literally) engender in men provokes, by men's own reckoning, men's violence:

> The extent of the violence that men mete out to women these days is also fuelled by their (men's) perception of women's rights. These days when a man beats his wife, he is often scared that if he leaves her alive she will take the matter to the police and he will definitely be condemned by the justice system which favours women. (Boyce, Jolly et al. 2003–2006)

Such narratives express frustration with the Constitution's 'prevention' of men enacting roles they perceive to be appropriate. The informant who speaks of women's rights as an incentive to increased violence against women provides information that appears to support the link between an increased sense of vulnerability as a man and the impulse to respond with violence towards women (Jolly and Jeeves forthcoming). This response is certainly underscored

---

1 I am grateful to Alan Jeeves for the conceptualization of rights from men's perspectives as a zero sum game.

by Isak Niehaus in his study of rape in the Bushbuckridge area of the Lowveld. He demonstrates that

> in many cases there was a significant disjuncture between masculine ideals and the real-life situation of rapists. Far from being 'men of men', men who rape often fail to meet the conventional challenges of masculinity: many were young, unemployed, petty criminals, cheated by their wives and lovers, or marginal elders. (2005: 83)

The 'not feeling good' referenced by our female research participant is not simply a matter of individual men feeling as if they are under intense scrutiny of law in terms of their relations with women and children. What comes out of the narratives is a sense of the pervasive scrutiny which men sense they come under from other men and the community at large, for not being able to act out dominant roles, as well as from the law, which many men view as having made illegal certain aspects of the performance of what is perceived to be a traditional male role, This is a reinvented version of the dilemma Bessie Head identified in her notoriously complex novel published in 1974. In *A Question of Power*, Elizabeth, the protagonist, a coloured woman, tells us that the best explanation for the emasculation of men under apartheid was given to her by 'an African man', who explains that being called a boy by a 'Boer' policeman renders him a boy, and not a man, in front of his girlfriend: 'How can a man be called a man when he is called a boy?' 'I was walking down the road the other day with my girl, and the Boer policeman said to me: 'Hey, boy, where is your pass?' Am I a man to my girl or a boy? Another man addresses me as boy. How do you think I feel?' (Head 1974: 45)

Here, in a profoundly gendered and racialized iteration of Althusserian hailing, the state, represented by the Boer policeman, interpolates the black man as 'boy'. Of course, the subject hailed in this instance cannot 'choose' not to understand that he is being hailed by the policeman, since immediate threat to him will ensue if he does not respond, albeit unwillingly. The subject, however, feels the gaze of a doubled panopticon: the stress, or 'not feeling good', comes from the state on the one hand, and on the other the female gaze of his girlfriend, whom he sees as perceiving him as inadequate in his inability to resist being interpolated as a boy.

We can identify the contemporary instance of such a doubled panopticon in current narratives that portray men as edging towards instantiation as subjects through desubjectification, and the shame that ensues. When men see themselves as trapped between the constitutional provisions on gender equality on the one hand, and on the other, the gaze of the community they perceive as expecting them to uphold an idealized version of masculine power, they find themselves under the scrutiny of both. Here, the Constitution and community take on the role of policing, the former supposedly enforcing constitutionally determined rights, while the community, which it is assumed comprises women and men performing traditional gender roles, expects masculinity, in exchange for the power it supposedly commands, to enact that power in the care of family and community. This power is ideally embodied in the male figure of 'an African man', and the community itself polices the adequacy with which men perform this role.

This gaze of the community, a panopticon policing of the performance of men in relation to an idealized expectation of manhood as both provider and reproducer, is explored in Siphiwo Mahala's novel published in 2007, *When a Man Cries*. Its narrator and protagonist, Themba Limba is, in the Althusserian sense of hailing, called to be a leader in the community – as a school principal and as a councillor for the township of Sekunjalo, adjacent to Grahamstown – yet is also instantiated as a disgraced subject. I will describe the reasons for this doubled movement of fortune in what follows. For the moment, however, Themba's description of his surprise at the nomination of him as a councillor by an elder – Old Man Jongilanga – demonstrates the fact that the gaze of the community on one's private life, whether approving or disapproving, is intense. Jongilanga nominates Themba because the elder recognizes Themba as one who knows both the poverty of the township and the educated ways of those in power. Themba goes up against a nominee who is perceived as a hero of the struggle, his rival Skade, but Jongilanga makes such a powerful nominating speech on his behalf that Themba wins the vote: 'It was clear that Jongilanga's words had pierced everybody's heart. It is amazing that as you walk around living your life people are actually observing and analysing you, documenting your actions and behaviour in their minds' (Mahala 2007: 68). This awareness leads Themba to realize that certain aspects of his life are best kept secret.

Themba's rise within the community is accompanied by opportunities to exploit and abuse the women with whom he comes into contact. Despite his marriage to Thuli, he revels in his temptation 'by' (as he sees it) a series of girls and women, among them Dolly, the mayor's secretary, whom he seduces with the promise of paying half the rent of her apartment; and the student, Nosipho, who comes to him for help in his capacity as headmaster, and whom he subsequently rapes. We later find out that not only is Nosipho HIV positive but she is also Themba's daughter, the product of a sexual relationship he had with Gladys, his aunt.

Gladys's current gold-digging boyfriend, Jack, tells her that Vusi, her husband and Themba's uncle, is having an affair. Gladys pays Jack to teach Vusi a lesson. Jack subsequently kills Vusi, inheriting, as it were, his wife, Gladys, and his prosperous businesses. Gladys takes sexual solace in the young Themba (at a time when he is drunk). She confesses to him her pact with her boyfriend, who has now turned violent. Themba returns to the house of his parents and discloses to them Gladys's conspiracy with Jack, which resulted in her husband's death, and Gladys is subsequently arrested. However, Themba never reveals to his parents his sexual relationship with his aunt.

The rehearsal of sexual power and domination in front of the community is represented in many narratives as key to the making of a man. As a youth, Themba seeks for places to take Thuli, his girlfriend, for sex, and settles on the room of his friend Sizwe. To reach this venue he and Thuli need to pass by a gang, the Mongroes, who challenge the couple to stop. Themba, thinking he sees a knife in a gang member's hand, drops Thuli's hand and runs to Sizwe's for sanctuary. One of the gang members throws a rock at his retreating head. He later tells Sizwe that he got in a fight with ten Mongroes. Sizwe responds that the Mongroes don't fight; they kill. Themba explains that he was attacked from behind but grabbed a stick and retaliated. Just when he remembers he deserted Thuli at the scene of the attack, she arrives unscathed: her brother is a member of the gang. She challenges Themba with desertion; he claims he went to fetch a stick: 'In the olden days having a scar at the back of your head was a sign of cowardice. That's because in those days men carried sticks wherever they went. As a modern man I did not carry a stick all the time. There was no shame in running to fetch one' (Mahala 2007: 33).

Themba takes care to explain to his readers, whom he assumes to be aligned with the panopticon policing of his masculinity, that he is not, in fact, a coward who deserted his girlfriend and ran away from his attackers.

This policing of masculinity is rehearsed when Themba turns up at the apartment of Dolly, the mayor's secretary – the one for which he pays half the rent. He goes there for solace after the mayor has turned down a challenge he has made in requesting the Council to spend money on his ward's drinking water and sanitation services, rather than a proposed park. He finds the mayor ensconced with Dolly, and later reflects that his relationship with Dolly has probably affected the mayor's negative decision in relation to his ward's appeals for services. Once again Themba, as narrator, defends himself to the reader, claiming that his loss of Dolly to the mayor does not mean that he, Themba, is a loser: he is still a 'man's man':

> Bongani Vanaza appeared to be the winner because he had the authority and the money, but that did not make me a loser. I believe in the premise that to compromise under certain circumstances does not make me a weak man. Compromise is not always a bad thing. It is at times the best thing. It is better to compromise a situation than to compromise an idea, for a man and his idea are inseparable. To challenge an idea is to challenge the man. I shall not compromise my ideas.
>
> When I walked away from Dolly's flat, I knew that I was never going to retrace my steps. My experience that day taught me she lacked self respect, and I did not want to associate with such a woman. (2007: 83)

In this performance, Themba reinterprets his loss of Dolly to the mayor not as a slight to his manhood but as an event that demonstrates that he is a principled man. This re-creation of self is concluded by his transference of his own potential loss of self-respect – for having failed to gain the support of the mayor by 'virtue' of his dalliance with Dolly – onto Dolly herself: she now 'lack[s] self respect' (83). This reading overlooks the fact that Dolly depends upon her favour with the mayor for her job.

Elsewhere in the narrative Themba ascribes a negative morality to girls and women who engage in transactional sex, even for survival. He labels Nosipho, the girl he has raped who later turns out to be his daughter, as a girl who 'open[s] her thighs for any man' (98). Subsequently we find out that Nosipho is being raised by her grandmother and, furthermore, that her uncle, who also lives with her grandmother, is sexually abusing her. All these situations make her appearance with taxi drivers and in the beer hall suggest a context of transactional sex for physical and, conceivably, for psychological survival. Yet Themba himself expects to benefit from transactional sex. After he is appointed school principal, a former woman friend from university, Thandi Maduna, is hired, and Themba is surprised when she refuses his sexual advances and reports him for sexual harassment.

## Childhood Sexual Abuse, HIV/AIDS and the Secrets of Performing Masculinity: The Social Significance of Fiction

One of the ways in which Themba, Mahala's narrator, expresses his masculine identity to the reader is through his voluptuous descriptions of the women with whom he has sex. Except in the case of Thuli, the girlfriend who becomes Themba's wife, these sexual relations – with Aunt Gladys, with Dolly, with Nosipho – are ones in which women's physical bodies are described in great detail, 'firm breasts' and thighs abounding. However, there is a paradox here: Themba's reputation as a man of the community will be lost should these sexual exploits – the incestuous relations with his aunt, the adulterous relations with Dolly, the rape (later, it is revealed, the incestuous rape) of the schoolgirl Nosipho, and the sexual harassment of Ms Maduna – come to light. In this sense, the reader is the recipient of the sexual secrets that Themba believes bear witness to his masculine desires and thus his manhood. The revelation of these secrets to the gaze of social sanction would, however – and, in fact, does – collapse Themba's social status as a man of power, father of a family, and protector of a community. This process begins when Themba's wife Thuli, who works as a counsellor, counsels Nosipho. Thuli thus finds out about the rape and is made aware that Nosipho has tested positive for HIV. When Themba refuses to acknowledge his rape of Nosipho, or to take an HIV test, Thuli deserts him, taking their children.

In her ground-breaking article, 'The Scandal of Manhood', Posel (2005a) describes the ways in which the scandal of baby rape has projected men's sexual behaviour, especially predatory sexuality, into the forefront through a combination of factors: the complete reversal in the contemporary era of the suppression of sexual matters under apartheid, including rigid censorship; the drive of AIDS campaigns to encourage citizens to test for HIV, 'know their status', and combat the stigma of HIV infection through acknowledgement of one's status to at least one's family, if not the community at large; and the introduction of confession as a moral and restorative imperative through an extension of the culture of the Truth and Reconciliation Commission to the broader spheres of public life. Indeed, Posel argues, this move has of necessity meant a change in what is considered private and what is considered public: the laws protecting women and children from abuse have opened the gaze of the law into that most private of sanctuaries, the home. Posel is careful, however, to indicate that the discourse of sexual exposé was, in fact, probably supported by a prominent few rather than a widespread majority, precisely because it threatened to derail the positive image of the nascent Rainbow Nation. She addresses Mbeki's reluctance to acknowledge any crisis in sexual abuse in South Africa, and his deep scepticism about the reliability of rape statistics in the country – scepticism that carries the implication that such statistics have been inflated to undermine the country's stature and represent racist stereotyping:

> The fact that the rape issue had amplified into an indictment of the fledgling nation – with family and fatherhood, two of the pillars of nationhood, both scandalized – was bound to intensify the resistance to its visibility among those who favoured other tactics of nation- building. So although there have been few declarations of dissent from 'ordinary' members of the public, there is probably a wider public sympathy for those political leaders who have expressed their scepticism, and anger and/or discomfort, at the growing public fuss about rape and abuse; and this sympathy is expressed as much in their refusal to participate in the clamour of acknowledgement as in their spoken responses. President Thabo Mbeki, in particular, was slow to respond to the rape of Baby Tshepang, prompting accusations of indifference [from the press and NGOs offering support to victims of child abuse] (Posel 2005a: 249–250)

Posel (2005b) has also explored Mbeki's AIDS denialism in the context of the politicization of sexuality in post-apartheid South Africa, linking it very closely to the reasons for Mbeki's downplaying of the 'rape crisis'. If the scandal of rape were to be acknowledged, she argues, Mbeki would, in his eyes, be accepting a stereotype of over-sexed black masculinity inherited from the racist discourses of colonialism. Rejection of this stereotype has resurfaced again and again in Mbeki's speeches, and appears most prominently in contexts in which he perceives the black body to have been 'over'-sexualized through racist, colonialist discourse. The issues of sexual abuse and HIV/AIDS obviously form two key contexts in which Mbeki's denialism specifically rests on a rejection of the pornographic sexualization of black bodies. Placing these twin denials of sexual abuse and HIV/AIDS in the context of Mbeki's attempt, in his promotion of the African Renaissance, to combat what he sees as the politics of despair initiated and sustained by colonization, Posel marks African masculinity as the site of potential crisis for Mbeki's politics. If African 'sex produces death, then the infant nation is stillborn', she argues:

> The fatality of sex is anchored in the family itself – the crucible of the nation. Metaphorically, it is the very intimacy of the home – mother, father and children – which has become contaminated. And it is men particularly – the fathers and sons of the nation – whose moral credibility is most acutely called into question. (Posel 2005b: 148)

Reading Mahala's *When a Man Cries* (2007) in light of Posel's observation, we can see that Themba's narrative depends precisely on keeping secret the two aspects of his life that have the potential, in Posel's terms, to cause his masculinity to be perceived as scandalous, to pitch it into crisis. These are, first, his sexual abuse of Nosipho; and second, her infection with HIV, which renders him potentially HIV positive, either because he had HIV before raping her and has transmitted it to her, or because she has transmitted it to him. (Biologically speaking, the former is more likely than the latter; in terms of the fiction's somewhat vague portrayal of the time between the sexual abuse and Nosipho's death, it is difficult to determine whether Nosipho has been infected long enough, should Themba have been the transmitter, for her to have developed full-blown AIDS and have died from it.) Indeed, these stigmas are intimately twinned in the persona of Nosipho, as she turns out to be his daughter through his liaison with his Aunt Gladys: she manifests the concatenation of incest, abuse and HIV positivity.

In keeping with the discursive 'logic' of confession outlined by Posel, Themba eventually decides to attend Nosipho's funeral and claim her as his daughter. Yet the limitations of confession are marked in Mahala's story, since the many who promote it as a gesture of healing for the nation may have less to risk personally than the smaller number of exemplary confessors to having raped or having been raped, referenced by Posel. Themba does not speak in public at the funeral of his sexual abuse of Nosipho – only to us, his readers, does he reveal this secret; Thuli, his wife, knows about it, not because he confessed to her, however, but because Nosipho revealed it when she sought Thuli's help. The novel concludes with a reconciliation between Thuli and Themba, as Themba confesses generally to the fact that he has treated Thuli poorly in the past, and says he will not do so in the future; and she declares herself proud of him for 'owning up to' his relationship as parent to Nosipho. Two obvious omissions from this confession mark the conclusion. The first is the fact that Themba's parenting was not only absent from Nosipho but that it was, when present, incestuous, marked by sexual abuse. The second exclusion is the glaring omission from the reconciliation scene of any reference to HIV/AIDS: the reconciliation takes place in the house of Thuli's aunt, where Thuli had been living with the children since she deserted Themba, and she had made an HIV test a condition of her return to Themba.

The withholding of HIV status from the reader is a recognizable trope in HIV/AIDS narratives. Exemplary here is Jonny Steinberg's *Three-Letter Plague* (2008), a work of investigative journalism tracing the implications of the epidemic in a rural Xhosa community, focused on the perspective of a young man, Sizwe. The HIV status of Sizwe remains both a lure that keeps the reader engaged in the narrative and an unanswered question: while we find out that Jonny Steinberg is HIV negative, we never find out Sizwe's status. A related trope is that of the male protagonist who knows he is HIV positive, knows he could be saved by anti-retroviral drugs (ARVs), but refuses to take them. Here the unanswered question, much speculated upon, but never determined in any one-on-one relation of cause to effect, is the reason for the subject's refusal of the ARVs. This is modelled in Liz McGregor's *Khabzela* (2005), a study of Fana Khaba, an exceptionally popular DJ on Yfm, Gauteng's most recognized youth radio station. Khaba declared his positive status on the radio and had financial access to ARVs and an entirely supportive work environment. Yet he abandoned ARV therapy to pursue alternative therapies, including those of traditional healers, miracle drug purveyors and the much-touted, immune-boosting foods that figure prominently in the recommendations of South Africa's erstwhile denialist Health Minister, Manto Tshabalala-Misimang.

While the material on Thabo Mbeki's denialism focuses on his ideology of the residual effects of the stigma of colonialist images of black sexuality, and of the immorality of blacks and their incapacity to govern effectively, investigative journalists such as Steinberg and McGregor perform the important task of linking the attitudes of the President to those of a majority of South Africans: 'Never, in all the acres of newsprint and film footage [...] [has there been] a word about South Africans' own deeply ambivalent views on the subject [of ARVs]', says McGregor (2005: 244).

These secrets surrounding sexual abuse, HIV status and the reasons for rejecting ARVs, either in totality or in terms of their sole use for therapy, are in no way morally or ethically commensurate with one another: sexual abuse of a minor is not of the same order of seriousness as keeping one's HIV status unknown to oneself, or private, once known. This is not to say that the maintenance of these secrets does not have ethical implications; it is to say that these ethical implications are distinct for each type of secret and will, in any event, vary from context to context. Nevertheless, what these secrets do have in common is that they act as markers of the limits of what the discourse of 'getting the nation talking about sex' can and cannot reveal, and even of the limits of what analysing a discourse generated primarily within the public sphere fails to touch upon. That is to say, there is a difference between how such discourse plays itself out in the public realm, even if it attempts to rewrite the boundary between private and public space, as Posel suggests, and how the focus on masculine sexuality actually impinges upon individuals' actions and responses in the intimate spaces of the home, within intimate, familiar relationships, and in terms of one's relation to one's gendered and ethnic identity.

Here fictions such as those by Mahala, Mpe (2001) and Sandile Memela's novella, *Flowers of the Nation* (2005), discussed below, have an important role to play in relating some key dilemmas of contemporary South African masculinity. Fiction enables exploration of intimacy without engaging the burdens of, on the one hand potential stigmatizing of individuals, and on the other, verifiability in quantifiable terms. The latter often acts as a gatekeeper in terms of disallowing a discussion of sexual abuse on the grounds that statistics are notoriously hard to collect, and are therefore often disregarded since they appear to create a problem where no such social pathology is believed to exist. The Mbeki response to the rape crisis scenario is a case in point. Yet, as I have attempted to demonstrate throughout this analysis of violence in relation to culture, to restrict one's purview to what is accurately verifiable in quantitative terms is often its own form of denialism. In terms of stigma, the outing of secrets to the reader cannot and does not carry the same risks that journalistic narrative does, even where these risks are mitigated by the subject's prior, public acknowledgement of his status, and the social capital commanded by the subject either before the journalistic revelation, or as a consequence of it, or both (as in the case of McGregor's subject, Khaba).

## Masculinity: The State of/and the Family

### Gender and the Fathers of the Nation

Haunting Mahala's narrative are the secret of Nosipho's sexual abuse and the fact that this abuse is incestuous (the father rapes the daughter); and the related secret of Themba's HIV status, since he may have given Nosipho HIV, or have been infected by her. Haunting Steinberg's tale is the unknown status of Sizwe (probably positive, by his own admission, but not verified by the text, even at the conclusion of the narrative). Haunting Liz McGregor's narrative of Khaba's illness and death is the unresolved question of the reasons for his refusal of orthodox antiretroviral (ARV) treatment. These narratives figure two pre-eminent 'scandals' of post-apartheid political leadership: the AIDS denialism of Thabo Mbeki; and the charge of rape laid against Jacob Zuma on 6 December 2005, which claimed that Zuma had raped the 31-year-old daughter of a former comrade at his residence in Forest Town, Johannesburg.

Using the capacity of fictional narrative to reveal the more intimate, familial dynamics of stigmatized issues – due to its capacity for objectivity (it locates stigma in a fictional persona, avoiding damage to actual individuals) and its release from the burden of justifying the importance of the topics it addresses – I can attempt to link Mbeki's denialism and the phenomenon of the Zuma rape crisis to the intimate spaces of other men's lives. Further, I shall do this so as to suggest that relations between leaders and followers are not one way, but compound each other in complex ways. While much has been written on Mbeki's HIV/AIDS denialism,[2] placing this alongside Mbeki's reluctance to admit to the extent of the problem of sexual violence in South Africa may give us a more nuanced sense of what this denial is about through its relation to potential stigmatization. Some exploration of the Zuma trial in the context of Mbeki's presidential role allows us to see how each of these leaders is appealing to a distinctly different family dynamic in terms of 'fathering' the nation, but also how these appeals can both be understood within the context of defending against a masculinity that is distinctly vulnerable. Both Zuma and Mbeki, I argue,

2   See, for example, Jolly 2007; Wang 2008; and A. Butler 2005. On denialism as a response to the sub-Saharan African epidemic globally, in terms of state governance, multinational capital, international finance and global governance, see Sitze's meticulous reading (2004).

have sought to contain and/or manipulate contamination of their respective notions of masculinity by forces they perceive to be hostile to the state/family of which they see themselves as exemplary members: Zuma mobilizes against a generalized black constituency, using a hyper-masculine performance of Zulu manhood to garner support; Mbeki seeks to perform a masculinity that rejects racist and colonialist stereotypes of blacks as promiscuous. A discussion that traces the predominance of gender in the rise of the hostility between Mbeki and Zuma is a necessary preamble to this argument.

Zuma was Deputy President of South Africa under Mbeki until his dismissal by Mbeki on 14 June 2005, in the wake of the statement by the judge who found convicted fraudster Schabir Shaik guilty, to the effect that the guilty party's relationship to Zuma was one of a 'mutually beneficial symbiosis' (Supreme Court of Appeal of South Africa 2006). In December 2005 he was charged with the rape of a woman reported to be the daughter of a prominent ANC family and an AIDS activist, who is herself HIV positive. He was acquitted of the rape charge on 8 May 2006 by the court, who upheld Zuma's defence that the sex was consensual. On 18 December 2007, Zuma was elected ANC Party President with 2,329 votes to Mbeki's 1,505. Under the Constitution, Mbeki cannot serve another term as the country's president. Zuma, supported by long-time left-wing allies of the ANC in the South African Communist Party, the Congress of South African trade Unions and the ANC Youth league, became President in May 2009. Zuma was charged with corruption by the National Prosecution Authority, and undertook a series of legal manoeuvres to try to make sure the case did not come to court prior to 2009 as, had he been convicted and sentenced to a term of more than one year, he would have been constitutionally ineligible for election to the South African Parliament and thus prevented from becoming President of the Republic of South Africa. Predictably enough, the charges laid against Zuma were and are interpreted by his supporters as elements of a plot laid by Mbeki to keep power out of Zuma's hands. On 6 April 2009, roughly two weeks before the election, the Acting Head of the National Prosecution Authority (NPA) announced that the case against Zuma would not be pursued. Despite sufficient evidence for the prosecution, the case was compromised by tapes produced by Zuma's lawyers revealing that a discussion in 2007 between the then head of Special Investigations and an investigator of the NPA dealt with how the timing of the case might be exploited to damage Zuma's run for the presidency.

Most analysts describe the leadership competition between Mbeki and Zuma as one between the liberal democratic values and acknowledgement of corporate capitalism represented by the former, and the African communitarianism of the latter, which motivates the left-wing support Zuma commands. Steven Robins does not see this as a choice between the modernism of Mbeki and the appeal to traditionalist politics of Zuma, or even, more specifically, as a choice between on the one hand the 'Xhosa Nostra' (as it is called by Zuma supporters), dedicated to seeing that leadership of the ANC remains in Xhosa hands after the traditions of Mandela and Mbeki, and on the other, the Zulu interests represented by Zuma. He has a different take on this. He has argued, persuasively, that the politics of gender and sex, rather than acting as a forum for these tensions, actually undergirds them:

> [The] vicious succession battle was expressed through a cultural politics of gender and sexuality that reflected profound tensions between constructions of 'traditional' African masculinity and a rights-based discourse on sexual rights and gender equality. While it appeared as if these concerns were simply background to the 'real' politics of the ANC leadership crisis, [Robins'] paper argues that the rising significance of sexual rights and sexual politics animated the tensions between the pro-Mbeki and pro-Zuma camps. (Robins 2006: 179)

While Robins makes the point that these either/or readings of Zuma and Mbeki overlook Zuma's capacity to represent himself as 'both a diehard African traditionalist as well as a modern revolutionary and former trade unionist' (2006: 165), he does not mention the fact that Mbeki's AIDS denialism detracts from any superficial reading of Mbeki as the embodiment of liberal modernity. While it may be true that Mbeki's promotion of gender equality and quotas for women in parliament fit the picture of the 'strictly corporate executive style and liberal modernism' that Robins attributes to Mbeki, Mbeki's position is as heterodox as Zuma's in terms of its mix of modernity and appeals to African distinctiveness, but differently so.

### Mbeki's Denialism: The Father's Defence of the (African) Family

Mbeki's denialism does not fit easily into the rather uncomplicated view of him as the epitome of a modern liberal state leader; nor, for that matter, does his silence, until very recently, on Robert Mugabe's human rights violations in Zimbabwe. His AIDS denialism pits him against the forces of rationality that supposedly characterize the approach of Western governments to the HIV crisis, or that of Museveni in Uganda or Festus Mogae of Botswana; and his failure to pronounce until recently against Mugabe is eccentric even within the African community, despite its differences with the international community on how to resolve the problem of Mugabe. These denialisms share a common character: they aim to counter the negative effects of a colonialist gaze on a family that is constituted as black African. To admit, as Posel has argued, that sex is the vector of death in the African AIDS epidemic – 'to concede the scientific orthodoxy' – is to allow public scrutiny of black, and particularly black male, sexual behaviour, in an apparent repetition without difference of colonialist obsessions with black sexuality. To recognize Mugabe's human rights violations is to acknowledge Mugabe's affinity to the stereotype of the banana republic dictator.

The term 'African' has a tellingly double usage in Mbeki's public discourse: it is referenced sarcastically and ironically when he is deriding colonialist visions of Africans – 'there are things in the African bush' (Mbeki 1998); and registered as a reclaimed term – 'African Renaissance' is the pre-eminent example. This double usage suggests yet another version of the dual panopticon: here the President must defend against colonialist errors of perception of the family 'from the outside'; but he must also make sure that 'the family' does not embrace behaviour that conforms in any way to such colonialist visions. The difficulty is that enacting vigilance simultaneously on both fronts can produce a contradiction in rhetorical terms, the effects of which are potentially devastating in actuality. The task of rejecting colonialist stereotypes of blacks, especially black sexuality, means denying that blacks conform in actuality to those stereotypes in any way. However, policing the behaviour of the family 'internally' – 'our African selves' (Mbeki 1998) – means condemning behaviour that might be taken to conform to such stereotypes; and this in turn means describing such behaviour as having been adopted by at least some elements of the family: an impossibility in terms of Mbeki's rhetoric against colonialist stereotyping that results in a performative contradiction in Mbeki's speeches.[3]

When Mbeki makes public addresses that explicitly entail a rejection of racist stereotyping, he employs a vocabulary and a sarcastic tone that imply the impossibility, the outrageousness, of any application of the colonialist image of black Africans as 'unable to subject passion to reason' and 'depraved and diseased' (Mbeki 2001). Such speeches are geared towards rejecting colonialist black stereotyping imposed on the family from outside, and also have a preventative component directed towards the family, in which Mbeki attempts to make the family aware of the history of such stereotypes and their crucial relevance to how Africans are perceived, neo-colonialistically, in the contemporary era. To militate against the family's invasion by external forces that are colonialist in nature, those whose actions imply any kind of conformity of actual family members' behaviour to such stereotypes must be heartily condemned as 'the enemy within'. We can see this in Mbeki's infamous attack on those whom he sees as 'selling out' to colonialism by identifying negative statistics associated with the black South African population, most prominently, in this case, against the Treatment Action Campaign's demands for treatment, based on a recognition that South Africa's HIV prevalence is among the highest in the world. The same speech also evinces the 'we' of black Africans as both subject (in terms of the President's identification of himself as such through the so-called royal usage of the first person plural) and vocative (in terms of black Africans as the addressees of the speech):

> There are those, *among us*, who have been 'taught from books of the same (racist) bias, trained by Caucasians of the same prejudices or by Negroes of

3 While I address Mbeki's denialism in the context of colonialism and apartheid with reference to the paternalistic structure of the family, Joy Wang does so with reference to Fanon's essay, 'Medicine and Colonialism', arguing that a 'closer examination of AIDS denialism has broader ramifications for a critical understanding of the relationship between medical intervention, postcolonial studies and human rights' (Wang 2008). What an analysis of fiction in addition to Mbeki's own text offers is a sense of the ways in which Mbeki's rhetoric seeks to provide a political framework and policies for attitudes toward Western medicine that stem from cultural ideologies that pre-date and exceed Mbeki's rhetorical framing of them. In this respect, Mbeki's infamous distance from the commoner appears as a simplification of his relation to the 'man in the street'.

enslaved minds, one generation of Negro teachers after another that have served for no higher purpose than to do what they are told to do'. To quote Carter Woodson, these have studied in schools of theology where the Bible is interpreted by those who have justified segregation; law schools where they are told that they belong to the most criminal element in the country; medical schools where they are likewise convinced of their inferiority by being reminded of their role as germ carriers; schools where they learn a history that pictures black people as human beings of the lower order, unable to subject passion to reason. Thus does it come about that some who call themselves *our* leaders join a cacophony of voices that demand that *we* produce statistics that will show that, indeed, *we* belong to the most criminal element in *our* country. And thus does it happen that others who consider themselves to be *our* leaders take to the streets carrying their placards, to demand that because *we* are germ carriers, and human beings of a lower order who cannot subject their passions to reason, *we* must perforce adopt strange opinions, to save a depraved and diseased people from perishing from self-inflicted disease. (Mbeki, ZK Matthews Memorial Lecture (2001), emphasis added)[4]

Prominent in this speech is the figure of the colonialist who has ensured that his teachings have been internalized by the oppressed black majority; but, in accordance with the performative contradiction I outline above, the move to dislodge the internalized inferiority Mbeki outlines in this speech involves Mbeki's own staging of South Africans as in need of moral regeneration, which they can only need if they are in some way morally degenerate.

In this context, Mbeki fashions himself as the leader-father whose task it is to explain to the family that their unruliness results in conformity to racist stereotypes. The task at hand is literally to protect the family from the exogenous influences of colonialism and neo-colonialism. The call for moral regeneration is based on an image of the society that Mbeki's own speeches describe as 'brutish' as a consequence of its colonial and apartheid heritage. That which whites perceived as a civilizing mission was, in fact, the imposition of 'the law of the jungle':

We seek to replace a society which, in many instances, has been and continues to be brutal and brutish in the extreme [...]. The society we seek to replace was, to a very significant degree, built on the law of the jungle of the survival of the fittest. [There] are those in our cities and towns who have lost all hope and all self-worth, who have slid into a twilight world of drug and alcohol

---

4   The rhetoric of this speech is reproduced in an infamous text of disputed origin that appeared in the public domain in April/May 2002, and was cited by Posel in her article 'Sex, Death and the Fate of the Nation' (2005a): '[...] thus does it happen that others who consider themselves our leaders take to the streets carrying their placards, to demand that because we are germ carriers, and human beings of a lower order that cannot subject its [sic] passions to reason, we must perforce adopt strange opinions, to save a depraved and diseased people from perishing from self-inflicted disease [...] Convinced that we are but natural-born, promiscuous carriers of germs, unique in the world, they proclaim that our continent is doomed to an inevitable mortal end because of our unconquerable devotion to the sin of lust'.

abuse, the continuous sexual and physical abuse of women and children, of purposeless wars fought with fists and boots, metal rods, knives and guns, everyday resulting in death and grievous bodily harm [...]. (Mbeki 1999, Premier's Address)

Reforming this society calls for nothing short of moral regeneration: 'We invite all those in our country who occupy positions of authority and responsibility to join in this new way of doing things, by engaging the people whom they serve and lead in the common effort to transform all of us into a people at work for a better South Africa' (Mbeki 1999).

This language, used in Mbeki's speech to open the 1999 session of the South African Parliament, is proliferated in speeches, documents, mission statements and principles of operation associated with a series of movements organized with varying degrees of governmental support and implication, which aim to effect this sort of moral regeneration. One of these is the African Renaissance itself. Others are the Moral Regeneration Movement, an idea first hatched by Mandela to address the issues outlined in Mbeki's speech, and subsequently made the responsibility of the then Deputy President of South Africa, Jacob Zuma; and the *Batho Pele* movement, which seeks to restructure government services to the people on principles of respect, equality, consultation, and the dedication and self-sacrifice of civil servants. The ethics of these movements is drawn in part from Steve Biko's Black Consciousness Movement, in which blacks are called upon to conceptualize truth and find solutions to challenges without departing from 'our fundamental beliefs and values' (Biko 1987: 92).

In the double-situatedness of Mbeki's position of responding to a colonialist gaze yet seeking to make the family aware of that gaze in order to make it police its own behaviour, we can see the threat of stigmatization, where stigma is recognized as involving the concurrent instantiation and desubjectification of the black subject. This dilemma is not properly described by the trope of the paradox, since a paradox can be sustained, whereas the doubled movement of instantiating the subject through desubjectifying him is *not* sustainable by the subject. My pre-eminent example of this scenario, described in Chapter 3, is the rape victim, whose only way to assert the violence that has been perpetrated against her is to assume a position of negative social worth. There is an analogy in Mbeki's conception of the effect of colonialist vision of the black as inferior and her/his sexuality as unconstrained. To demonstrate the harm that colonialism and racism have inflicted upon the majority of black South Africans, Mbeki has to illustrate that black South Africans have inhabited but, much more problematically, continue to inhabit positions of negative moral and social worth within a neo-colonialist global economy of value. In the case of Mbeki, his carefully intentioned attempts to warn against colonialist values have literally threatened the very subjects he intends to protect. The denialism of the connection of HIV to AIDS; the subsequent foot-dragging of the government on rollout of prevention of mother-to-child transmission drugs; the initial refusal to rollout ARVs and subsequent barriers to access them; and on-going debates about the effectiveness of these drugs in view of their negative side effects; these have all had a profound impact on the ability – logistical, psychological and/or cultural – of a vast majority of South Africans to go on ARV treatment. In the context of the nation as a racially embodied family, Mbeki has literally become complicit in the 'letting die'[5] of some members of his family. Yet to hold him up as solely responsible for reluctance to test for HIV and/or to take up anti-retrovirals, to give one example, is to suggest that 'his' subjects have no say in the matter, no resilience.

*The Agency of Familiar Subjects: Johnny Steinberg's* Three Letter Plague[6]

This erasure of the agency of 'ordinary' South Africans in the discussion of Mbeki's denialism overlooks the nature of the affiliations between African political leaders and their constituents. It is perhaps difficult to convey the intimate sense in which many South African communities construct their felt affiliations in relation to those they consider their leaders in the constitutional democracy.

This context of affiliation is captured by Jonny Steinberg in his *Three Letter Plague* (2008), in a chapter entitled 'Voting Day'. Steinberg does not vote in the municipal government election as he lives in Johannesburg, and he is in the ward of Lusikisiki, accompanying Sizwe, his translator-protagonist, to the polling station. Despite the failure of the municipal government to deliver services, or to stand up to the chief and his advisers, who will only take actions that benefit themselves, the community turns out in full force to vote for the admittedly ineffective ANC ward councillor. This is Steinberg's explanation of this phenomenon, which is worth quoting at some length:

> In the line, Sizwe greeted an elderly man with his broadest and most generous smile.
> 'Molweni, Zizi,' he beamed.
> The old man clearly enjoyed the appellation, and soon the two were chatting happily. Once he had left us and made his way to the voting booth, Sizwe turned to me.
> 'Do you know what is Zizi?'
> 'It is the name you use to address a member of the Dhlamini clan.'
> 'Yes,' he said. That is exactly what it is. And do you know who else is Zizi?'
> 'Thabo Mbeki.'
> He took out his broad grin once more.
> 'You are so right, my man, you are so right. We have Zizis here in this village, and Zizis there in the government in Pretoria.'

5   This phrase is taken from South African satirist Pieter-Dirk Uys's observation: 'In the old South Africa we killed people. Now we're just letting them die'. The 'joke' is cited by Catherine Campbell and used in the title of her study of the failure of HIV/AIDS prevention programmes (2003).

6   This work is published in North America as *Sizwe's Test: A young Man's Journey through Africa's AIDS Epidemic* (New York: Simon & Schuster, 2008). As with Krog's *Country of My Skull* (1998), a certain spectacularization and exoticization is evident in the differential marketing of North American and South African editions of these texts.

I marvelled at Sizwe, at the invisible strand that linked him to the president via the old man, at the bond that had wrapped itself around everyone standing in the line. Democracy had not treated this village especially well. When the adults of Ithanga converged on the school to vote for the first time in April 1994, they had been told, on radio, and on election platforms, that their vote would bring them running water, electricity, proper roads, perhaps a clinic. More than a decade later, there isn't a soul here who has forgotten that every one of these promises was broken.

Nor is anybody especially naive about the character of local politics. When I asked Sizwe whether he knew the ANC ward councillor for whom he was about to cast his vote, he spoke of a well-off man who lived in a smart, brick-and-mortar house some twenty kilometres away, in a village with electricity and running water.

'Will he be good for Ithanga?' I asked.

'He is not smart enough to be good for Ithanga,' Sizwe replied ....

And yet these acidic observations cannot burn the thread that binds the Zizis in Ithanga to the Zizis in the Union Buildings in Pretoria. (Steinberg 2008: 165)

It is this thread that is ignored when readings of Mbeki, or Zuma for that matter, assume that the communication along these lines of affiliation are one-way, from political 'top' to 'bottom'. Liz McGregor is remarking on an aspect of this when she claims that, in all the debates regarding Mbeki's denialism, little or no time has been spent documenting and seeking the reasons for ordinary South Africans' 'deeply ambivalent attitudes' (2005: 244) on the subject of ARVs.

Jonny Steinberg's *Three Letter Plague* provides a stellar counterpart in this regard to Mbeki's 'high'-level denialism in his description of Sizwe's attempt to test the HIV herbal cure proffered by Mabalane, a local *nyanga* (a traditional healer). Sizwe discovers that his niece is HIV positive and goes to get the herbal remedy from Mabalane. Steinberg describes Mabalane's compound as poor and small, surrounded by a knee-high fence. Upon reflection, Sizwe decides that, because Thandeka's boyfriend is untested, he, too, must take the remedy. After two weeks, both Thandeka and her boyfriend go to be tested, the boyfriend for the first time. Thandeka is still HIV positive, and so is her boyfriend: they have CD4 counts above 400 and ARV treatment is considered appropriate at CD4 counts of below 200. Sizwe phones Steinberg to tell him the news; Sizwe is happy with Mabalane because the intervention of the herbal remedy has led Thandeka's boyfriend to test, so Thandeka and her boyfriend will be counselled together regarding the dangers of reinfection and their future care.

In a moving passage, Steinberg describes how Sizwe, in a position analogous to that of Mbeki, sees the *nyanga* and the *nyanga*'s house through the eyes of Steinberg, and reads in Steinberg's version of events a panopticon gaze that is racialized and contemptuous. Reading the chapter on Mabelane written by Steinberg, Sizwe responds with anger after the fact, taking offence at the passage in which Steinberg describes the fence around Mabalane's humble dwelling as 'knee-high', and asking why Steinberg described it as such. Steinberg asks if the fence is in fact knee-high, and Sizwe responds that 'It is about the height of the stomach. You exaggerated. You wanted to show that the man's place was fucked up. What fool wastes his time and money building a knee-high fence? Anything can get over it, even a small dog' (2008: 224). Steinberg responds, reflecting on the defensiveness he believes motivated Sizwe, at least in part, to praise Mabalane and his herbs:

> Now he [Sizwe] is telling me he has seen his world through my eyes, and what he saw was people with useless fences around their gardens and useless bottles of herbs in their rooms....
>
> I recall his defensiveness on the phone when I asked him whether Mabalane's cure had worked, and I think I see what he is protesting against when he shields his cousin from me. He is protesting against a collective humiliation. Black people have gotten sick in droves and line up outside a clinic to get the medicine the white doctor has brought. It is humiliating. Before the gaze of their community they are outed as bearers of a disgraceful disease; they must sit in support groups run by fiery young women and for the rest of their lives they must swallow ghastly pills that serve only to remind them that they are sick and that each cough or bout of diarrhoea could lead to death.
>
> He wants very much for an end to this, and for the end to be delivered by a dose of Mpondo medicine; a gift from the ancestors that heals one now and forever and puts an end to the lines outside the clinic and the counsellors in the school hall.
>
> I have rubbed his face in it. I went to Mabalane's place, and what I saw was a knee-high fence. (Steinberg 2008: 224–25)

This passage has the potential to shed a different light on Mbeki's denialism: the claims of Mbeki to have distanced himself through intellectual reflection rather than having sensed the dilemma of 'ordinary' South Africans have, perhaps, been exaggerated and overlooked in the spectacular rendering of his denialism.

### *An Appeal to the Father: Sandile Memela's* Flowers of the Nation

Complicity in letting subjects die, and resistance to it, is explored in Sandile Memela's novella, *Flowers of the Nation* (2005).[7] The novella tells a story of two young girls whose father, Sizwe, is dying of AIDS. The family live in impover-

---

7   It is important to note here that the 'Flowers of the Nation' is also the name of the virginity-testing campaign, which is the traditional Zulu leaders' response, under the direction of King Goodwill Zwelithini, to the HIV/AIDS epidemic. The Children's Bill has, in fact, outlawed virginity-testing for girls under the age of 16; for girls over the age of 16, virginity-testing can only take place if the candidates are properly counselled, the results are not made public, and the candidates' bodies are not marked in any way. The Gender Commission has recommended that virginity-testing be relinquished altogether. In July 2008, I was invited to a celebratory occasion to be held in August: a virginity-testing event. The local Nkosi pointed out that security at these events to protect the newly pronounced-upon virgins is essential and expensive. The irony here is that in the era of the HIV epidemic a girl who is pronounced a virgin becomes a desirable sex partner with or without her consent, and not necessarily because of the virgin cure myth; in terms of even the most basic HIV education, she is a safe bet.

ished circumstances in Soweto, with their paternal grandmother and Sizwe's wife, Winnie. The girls, Zenzele and Mpumelelo, decide that without the knowledge of their mother and grandmother they need to seek the help of their rich uncle Vusi, who lives in Pretoria. Vusi is the epitome of a black economic empowerment (BEE) success story. Memela's dedication of *Flowers of the Nation* to Thabo Mbeki could, perhaps, be read as a purely ironic act of political criticism. However, Memela's position as a spokesperson for the Mbeki government's Ministry of Arts and Culture, as well as the fact that the dedication is to both Mbeki and the children of the children of the 1976 riots, suggests we consider the dedication in a different light: as an appeal to Mbeki to protect the children of the nation. The invocation of the 1976 schoolchildren's riots suggests that Memela sees his petition as mobilized by the ethic of those riots: the children are demanding that from which the parents will benefit.

The appeal to Mbeki in the dedication of the story is counterbalanced by his denunciation in the first sentences of the novella. The failure of the father – in terms of the plot, the sick Sizwe who refuses to reconcile with his rich brother, and the rich brother who initially fails to come to Sizwe's aid, but by implication, also President Mbeki, who refuses help to those sick with AIDS – casts the responsibility for action on the children, in a replaying of 1976: 'It was the children who had to do something. Action does help. After all, most of the adults were paralysed by fear and worship of the cult of personality. They were awed by the great Renaissance Leader' (Memela 2005: 1). With the help of two models of masculine supportiveness, Bra Mesh and the tellingly named Steve, who works for the Johannesburg Development Project, the girls find their way to Pretoria, succeed in initiating a full reconciliation between the two brothers, Sizwe and Vusi, and save their father's life: Vusi pays for Sizwe to be hospitalized in a private institution, and pays for his drugs. Zenzele, through whom the novella is focalized, constantly wonders why the rights of the poor are not equal to those of the rich.

The novella ends successfully in terms of Sizwe's return home, but we are left with a figure with which we are familiar from the days of Mpahlele's 'The Suitcase' (1989): this time it is an HIV-positive baby brought to the private clinic by its mother. They are refused treatment because the mother has no money. The mother deserts the baby at the clinic, but not surreptitiously: she tells the nurse into whose lap she drops the baby that if, as the nurse had told her earlier, she wishes to save lives, she must do what she can for the baby. The text tellingly links the economy of transactional sex to the nurse's attack on the mother for her supposed promiscuousness, through reference to the 'rights' only of the rich to access HIV/AIDS care. When Zenzele and Mpumelelo make their way from Soweto to Johannesburg, where they meet Steve, they are vulnerable to attack, particularly sexual attack. When Zenzele is hailed by a boy and refuses to respond, he threatens her: 'You think you are an African queen. I will get you, one day' (Memela 2005: 10). Similarly, when Zenzele accepts food from a rural Zulu boy, she is suspicious of his motives, and states: 'There is nothing for *mahala* [free] in Jozi […]. What is it you will demand from us?' (14).

The food seller assures her that he will demand nothing in return for the food, assuring her he is not a jackroller,[8] but she restates her terms several times before she agrees to take food for herself and her sister.

When the well-dressed clinic manager explains that he cannot treat those with no money, he explains: 'We are trying our best to provide the best for people. But we must learn that nothing is for *mahala*. What kind of people shall we be if we expect to get things for free?' This capitalist logic has a morality attached to it: if sex always has to be paid for, and health care always has to be paid for, those (presumed to be) seeking the sex that produces both material goods and babies should think first before they assume sex comes without a price. The nurse harangues the mother who drops the baby in her lap: 'The clinic was not there when you were enjoying yourself. You must face up to the consequences of your own actions. Your choices have affected your life. Come, take your baby, Miss Soweto!' (82). In terms of the interpretation of the novel as a story of the nation figured as a family that requires reunification – the last chapter is entitled 'Family Unity is a Nation's Strength' – President Thabo Mbeki fails to father the abandoned baby appropriately.

The novella relentlessly promotes the Renaissance African – a new kind of man who will effect a second liberation – but this new Renaissance entails negotiating an unresolved contradiction. One element of this contradiction is epitomized by the morality of self-restraint and self-sacrifice, evinced by Zenzele's promise to herself not to get involved with men, not to have sex until she is married and not to get married until she and her future husband have been tested for HIV; and by the ethic of hard work embodied by Vusi and rewarded by his material success within a Black Economic Empowerment context. The other is manifested in the novel's repeated calls for the government to abandon rampant capitalism and assist the poor, particularly in terms of employment opportunities, health care and other social services. If the former appears to reflect the ideology behind Mbeki's (neo-liberal) African Renaissance, the latter appears to share its appeal with the populist politics associated with future President Jacob Zuma.

## Unsettling Patriarchal Sexuality in the Era of AIDS I: Gendered Realities and Phaswane Mpe's *Welcome to our Hillbrow*

The self-cancelling dynamic of Mbeki's denialism has been phrased in different ways. Memela's novella suggests that Mbeki's dedication to liberal economic policy, upheld in the service of demonstrating the responsibility of the post-apartheid government globally, kills, except in the few cases where private capital can step in to make up for his failure. Mandisa Mbali has argued that '[Mbeki] is still trapped in intellectual boundaries defined by coercive and racist

8 Jackrolling is 'the undisguised use of sexual violence against young women in the township by young armed men' (Simpson 1992).

arguments common in colonial and late apartheid public health. He is fighting an enemy that no longer exists at the expense of the lives of his own people' (cited in Hoad 2005: 119). Against this, Neville Hoad suggests that Mbali overlooks the fact 'that reports of the death of racism have been somewhat exaggerated'; and argues that instead of abandoning his 'critique of the pornographic spectacle of blackness', Mbeki should extend it (2005: 119). He should do this by rejecting the moralities of sexual constraint called for by his own contestation of the scientific racist notion that blacks are incapable of subjecting their passions – most particularly sexual passion – to reason.

Hoad argues that Mbeki's approach entails, in its rejection of colonialist stereotyping of black incontinence – sexual and otherwise – a profound paradox. In order to refute the racist stereotype of black sexuality, Mbeki proliferates a vocabulary that does not reject the Manichean allegory in which black represents embodiment – as opposed to intellect and/or spirituality – and sexual incontinence, polygamy and (non-human) animalistic behaviour, while white represents the reverse values. Instead, it merely seeks to attach to black identity the values white racism attached to white identity – or, as Hoad puts it,

> [...] the valorized forms of racist white embodiment, the spiritual, the monogamous, the respectable, and the aestheticized are equally part of the sexual history of racism, and to look to them for safety marks a complicity with racism in another way [...].
>
> A critique of racism that invokes the aestheticized, spiritualized, sexually continent face of whiteness as the response to the racist stereotype of overly embodied self-destructive blackness is [...] a critique that is doomed to repeat the failures of its object. (2005: 119; 126)

Hoad holds up Phaswane Mpe's famous novel of HIV/AIDS and sexual stigma, suffering and death, *Welcome to Our Hillbrow* (2001), as an example of an alternative, South African contribution representing the vulnerability of all to HIV through an expression of erotic relationships that do not invoke the moral sanction of the narrator. Yet in his call for the representation of an African eroticism that draws upon the everyday lives of men and women 'working through problems of sexuality and the material and ideological legacies of imperialism' (2005: 127) Hoad appears to risk, in his rejection of 'the silencing phantasm of sexual respectability' (126), the differential stakes, gender-wise, for those implicated in the task he describes.

*Welcome to our Hillbrow* describes the lives of the poor-but-nevertheless-on-their-way-up-the-ladder community of educated youth in Hillbrow. They were the first generation of their families to move from the rural area of Tiragalong to be educated in the city of Johannesburg. The narrative is well known for its use of the unusual second-person voice by its narrator, a rhetorical feature that aligns the protagonist – 'you' – at any particular point in the story with the reader in an intimate 'embrace'.

Refentše, our first protagonist, comes to Johannesburg and falls in love with Lerato, whom he invites to move in with him. Prior to this, he has betrayed his best friend, Sammy, by having sex with Sammy's girlfriend, Bohale, when comforting her after Sammy took to drink and drugs. Refilwe, Refentše's cousin, comes to Hillbrow and asks Refentše for a reference. She is his former lover and would like to seduce him away from Lerato. However, Refentše resists her advances, aware that his betrayal of Sammy in the past speaks to his potential temptation by Refilwe and betrayal of Lerato.

Refentše's mother sees Lerato as an evil town girl and when he returns to Tiragalong for a weekend, she tells him she will disown him if he does not leave Lerato. After his home visit, Refentše loses interest in his food and his relationship with Lerato – indeed, in Hillbrow in general. Lerato calls Sammy to help her work out what is wrong with Refentše, and in a mirroring of the incident between Refentše and Sammy's girlfriend, Bohale, she sleeps with Sammy. The difference is that Refentše walks in on Lerato and Sammy. (Sammy has never found out about Refentše's sexual liaison with Bohale; on her way to see Sammy in hospital and tell him, Bohale is run down by a stolen car. After her death, Refentše never tells Sammy about the event.) Refentše broods about Sammy and Lerato, fantasizing that their relationship is not a single incident borne of desperation, but a long-standing betrayal of him. He commits suicide, and Lerato follows suit.

What Hoad picks up on in his admiration of the fiction is that in rendering everyone vulnerable – rural folk, Hillbrow inhabitants, much-resented migrants from other African countries resident in Hillbrow, and the global ebb and flow of humans moving between continents – Mpe steadfastly deconstructs modes of morality that seek to locate illness and misfortune within a locatable persona, externalizing them from the 'family' of the safe, and thus projecting that family as morally upright. In a series of revisions of his actions and those of other characters, which are sent down from 'Heaven', Refentše revises the hypocrisy of a judgementalism that leads to human misery with each passing narrative event. He leaves Refilwe originally because she, as a youngster, has relations with boys other than him; his subsequent betrayals of Sammy (by sleeping with Bohale) and Lerato (by terminating any opportunity to discuss her betrayal of him with Sammy, instead taking up the 'seductive' option of suicide), lead him to reflect on the retroactively constructed hypocrisy of his desertion of Refilwe. Here sexual 'promiscuity' is reconstructed as generosity, just as the sexual relations between Refentše and Bohale, and Lerato and Sammy, arise from acts of sympathy. The narrator addresses Refentše and the reader on this topic:

> [Refilwe] was a kind-hearted and generous soul. Her open-thighedness was the only side of her generosity that you [Refentše] did not like. For that you could not blame her too strongly, though, you yourself having subsequently committed the sexual error that you never imagined you could commit at the time when you judged her so strongly, after your remarkable discovery of her infidelity. You also reasoned that her sexual life would not hinder her from doing her work. It never did. (Mpe 2001: 32)

After Refentše's suicide, Refilwe builds on the story of Lerato's infidelity to him to portray Lerato in Tiragalong not only as an evil city woman but also as the daughter of a Nigerian, a *Lekwerekwere*. *Makwerekwere* (plural) are black foreigners from other African countries seeking a living in South Africa, most particularly in the urban areas, who have always been the target of xenophobic violence, and who are seen as a source of HIV infection. It turns out that Lerato's mother resides in Alexandra township, Johannesburg, and her father is, in fact, Piet, a migrant from Tiragalong itself to Johannesburg. Nevertheless, Refilwe perpetrates the myth of Lerato, the evil woman from the outside, be it Johannesburg, or Nigeria, or both, who corrupts Refentše, exploiting his naiveté and driving him to suicide.

The narrative concludes with Refilwe, who is now studying for a Master's degree at Oxford Brookes University, falling in love with a Nigerian who looks like Refentše. Upon learning that he is HIV positive, her lover returns to Nigeria so as not to burden Refilwe or her family. She returns to Tiragalong – to die, because she is also HIV positive; both she and the Nigerian have been infected for over a decade. The cure for xenophobia is shared vulnerability. The narrator tells us, addressing Refilwe this time, that

> You can no longer hide behind your bias against Makwerekwere. You do not blame them for the troubles in your life, as you once did. You have come to understand that you too are a Hillbrowan. An Alexandran. A Johannesburger. An Oxfordian. A Lekwerekwere, just like those you once held in such contempt. The semen and blood of Makwerekwere flows in your Tiragalong and Hillbrow veins. (Mpe 2001: 122–23)

Hoad portrays Mpe's description of the sex lives of his young black urban protagonists as countering Mbeki's focus on the rhetoric of black promiscuity of Cuvier and other racist scientists of the nineteenth century – a focus, he points out, that risks re-inscribing that which it wishes to dislodge. Nevertheless, Hoad idealizes the relationships between these protagonists, making a case through what are his misreadings of the text. He uses a passage in which Mpe describes sex between Refilwe and Refentše to make his point. I quote from Hoad to illustrate how he builds his argument:

> There is a lyrical matter-of-factness to Mpe's descriptions of the sex lives of his young black urban protagonists: 'She was rolling her tongue around Refentše's, with her soft hands brushing his chest gently. He held her tightly, not wanting to lose her. They kissed with mouths and tongues as well as with the southern hemispheres of their bodies.' At the risk of overreading 'kissing southern hemispheres,' we might see here a deft and ironic reworking of Cuvier's racist geography of lust: our protagonists have sex with each other with southern hemispheric tenderness. (Hoad 2005: 120–21)

Hoad goes on to juxtapose the positivity of Mpe's scene with the gossips from the rural areas, from Tiragalong, who, Hoad claims, say that Refilwe's mother is 'one of those women who could not say no to any drop of semen flowing aimlessly in the streets. So she had courted a stranger's sperm, as it flew its way around the streets of Hillbrow' (Mpe 2001: 82).

There are two problems with Hoad's reading. The first is that Hoad neglects the fact, or at least, neglects to alert his readers to the fact, that the scene he cites as evidence of a tender, 'southern hemispheric' sexuality does not take place in the plotline of Mpe's story: Refentše and Refilwe never have sex. Significantly, the scene is part of a dream fantasy of Refilwe, who dreams that Refentše is alive again and that she is having sex with him. She wakes from this dream to pursue the man who looks like, but is not, Refentše: the Nigerian whom she meets at the Jude the Obscure pub in Oxford. Furthermore, what Hoad claims is said about Refilwe's mother is said of *Lerato*'s mother and, in fact, reflects negatively on Refilwe. This gossip – that Lerato's mother is a promiscuous woman who had sex with a *Lekwerekwere*, the father of Lerato – is initiated by Refilwe, who returns from Johannesburg to Tiragalong after Refentše's suicide, intent on revenge against Lerato for having 'won' Refentše, confounding Refilwe's plan to get him back for herself.

Hoad's point, that this is a moment of tender sexuality, stands; but the implication that tender sexuality is a fantasy has far-reaching consequences for a reading of the novel's depiction of gendered relations and of the transmission of HIV/AIDS.

If we look back at the actuality of the protagonists' sex lives, we see relationships that, unlike the fantasized ideal, have their potential brutally terminated by patriarchal gender relations and by HIV/AIDS. In particular, the acts of sexual consolation that Refentše and Bohale engage in on the one hand, and Sammy and Lerato on the other, may be viewed as 'acts of well-intentioned generosity', but become acts 'that we call betrayal' when the politics of patriarchal gender are brought to bear on their interpretation (Mpe 2001: 67). When Refentše decides to commit suicide, it is because he has seen his friend Sammy having sex with Lerato and fantasizes that this has been an ongoing event, not a one-time betrayal. This speaks to a certain approach to masculinity, in which to be cuckolded means to lose one's status as a man.

This scene of cuckoldry is played over and over as a site of unseemly emasculation. The inability to have and control a female partner, when it is performed in view of another male, appears and reappears as the key site of masculine failure. Whether black hyper-masculinity is proffered as a response to the threat to masculinity posed by apartheid, as in Bessie Head's *A Question of Power* (1974), when Elizabeth's male informant tells her why he 'can barely retain' his own manhood, or whether the scene is found in its post-apartheid iteration, this failure to perform masculinity successfully is described as defacement, and the threat of it is ubiquitously portrayed.

In *When a Man Cries* (2007), Mahala's young Themba goes to the police station to inform on his aunt, his former sexual partner. This is framed as a scene in which the timidity of the adolescent Themba is converted into an assertion of his male identity through his implicit denial of his sexual liaison with his aunt, an older female whose fate he decides in his betrayal of her to the police. His initial timidity is noted by the policeman, who orders Themba to speak up, asking him if he is speaking so softly because he found another man with his girlfriend on the previous night. As if this joke were too subtle, the policeman repeats: 'C'mon, speak up boy. Do you think I'm your woman or something?' (Mahala 2007: 26). The chapter is entitled, with potential ironic significance, 'To be a Man'. Themba in fact becomes a man by betraying his aunt. He feels guilty for turning his aunt in, but takes solace in the fact that he has 'stood for the truth even if it mean[t] my integrity as a man would be questioned' (27). This integrity will, of course, only be questioned by a reader who sees Themba's act of literally 'shopping' his aunt for his manhood as a betrayal of that manhood; otherwise, as yet, no-one knows of Themba's sexual intercourse with his aunt. When the community finds out, it does so at Nosipho's funeral, when Themba publicly claims Nosipho as the daughter of himself and his aunt. This act of claiming fatherhood once again restores rather than denies Themba's manhood, as his sexual abuse of Nosipho remains a secret to all but his wife. Thuli is the only person, other than the reader, who, it is implied, can be trusted to keep secret of Themba's incestuous sexual abuse of Nosipho for the sake of the family. Thuli holds in her hands the power to deface Themba, but once he grovels before her with contrition at the conclusion of the novel, it is implied that the reunion will ensure the safety of Themba's secret.

*Welcome to Our Hillbrow* holds to no such ambiguity regarding the negative consequences of upholding patriarchal masculinity. Refentše comes to see his response to Lerato's 'betrayal' – his suicide – as giving in to a negative model of action. Suicide is synonymous with relief (Mpe 2001: 41), and the relief comes from not staying alive to learn how to interpret sexual relationships in other ways, outside the economy of patriarchal constraints on gender. The refusal to experience the episode with Sammy and Lerato as an opportunity for re-vision, marked by Refentše's suicide, is specifically linked in the novel to the capacity to be a good creative writer, to see other-wise: 'every act of listening, seeing, smelling, feeling, tasting is a reconfiguring of the story of our lives. Yet when Lerato and Sammy provided you [that is, Refentše] with the chance to add to your storehouse of experience, you could not rise to it' (2001: 61). When the narrator tells us that Refentše, with the benefit of hindsight, from his position in Heaven, sees his act of suicide as giving in to temptation, the narrator also tells us that Refentše, from Heaven, identifies the character who attempted to entrench Lerato's and Sammy's infidelity in his mind, and thus contributed to his temptation. He was the aptly named Terror, Refentše's childhood enemy.

Terror, who makes 'a career for himself as a rapist', approaches Lerato because, the narrator tell us, 'Terror wanted to take Lerato's thighs for a playing field, in which his penis would be player, referee and spectator simultaneously. He wanted to be able to say, later: "But what can you tell me now! I have eaten her! She is just as cheap as they all are!"' (65). Lerato repels Terror, who then attempts to persuade Refentše that Lerato and Sammy can never be trusted with one another. Refentše banishes him from the apartment, claiming that he is a rapist who takes advantage of women wherever possible, and says of

Terror that his 'respect for his manhood was so shallow, that he left it to swim in the pools of AIDS spilling into the night streets of our Hillbrow' (65). After Refentše's suicide, when Sammy's mental health has degraded and he has let out bits and pieces of the history of his relations with Lerato and Refentše, Terror picks up on these to literally terrorize Lerato into suicide. Lerato's mother was very fond of Refentše and considered him her son-in-law. Terror threatens to reveal that Lerato slept with Sammy to the communities of Johannesburg and Tiragalong, starting with Lerato's mother, unless Lerato sleeps with him. Because Lerato does not believe that her mother will understand her lapse with Sammy, envisaging herself being characterized as a 'murderess' and stigmatized for her 'sexual looseness' in the wake of Terror's threatened revelations, and because she cannot bring herself to be sexually blackmailed by Terror, she commits suicide. Terror, then, acts not only as a character in the novel, but characterizes the element of patriarchal sexual violence within it.

Associated with this patriarchal violence is the narrative of bewitchment in the novel. Because Refentše's mother disapproves of Lerato as a loose city woman, when Refentše dies she is accused by the people of Tiragalong of having used potions to keep him away from Lerato, but of having gone too far. This view is confirmed when she falls into his grave at the burial, as 'only witches could fall into a grave upon a corpse's burial'. So 'the Comrades of Tiragalong, in order to cleanse the village, had necklaced your mother to death. They put large tyres round her neck and poured generous quantities of petrol onto them and onto her whole body. Then somebody gingerly lit a cigarette before throwing a match into her hut […]' (43). That this is not an isolated incident is reinforced by the tale, told immediately after the story of Refentše's mother's necklacing, of Tshepo. He is Refentše's role model and he dies when he is struck by lightning.[9] His mother dies of grief when she hears of this. The community of Tiragalong decides that an elderly neighbour is the witch who is responsible for this, claiming that she bewitched her husband and her illicit lover.[10] The elderly neighbour is then necklaced, although the tales of her killing her husband and lover later turn out to be false.

9    Hoad explains that in Mpe's novel, AIDS is seen as caused by 'an almost fatalistic explanation of contingency, misfortune, and bad luck', citing the narrator's claim that 'at least AIDS came by accident, unlike such malicious acts as sending lightning to strike Tshepo' (2001: 124). While Tiragalong does indeed attribute the death of Tshepo by lightning to the witchcraft of the jealous neighbour who, like Refentše's mother, is cruelly 'necklaced', the narrator says of this that 'it was only after the witch had found her punishment by necklacing, that Tiragalong was given cause to realise its *mistake* in concluding the book of her life in that manner' (2001: 45; emphasis added). Thus the 'witchcraft-induced lightning' is not, in fact, seen by the narrator as witchcraft-induced, or as an act of human agency (Hoad 2005: 124) .

10   In view of this, we can see how Themba's aunt, in Mahala's *When a Man Cries* (2007), fits the trope of a witch: her husband dies in mysterious circumstances, amid much gossip, and she is betrayed by Themba to the police for having colluded with her illicit lover to kill her husband. Her punishment is inflicted by the state, rather than the community: she is imprisoned in the wake of Themba's accusation of her.

That which is other, that which is female: both are implicated in the literally terrorizing aetiology of HIV/AIDS. Witches bring on unexplained illness and women and *Makwerekwere* are associated with bringing the pollution of HIV/AIDS and death into the community.[11]

## Unsettling Patriarchal Sexuality in the Era of AIDS II:
## Jacob Zuma and the Appeal of 'Ethnic' Hyper-masculinity

In his remarkable description of the lines of affiliation that work in both directions to tie the constituent in the rural village to the President in the Union Buildings, Steinberg concludes that 'It is axiomatic: to be black, here and now, in the early years of the twenty-first century, is to vote. And to vote is to vote ANC' (2008: 165). He speculates on what might happen to a villager if that villager were to fail to vote in the municipal government elections on 1 March 2006. His prospective non-voter is, tellingly, female: 'if there is anyone in this village who did not go down to the school to vote, I doubt she would have shamed herself by saying it out loud' (165).

Zuma's role as Deputy President was terminated by Thabo Mbeki in June 2005. He resigned as Deputy President of the ANC in the wake of the corruption charges related to Schabir Shaik, but his strong support from the left wing of the ANC ensured that he was reinstated and given a salary for his service. This was the first time a deputy president of the ANC had received recompense. From a certain perspective, one might speculate that in the wake of the rape charge laid in December 2005, from which Zuma was not acquitted until 6 May 2006, a woman voting in the 1 March 2006 municipal government elections may have had more cause than the failure to deliver basic services for considering not to vote for the ANC.

The complication that developed since Steinberg's astute observation of the

11  This strategy of enacting containment via scapegoating has reasserted itself in the largest riots ever against *Makwerekwere* in South Africa in May 2008. An estimated 62 people were killed and 25,000 displaced. As I noted in the Introduction to this work, the riots marked the first deployment of the South African military within South Africa since the transition. As Mpe's *Welcome to our Hillbrow* (2001) states, many of the stereotypes of *Makwerekwere* – that they are diseased, for example, or 'loose' sex workers, or blacker than indigenous black South Africans, and/or predatory upon them – are, like all stereotypes, unreliable markers of identity: many South Africans were killed and wounded in the xenophobic riots. The reasons for those riots are various, with complex interactions between them. Among the most prominent are the loosening up of border controls after the transition and, in particular, the opening up of borders within the South African Development Community; the growing gap between a black elite and its increasing and increasingly spectacular wealth, and the vast majority of impoverished black South Africans; desperate rates of unemployment; and the ability of employers to profit from well-trained illegal immigrants by working outside South Africa's labour legislation. Undergirding each of these reasons, with monolithic structural determinism, is the failure of the post-apartheid government to deliver acceptable and affordable services to the black majority.

March 2005 municipal government elections was the ANC 'family' feud: the Mbeki-Zuma split. The tensions between the two factions were cemented at the annual leadership convention of the ANC at Polokwane in December 2007, when Zuma, despite his past acquittals for rape and corruption and a pending charge of corruption, won the presidency of the ANC handsomely. The support Zuma has amassed during the rape and corruption charges and their related judgements and rulings suggests that, if the relationship between constituent and President is configured as between family and father in terms of the family as national metaphor, the politics of affiliation within the clan can translate what was a national metaphor into the less comfortable figure of synecdoche. Ardent and plentiful supporters of Zuma expressed their support for him during the rape trial by joining his hyper-masculinist performance; among them, disturbingly, were numerous women who joined in the highly public, misogynistic condemnation of his accuser. These events have been documented with a keen eye and in great detail elsewhere. I repeat some of them here not in the cause of labelling Zuma's (literal) call to arms aggressively patriarchal (that, too, has been accomplished by others), but to highlight what it is about the Zuma performance that is so popular. What is the attraction of his questionably 'traditional Zulu' hyper-masculinity that appeals to his supporters, Zulu-speakers and others? How does this performance help bind Zuma, the president of the ANC and president of the country, to his supporters, along the 'thread' that links local municipalities to the Union buildings? And how does this performance 'read' in terms of the threat posed by the potential stigmatization of masculinity?

The Zuma trial revisited that scene of trauma which is kept secret, with the complicity of the wife, in *When a Man Cries*: the rape of a daughter. The woman who accused Zuma, named Khwezi (Star) by her supporters, was not Zuma's daughter, but the daughter of a close friend of his from his days in exile. He was 64 at the time; she was 31. He claimed that the sex was consensual, an argument that Judge Willem van der Merwe accepted. The plaintiff referred to Zuma throughout as *umalume*, or uncle, even during intense cross-examination, arguing that Zuma was 'as a father' to her; Zuma and his defence team strongly denied this claim. Of significance to my argument is Zuma's hyper-performance of a supposedly authentic masculinity; the discourse surrounding the 'insanity' of the plaintiff; and the virulence with which Zuma's supporters (both male and female) rendered the plaintiff abject.

Steven Robins has commented on Zuma's 'Zulu performance':

> [Zuma] spoke in isiZulu throughout his cross-examination and repeatedly drew on traditionalist idioms and 'cultural rules' to buttress the defence's argument that he had consensual sex with the 31 year old woman accusing him of rape. For example, he spoke of how in Zulu culture 'leaving a woman in that state [of sexual arousal]' was the worst thing a man could do. 'She could even have you arrested and charged with rape,' he told the court. He addressed the judge as '*nkosi*' – *yenkantolo* (the king of the court) and referred to his accuser's private parts as *isibhaya sika bab'wakhe* – her father's kraal. He also conceded that he entered the kraal without *ijazi ka mkhwnyana* – the

groom/husband's coat, or … a condom. These translations of isiZulu idioms
are usually associated with 'deep' rural KwaZulu-Natal. (Robins 2006: 163)

In addition, Zuma argued, should the plaintiff have wanted him to pay *lobola*, or
a bride-price, for the woman, he would have been, and still was, ready to do so.
Outside the court, Zuma supporters wore T-shirts with the caption '100% Zulu
boy'; supporters burned posters with an image of the plaintiff and her name
on them, crying 'Burn the Bitch'; and women burned G-strings to demonstrate
against the supposed sexual promiscuity of the plaintiff. Also in evidence were
anti-rape demonstrators of the 1-in-9 campaign, illustrating that so few women
are prepared to report their rape to the police, with whom Zuma supporters
clashed. Following the trial, the plaintiff went into exile in the Netherlands, as
she feared her safety could not be assured within South Africa. During the trial,
Zuma supporters made her real name public; they also stoned a woman they
believed to be her.

Steven Robins has pointed out that 'this situated performance of Zulu masculinity' was not just mediated 'to South Africans and the wider world' via local
and international media 'fascinated with primordialist fantasies of Zulu culture
and sexuality' (2006: 164). This masculinity is also historically constructed via
the manipulation of 'tradition' by the colonialist and apartheid regimes to forge
coalitions between colonial officials and tribal elders through the promotion of
patriarchal interests. In this respect, Mark Sanders' distinction (2007: 77–98)
between custom and 'customary law' is salient: custom describes a way of doing
things and customary law codifies and dehistoricizes that way of doing things
in the interests of what Kopano Ratele (2006) has called the 'ruling masculinity'.
Sanders' concern with the potential contradiction in terms of a constitution
that grants equal rights to women, yet preserves 'Customary Law' to account
for elements such as polygamy, is of specific import in the Zuma case. Such a
constitution in fact has the potential to undermine women's actual customary
practices – an aspect of their defacement in terms of my argument. Zuma is a
polygamist, who has four wives and three women for whom he has paid *lobola*,
but whom he has not yet (at the time of writing) married. Women's constitutional rights theoretically trump the concessions to customary law in cases
of appeal. In this respect, the central role of the question of *lobola* in Zuma's
defence can be seen as an acting out against the constitutional provisions on
equality. Moreover, this act may appear to present Zuma as an 'authentic' Zulu
male or '100% Zulu boy', but in fact depends upon an exoticization of Zulu tradition that is neo-colonialist in its import.

Simphiwe Sesanti has argued for an Afrocentrist interpretation of the South
African Constitution, citing Thandabantu Nhlapo's claim that 'if a "culture of
rights" is to take root in South Africa – and in a sustainable fashion – the association of human rights with Western thought and world views is not helpful for
the general populace' (Sesanti 2008: 369). However, Sesanti's article points out
that Zuma was able to sell several of his actions as having resulted from his
'Zuluness', despite the fact that these actions would be condemned by many

Zulus precisely for their betrayal of Zulu notions of communal and familial duty and reciprocity – many of which notions are shared across the other ethnic groups of South Africa. For example, both Sesanti (2008) and Mmatshilo Motsei (2007) point out that the familial claim made by the plaintiff was rejected by Zuma in direct contravention of the conventions that govern conditions of respect between generations within a community. Further, according to Sesanti, while there is indeed a tradition of polygamy in Zulu communities, there is no way in which this negates adultery as a violation of custom. Indeed, the lack of commentary on this aspect of Zuma's behaviour may be the result of a public so impressed with exotic images of a conveniently manufactured ethnicity that it assumes that there can be no adultery in a polygamous marriage: an assumption that could be interpreted as highly insulting under the circumstances. Zuma further claimed that the traditional khanga, a garment worn by women across Africa, represented the tempting short skirt of international notoriety as a symbol of women having 'asked for it'. This argument, too, Mmatshilo Motsei demolishes with her customary expertise (2007).

On the issue of a Zulu man not being able to leave a woman in a state of desire without acting on her (presumed) desire, Sesanti (2008: 373) cites Professor Sihawu Ngubane, director of the isiZulu programme at the University of KwaZulu-Natal, telling The *Mail & Guardian* that he has never heard of such a phenomenon. This rejection of Zuma's appeal to Zulu culture to explain his engaging in sexual intercourse with the plaintiff was repeated by a variety of informants. Motsei persuasively reads this moment as evidence of how blacks have internalized the stereotype of the black man's lack of control, especially when it comes to sexual appetite. Indeed, Motsei references the history of the representation of black men as rapists, not in relation to the nature of the complaint brought against Zuma but to the manner in which he defends himself as a Zulu man whose duty it is to satisfy his woman: 'As a people, we have internalized these stereotypical notions of black men's sexuality', she says (2007: 27).

Ultimately Judge van der Merwe found against the plaintiff, in large part resting his argument on her lack of credibility. This supposed lack of credibility emerged from arguments that van der Merwe found convincing over the irrationality the defence attributed to the plaintiff's behaviour, both within the Zuma household and prior to the incident. The judge allowed the complainant's past sexual history to be introduced, permitting the defence to lead testimony on this subject. The defence argued that she had a history of false rape accusations going back to her childhood. This in turn labelled the defendant as mentally unstable. We have already traced the mechanism whereby women protesting against conditions of extreme oppression within the patriarchy are labelled as 'insane', with reference to Butler's theory of the relations between the realm of the unspeakable and the instantiation of subjects. In the trial, the language of sanity/insanity played a key role, and not only in relation to the plaintiff. The defence claimed that a 'sane man' would never have raped a woman with a policeman on the grounds and his daughter sleeping in the same house. The defence reproduced the trope of insanity as tautology in reference to the rape victim when, having claimed that the plaintiff was insane, rendering her claims to having been raped before therefore false, it nevertheless proposed that when the plaintiff testified to having 'froze' upon seeing the naked Zuma with an erect penis next to her bed, she should have had some experience of how to defend herself against the assailant, precisely because she had been sexually assaulted in the past.[12]

What some observers found disturbing was the large number of female Zuma supporters, and the vehemence of their performance of that support. Ms. Euginia Yantcho of Bellevue East claimed that behaviour such as the plaintiff's 'destroys our men'. She took part in the burning of the G-string bikinis, saying that the purpose of the demonstration was to take a moral stand against women who accuse men of rape 'too easily': 'Our daughters are asking to be raped' when they wear G-strings, she claimed (Nel 2006). Another woman wore ANC colours while carrying a placard saying 'No Woman President' (Motsei 2007: 30). This is a reference to the fact that Mbeki had called for a female to be made president to demonstrate the embrace of women's constitutional equality at the highest level. This was interpreted by pro-Zuma supporters as Thabo Mbeki proposing that his Deputy, Phumizile Mlambo-Ngcuka, should be president after him, to prevent Zuma from becoming president. An infamous supporter of Zuma, Ma Mkhize from Umzimkulu, claimed that if she had been raped by Zuma, she would feel so honoured she would not have bathed her bosom that had come into contact with his for days (Motsei 2007: 31). Lindiwe Tshabalala, 46, an office manager from Pimville, Soweto, claimed that 'If it really happened to her, I feel sorry for her, because she's ruined somebody else's life politically'. She said, referring to the plaintiff, that 'she should have screamed if this was really rape': 'Even with a gun, you have to come out of that without being raped. Even if he slaps you – you run away, you scream, you do whatever you can to stop him' (United Nations Office for the Co-ordination of Humanitarian Affairs 2006).

While Motsei attributes these sentiments to an internalization of the values of the patriarchy, the phenomenon of women's apparent collusion in their own oppression requires more specific contextualization in terms of how the introduction of women's constitutional rights put some South African women in an exceedingly difficult position. AIDS activists and researchers have pointed out that even if women are educated regarding AIDS and understand the principles of abstaining, being faithful, and condom usage (the ABC campaign), their ability to act on that information is constrained by their lack of social power. The women with whom I have worked since 1996 find themselves in an analogous dilemma with regard to their rights. For example, they know, from educational workshops, that it is their right to say no to sex, even within marriage; but in many situations attempts to enact these rights will result in violence against

---

12  Had the plaintiff really been of unsound mind, Motsei argues, the fact that Zuma had known her since she was five means that he would have known of her mental instability. Having foreknowledge of the plaintiff's supposed fragile mental condition would have made him particularly ill-advised to follow through with a sexual encounter.

the woman asserting her rights, and termination of a relationship which may be providing her with the income to support her family. Here the law appears to be destabilizing relations between men and women rather than warding off violence (Jolly and Jeeves forthcoming). By inducing 'lack of respect' between men and women, and failing to support women through enforcement, human rights legislation causes guilt to accrue to women, who know they have the legal and moral right to protect themselves, but are, in fact, unable to do so:[13]

> Men do not like us to use our rights, even though we know our rights and are told how to use them, but they maintain that men are still men, they have to be listened to. Even though you [as a woman] know you have rights and you know what to do, you get abused because you cannot use them because you are afraid of a man. (Boyce, Jolly et al. 2003–2006)

This extends to the question of rape within marriage, which may be illegal but is considered a man's right, even in the eyes of many women: 'It is possible you are getting raped [within marriage], even when you don't like it [the sex], you have to sleep with him because he is a man and he has his rights' (Boyce, Jolly et al. 2003–2006). Even where a woman does not respect the husband's right to sexual intercourse on demand within marriage, she hesitates to exercise her right to report his behaviour because she risks loss of his financial support and the termination of the relationship: 'When you [a woman] open a case, you will not be on good terms with him, he may even ask you to part ways, he will say, how can I love someone who threatens to put me in jail, because he won't be free to beat you up anymore' (2003–2006).

Or, as another woman put it, a woman cannot risk the security a man offers her and her children by reporting him for abuse, even if she knows it is her right to report him (I quoted this research participant in Chapter 3 in relation to women's commitment to a better future for their girl children):

> What is problematic nowadays is that we as women are enlightened, when there is a problem and you realise that you are being abused, you want to find the solution for that problem, whilst trying to find the solution, there is that pressure coming from men, they oppress you at that point and that makes it difficult. (Boyce, Jolly et al. 2003–2006)

Rather than suggest that women internalize the values of patriarchal masculinity for customary reasons, these statements suggest that women who both understand and accept their rights under the Constitution live with a sense of victimization, fear and guilt, their hope being that their children will live in times when the gender order will not put men and women under the pressure of conformity to patriarchal gender relations.

We are living in the period of transition when, to tell a woman who has lived in a marriage in which patriarchal gender roles have applied or apply now, that

---

13   I am indebted to Alan Jeeves for his identification of this element of guilt in women educated as to their constitutional rights, yet unable to act upon them for fear of reprisal.

if her husband has demanded sex from her and she did not want to have sex, she has been raped through the course of her marriage (whether *lobola* has been paid or not). This puts that woman in the position of re-envisaging herself as a victim. The negative consequences of this have been explored in some detail in Chapter 3. Thus, when we have women at Zuma's trial performing what may seem to be their own abjection, they may be engaging in denial as a survival strategy. To accept patriarchal gender roles and the potential violence that may ensue from them is better for some than the stigma of shame and the experience of isolation attendant upon transforming oneself into the modern woman proposed by the Constitution, without the requisite social power to live that way. The techniques of modernity required to perform a liberated gendered self are not (yet) customary. The fact that the plaintiff is a lesbian, and declared herself to be so in the course of the trial to indicate her lack of desire for a masculine partner, may well have increased the rage against her for this reason. That is to say, comments such as Ma Mhkize's represent not simply an affirmation of Zuma as a Zulu male, but of the compulsory hetero-normativity that the patriarchy dictates. Lesbianism could be seen as 'opting out' of that which is compulsory, including the oppression of women that the compulsory necessarily entails.

I have proposed that Mbeki's denialist policies as they relate to HIV/AIDS, gender-based violence and (until very recently) Mugabe's human rights violations, and the appeal of the populist Zuma, when all are taken together, portray a particular and consistent logic in the linking of gender to racialized masculinity, despite the facts that each leader's response has been distinctly different, and that each leader's response may well be attended by differential levels of self-awareness of the consequences for the broader public (although measures of self-awareness cannot be verified.) If Mbeki's related denialisms are seen as part of a conceptual approach constructed to counter racist representations of black women and men as barbarous – 'as human beings of a lower order, unable to subject passion to reason' – and his African Renaissance and initiatives related to countering moral degeneration can be seen as an attempt to persuade the society not to conform to this racist image, then Zuma's hyper-masculine, hyper-'Zulu' performance can be seen as a rejection of the very notion that moral regeneration is required.

This explains why, when Judge van der Merwe reprimanded Zuma for failing to control his sexual desires and failing to have sex with a woman he knew to be HIV positive without wearing a condom, Zuma's apologies in the press appeared to lack sincerity. Zuma, former Chair of the South African National AIDS Council, told the court that he had showered after having had sex with the plaintiff to reduce the chance of infection. In his press conference the day after the acquittal he apologized for having 'made a mistake' (Clayton 2007) in having unsafe sex with a woman he knew to be HIV positive. Van der Merwe's paraphrasing of Rudyard Kipling when reprimanding Zuma for allowing his desire to get away with him – 'If you can control your sexual urges, then you are a man, my son' (Hope 2006) – not only replays the very white, colonialist morality that labelled black sexuality excessive in the stereotypes Mbeki seeks to dislodge; it also gives Zuma and his supporters an opportunity to stage their rejection of such morality. While Zuma said that he found the trial judge fair, the flippancy with which he dealt with criticism in the press of his comments regarding the plaintiff's HIV status, and his supporters' vehement rejection of the Christian morality that the judge was seen to reference in his judgement, suggest that this occasion to flaunt both conventional sexual mores and the precepts of basic HIV prevention play into a performance of masculine status that resembles Themba's boasts of his sexual prowess to the reader prior to his demise in *When a Man Cries*. As Themba deflects his loss of status when he loses Dolly to the mayor onto Dolly herself – she is said to have lost self-respect – so does the Zuma trial perform the transference of a potential loss of self-respect attributable to Zuma onto the plaintiff. For those for whom this hyper-masculine performance works, that is to say, is attractive, the vehemence with which she has been castigated as one who has falsely 'cried rape' is in inverse proportion to the stature that accrues to Zuma as the ideal leader, and vice versa.

In this respect, Zuma's populism does not make those men who fear the constitutionally decreed equal rights of women, or, indeed, the women who fear such changes, 'feel bad'. Nor does the performance suggest that the impoverished masses should engage in behaviour modification that appears to conform precisely to the white, Christian morality brought to bear on the colonial and neo-colonial surveillance of black masculinity in the first place, even if some perceived conformity to this morality may be required for protection against HIV transmission. The reassuring familiarity that Zuma offers his supporters no doubt constitutes in large measure his extraordinary popularity with the masses, who see Mbeki as notoriously distant from the ANC rank and file and, by extension, from them. They regard Mbeki as a leader with intellectual tendencies who has lost touch with the quotidian experiences of the impoverished majority. The comfort of familiar gender roles, those inherited from the colonial and apartheid entrenchment of black patriarchy and female subservience, is central, not peripheral, to Zuma's appeal.

Mbeki's apparently contradictory manoeuvres – rejecting colonial and neocolonial racism by denying a certain ontology, at the same time introducing programming to ensure that ontology does not appear verified – come close to a situation in which the instantiation of the black subject as gendered (and how can *he* not be, having constructed 'female' completely *within* the confines of the patriarchy?) occurs simultaneously with the threat of his defacement – his stigmatization. Zuma's excessive flaunting of the moral gaze upon his own sexual behaviour represents a rejection of the terms of Mbeki's dilemma altogether. But while Hoad's reading of *Welcome to our Hillbrow* risks invoking the ideal, that ideal is actualized in Zuma's performance. Here, the appeal of/to an ideal – *there is nothing wrong with me/us; and thus I/we have done nothing wrong* – resurrects the subservient female subject, constituted by the colonial and apartheid eras, as the original, the authentic, subject. This performed denial of her oppressive history and current dilemma in the assumption of her subservience as authentic – *Zuma*'s denialism – is, therefore, not a peripheral side effect of his politics, but central to its appeal. The instantiation of the (male) black subject in this context depends upon the female (black) subject's defacement.

Njabulo Ndebele pointed this out, most importantly emphasizing that this dynamic is evident in Zuma's performance, without the question of his innocence or guilt of the actual rape charge even being addressed. Ndebele's piece, entitled 'Jacob Zuma and the Family: How Zuma's Bravado Brutalized the Public (2007b: 230–32)', was written in response to Zuma amassing support for himself during the trial by invoking the militaristic masculinity of the apartheid struggle. The piece was composed prior to Zuma's acquittal for rape, and affirms the fact that Zuma should be considered innocent until he is proven guilty. In Ndebele's eyes, what Zuma was guilty of when the piece was being written, was performing, symbolically, the power of aggressive patriarchal sexuality through his association with the liberation song *Umshini wami*, '(Bring me) my machine gun'), in which the militant calls for his AK47 machine gun, in the context of a rape trial: 'Was he knowingly and defiantly inviting me to make horrible connections between the AK-47 and the invasive penis?' (232). Ndebele calls upon Zuma to constitute his ANC 'family' without invoking the persona of the raped woman as enemy. He reflects that 'as [Zuma] sang and danced with his supporters, images of South Africa's raped mothers, sisters, daughters (some of them infants), nieces, aunts, grandmothers, raced through my mind, torturing me. Are their pain and the broad sense of public morality of little consequence in the settling of "family" scores?' (232)

The irrelevance of the question of Zuma's actual guilt or innocence in the face of such hyper-masculine performance is, paradoxically, another tragic effect of the dynamic's (d)effacement of the female. The performance demonizes the plaintiff, who becomes a spectre of herself in the process. Certainly, her desire is an irrelevant criterion: it disappears in resounding silence. The silence of Zuma's wives during his trial; the silence of Thuli over the issue of Themba as a paedophilic and incestuous rapist, and the issue of his HIV status; the silence of the *Flowers of the Nation* over the fact that the desire women must repress in order to save themselves for marriage, family and the nation, and from HIV, will not be sufficient in the face of jackrollers: these silences render female desire unspeakable in the face of hyper-masculine performance. Motsei figures this silence in her concise reversal of the trial judge's pronouncement on the Zuma complainant. Motsei points out that in a society in which the sexual assault of women is socially sanctioned, women's presence can be read as consent. In such a context, she argues, 'just like the complainant who might, according to Judge van der Merwe, "perceive any sexual encounter as rape", Zuma might perceive all acts of patriarchal sex as consensual' (2007: 23).

## Non-hegemonic Masculinities: Negotiating the Abject

My aim in this chapter is not to suggest that South African masculinity is monolithic; or that the varieties of masculinity that appear as practised or as ideal are uniformly patriarchal. My concern is, however, to point out that political figures of the status of Mbeki and Zuma manifest formative political concepts that embody certain senses of gender; that these senses of gender are not incidental, but central to those concepts; and that these senses of gender influence and are influenced by quotidian masculinities, both ideal and practised. The performances of masculinity that Mbeki and Zuma undertake are, I argue, responses to the threat of a situation in which men enter into the realm of the speakable by occupying a position of negative moral and social worth. In the case of Mbeki, his denialism of HIV, of gender-based violence and of Mugabe's human rights violations stem from a fear of the return of racism, in which blacks occupy the position of the abject. His drive to censor any scene that may appear to conform to colonialist and neo-colonialist stereotypes, such as the spectre of AIDS ('a diseased and dying people') or the spectre of the black male as rapist ('[a being] of [a] lower order that cannot submit [his] passion to reason') is constructed around fear of the black African being rendered abject.

Zuma, I argue, undertakes a calculated performance of hyper-masculinity that appeals to both men and women who sense that constitutional democracy, and the rights it seeks to entrench, are a threat to what they assume to be customary gender performance: hetero-normative relations between male and female, negotiated via the patriarchy. It should be pointed out, however, that this ideal of hetero-normativity in gender roles is precisely that – an ideal. The fact that it is an ideal that conforms to notions of gender performance that may be more popular in many communities of South Africa than those to which the Constitution gestures does not mean that the hetero-normative ideal is readily attainable. Zuma may be able to perform the fantasy of the man well in control of, and able to provide for, his family, from paying *lobola* (or readiness to pay *lobola*), to a man in charge of the gendered norms that supposedly govern this idealized family, but the resources he has to do so are exceptional. In any event, this performance cannot be assumed to correspond even to Zuma's lived reality.

Current research on masculinities in South Africa suggests that the most violent responses to change come from severely marginalized men who use violence against women as a way of breaching the gap between the masculine ideal and their lived realities. The difficulty with Zuma's performance is not only that its hyper-masculinity and his status rally extant support for the unattainable hyper-masculine ideal, but also that they lend that ideal further allure and quotidian currency. As a mechanism that contends with the fear of masculinity being rendered abject by displacing the figure of that which could become abject onto woman, in the name of instantiating her 'proper' or 'authentic' subjectivity, the Zuma performance replicates the figure of hyper-masculinity that Mahala offers us in Themba, the protagonist of *When a Man Cries* (2007). Themba projects his own fear of losing self-respect onto Dolly: her supposed lack of self-respect, which renders her unavailable, simultaneously resurrects Themba as a principled man. The characters of Nosipho and the plaintiff in the Zuma case also have narratives that mirror one another in an eerie parody.

My analysis does not suggest that the damaging effects of a patriarchy reacting in fear to the threat of a masculinity perceived to be at risk of itself being rendered abject is in any way essential or non-negotiable. On the other hand, like Tina Sideris (2005) I wish to avoid the suggestion that identifying a minority of men who have attempted to renegotiate their relations with women differently is cause for widespread optimism. In *Welcome to our Hillbrow* (2005), Phaswane Mpe makes the point that invocations of the ideal, rather than being strategies for re-envisaging and renegotiating our relations to the actual, can be violently exclusionary in their absolutism. The realm of the ideal is absent from the novel not just in terms of plot but even of the retrospective knowledge gained by those who die and enter Heaven. Heaven in Mpe's fiction is not a place that confirms the dead person's morality as superior; it is not a place of omnipotence; nor are the inhabitants of Heaven without regret, as they spend their time viewing the actions of those still living with concern. The well-being of the inhabitants of Heaven depends on how they are remembered by the living and their descendants. Here, Mpe suggests that the ways in which people on Earth selectively reconstruct the lives that those in heaven lived when on Earth, in order to make those lives 'fit' the fears and aspirations of the living, have the greatest potential to disturb Heaven's inhabitants:

> Heaven is the archive that those we left behind keep visiting and revisiting; digging this out, suppressing or burying that. Continually reconfiguring the stories of our lives, as if they alone hold the real and true version […]. Heaven can also be Hell, depending on the nature of our continuing existence in the memories and consciousness of the living. (Mpe 2005: 124)

What those in Heaven appear to have the capacity to do is rehearse their former actions in a critical light. Thus the narrator reflects that Refentše's suicide is 'seductive' in its easiness, its absolute judgement of Refentše himself and Lerato. What Refentše relinquishes in suicide is the opportunity to reinterpret the story of his and Lerato's infidelities as human, rather than exceptional. This opportunity is explicitly linked to the ability to interpret an archive of life stories differently:

> There would always be another story of love, betrayal, friendship, joy and pain to add to our narrative granary. There would always be the need to revise, reinforce, contradict…. Every act of listening, seeing, smelling, feeling, tasting is a reconfiguring of the story of our lives. Yet when Lerato and Sammy provided you [Refentše] with the chance to add to your storehouse of experience, you could not rise to it. (Mpe 2001: 61)

Refentše's response – suicide – matches precisely the kind of absolutism demanded by the hyper-masculine ideal of complete control. Despair at his exposure as a cuckold by Sammy, and his fear-driven fantasies of Lerato repeatedly betraying him, fed by the aptly named Terror, led Refentše to choose death rather than renegotiate his relationships with others and himself.

*When a Man Cries* describes some renegotiation between Themba and his community through his reconciliation with his former rival, Skade, and the community at Nosipho's funeral, although the substantive element of the renegotiation of his relationship with his wife remains unrepresented. Tellingly, in order to come to the point of apologizing both to the community and his wife for his failings, Themba first identifies with that most abject of creatures, the Sekunjalo bitch, the proverbial mad dog, who comes to raid his rubbish bin. Despite the fact that the community associates the feared bitch with witchcraft, Themba invites the flea-ridden, emaciated creature into his house, feeding her and embracing her:

> I do not have a dish for the dog so I spill the food on the floor and the bitch readily cleans it with her tongue. Part of the food falls onto my feet and the tongue starts licking the porridge from my toes and the sandals I am wearing. I feel her tongue rubbing on my skin and it tickles. For the first time in a long time I find myself laughing. I go back to the kitchen and put the now almost clean pot back in the sink.
>
> I come back to the sitting room and find the dog lying flat with her belly on the floor rug. She wags her tail as I appear from the kitchen. I feel good that some creature out there is happy to see me, appreciates who I am; and is able to make me laugh. I sit on the floor next to the bitch. I lie with my belly on the floor and rest my chin on my right fist. I stretch out my left hand to reach for the body of the bitch. I start cuddling her silky body. I am lying next to one of the most famous and feared figures in Sekunjalo and yet I don't have the fright that I used to have when I heard people talking about the deadly venom of the bitch. The bitch is known all over the township, but I never heard anyone calling her by name. They call her, excuse me, we all call her 'the bitch', but today I am going to give her a new name. (Mahala 2007: 141–42)

Themba names her Lily, because he reflects that she has healing power, just as the leaves of the lily are used to cure septic wounds and insect bites. If his renegotiation with his wife remains to be proved, that with Lily does not; he 'marries' Lily in what the community would see as an abject state, but the 'marriage' is the one that frees him from the panoptical censorship of 'proper' masculinity, enabling him to go to the funeral and meet with his family. The human-canine 'marriage' is clearly described:

> Lily closes her eyes as I continue caressing her silky soft body. I come closer to her face and she seems unfazed by my closeness to her. I come closer and touch my nose with hers. Her body is warm but her nose is as cold as ice. She opens her eyes slightly and releases a pleasant whine that sounds like 'I do'. (2007: 142)

Themba later has to wash off the fleas he has picked up from Lily, the first shower he has had in a long time, in which he reflects that his sexual associations of the past, undertaken simply to add another name to his list of 'sexual victims' (142), have had consequences 'that will haunt me to the grave' (143).

The image of Themba embracing the most feared and hated creature in Sekunjalo is an apt one with which to close this narrative journey. The image points to possibilities for renegotiating a number of violent relations, by relinquishing fear of social sanction and embracing that which the majority of the community deems to be abject. The 'Sekunjalo bitch' is a most hated and feared figure of witchcraft, believed incapable of metamorphosis, suggesting that there is nothing to fear so much as change, especially where the female figure (human or dog) is associated with that change. Yet Themba literally adopts Lily, and in so doing relinquishes his fear of occupying a position of negative moral and social worth: he sees himself as both man and abuser of women and girl-children. That this position will be fraught with opposition is indicated by the old woman at Nosipho's funeral, who labels Themba 'human waste' (156) and a 'sorry sight' (157), and calls upon the community to beat him. Her aggression is reminiscent of Zuma's supporters at his trial for rape: she defends speakable masculinity with tenacity. Nevertheless, the bitch of Sekunjalo reconfigures the position of the plaintiff: the 'bitch' of 'Burn the Bitch' becomes, in *When a Man Cries*, both the catalyst and the means through which violent sexual relations are seen to be violent by the perpetrator. In this embrace of what was formerly seen to be abject, and feared as such, the narration renegotiates its relations with those who have been figured as abject within the realm of the speakable: non-human; child; woman.

# CONCLUSION

# Constituting Dishonour

Since the institution of their finalized democratic Constitution in 1996, South Africans of all walks of life and in all places have been flooded with workshops that were established with the goal of educating citizens to 'Know Your Rights'. Driving this approach is the notion that citizens have rights of all kinds that the state should support, and that the state is capable of supporting these rights to the degree necessary to assure them. The citizen's responsibility is to remind the state of *its* responsibility to protect the citizen, in an interesting transference – interesting for the breadth of its scope – of accountability for the self to the state. One thinks here of the extent to which subjects of the Western democracies depend upon the state increasingly to mediate interpersonal relationships of all kinds. An unsettling irony appears: the subjects hand over responsibility for an increasing sphere of their existence to the state in the name of democracy. This is not to deny at all the fact that rights-based discourse has led to some crucial victories in South Africa in the area of HIV/AIDS care, women's and children's rights. However, the problem of the ability of the state to single-handedly construct an environment in which basic human rights are exercised, rather than the actual exercise of these rights remaining in the realm of the ideal, runs as a fundamental question mark through the fabric of post-apartheid culture, *alongside* the assumption of the achievability of this ideal state.

This tension is evidenced in the difficulty men and women experience in their attempts to renegotiate marital and sexual relationships in contemporary South Africa. Alan Jeeves and I have pointed out that communicating women's rights under the Constitution to women in a context in which they are unable to exercise those rights results in women educated as to their constitutional 'privileges', but feeling guilty in terms of their inability to act upon them. Similarly, men are aware of women's rights under the Constitution, and some may indeed wish to renegotiate their relations with their female partners, but there is no

157

customary, or speakable, language with which to initiate this process. When we interviewed women about negotiating rights within marriage, such as the right to decline to have sex with one's husband, or to be free of abuse, it became clear that women see the language of claiming right(s) as one far more likely to provoke violence than deter it (Boyce, Jolly et al. 2006).

The participants in the interviews suggested that a language of respectful negotiation, rather than demand, would be necessary to implementation of some of these rights successfully. However, the overwhelming sense was one of a radical disjuncture between the lived experience, or habitus, of marital and/or established partner relations and the discourse of claiming rights:

> Interviewer: Have human rights laws affected men's relations with women?
>
> Person B: It depends on how that man perceives that, or how you as a woman have shown him that you know your rights. If you rudely[1] show him that you know your rights, he will see that as a problem. But if you tell him nicely, or even before he does something abusive, you tell him about your rights, make him aware that you know your rights, he may understand your rights.
>
> Person C: Yes there are rights but sometimes they don't work because then you don't rely on each other for anything, there's no time to persuade each other. You go your own way and he does the same. There's no dependence on each other. (Boyce, Jolly et al. 2003–2006)

The men's interviews illustrated men's agreement with this analysis. The relevant quotation is worth repeating in full:

> The extent of the violence that men mete out to women these days is also fuelled by their [men's] perception of women's rights. These days when a man beats his wife, he is often scared that if he leaves her alive she will take the matter to the police and he will definitely be condemned by the justice system which favours women. I think that the reason why men are so brutal to their partners, is because women are failing to use their rights in a responsible manner.[2] (Boyce, Jolly et al. 2003–2006)

In this context, as we have observed elsewhere, women understand perfectly well that 'rudely showing [the man] your rights' precludes negotiation and disrupts the relationship: 'You go your own way and he does the same'. With men fearing abjection as they perceive patriarchal power to be diminishing, the female participants were informing us that the language of gender equality could destroy the mutuality of the relationship in a heartbeat.

1 The word 'rude' in this context is strongly correlated to the refusal or failure to practise *hlonipa*: a system of showing respect for familial and community hierarchies through specific practices of gesture and speech (see Finlayson 2002). Since the practice of *hlonipa* is a means of both creating and representing the bonds between members of family and community, this lends more rather than less import to the participant's claim.
2 This suggests that the practice of *hlonipa* and the exercise of women's constitutionally defended rights are viewed as mutually exclusive.

There are, I think, two different levels at which one can read this story. At one level – a level that does not get to the core of the issue – one can argue that such couples simply have a problem at the level of knowledge: men and women should be educated as to the 'correctness' of the equitable gender relations manifest in the constitutional provisions on gender equality. However, the dilemma at the level of the man and the woman attempting to renegotiate, rather than terminate, their relationship, remains. The situation allows for no nuances. Either the woman accepts the violation of her rights, or she risks violence and/or the termination of the relationship. The man either relinquishes his experience of what it means to be masculine within his community by becoming a subject knowledgeable in terms of the current law, or responds to his wife with termination of the relationship and/or violence.

The difficulty with assigning the failures of the Constitution to citizens' lack of knowledge is that it overlooks the limitations of the kind of subject the Constitution assumes in the first instance. In the discourse of 'know your rights', the state should take care of its subjects; and when it does not, the subject should claim her right(s). On the other hand, the man who fears the diminution of his power, and his partner, who lives between guilt over not asserting her rights and fear of asserting them, constitute improper subjects of the Constitution: they haven't got the idea (yet). But is the dilemma as simple as practices on the ground 'catching up' with constitutional provisions? At a different level, I suggest, one can read this story as not about the inadequacy of the subjects of the state in terms of their lack of knowledge and/or faulty performance, but about the limitations of the kind of subject assumed by constitutional law in (lack of) respect of those who fall outside its habitus.

The central difficulty we return to in over-reliance on the Constitution to think through and effect human rights practices can be phrased in the form of a fundamental paradox. Humanitarian discourse and human rights legislation phrase the relationship to their rights of those subjects who are expected to command rights as a relationship of ownership. To 'have' rights is the formula we use for the abstract expression of this relationship. Yet when it comes to the attempt to ensure that those rights are asserted, one cannot logically use the language of possession: if one has the right (already), why would one need help to assert that right? Of course, one can answer this by arguing that the right is there in the abstract, but the subject who is supposed to command that right 'needs assistance' to exercise the right, to make the right a reality. This form of the argument presupposes that all that has to happen in South Africa for the Constitution to be effective is for practices on the ground to 'catch up' with its provisions.

However, performatively speaking this poses the problem of the subject who (is supposed to) command rights – say, for example, our woman attempting to negotiate change – not as one who actually commands rights, but as a supplicant before the law. In Kelly Oliver's terms, discussed in Chapter 3, she is forced to seek recognition within a hierarchy that regards her as marginal. Furthermore, the law would conceive of the male partner – the one who feels threatened by the introduction of women's rights – as a perpetrator *with* access to forms of negotiating his relationships that are alternatives to the hyper-masculine. This would be a harsh judgement, considering the evidence of the final chapter of this work; but perhaps more importantly, not a judgement that would necessarily produce change. It is interesting that in either case the law constructs these two subjects as *shameful*: she because she cannot exercise agency on her own behalf, despite her knowledge of it; he because he is incapable of mastering the post-apartheid discourses of gender equality and is, in that sense, not a man in the eyes of the law.

In *Diary of a Bad Year*, J. M. Coetzee, through his author protagonist who is also named Coetzee, poses two fictional scenarios, one in which citizens envisage opting out of the state; and another in which honour and its correlative, shame, have become obsolete. In terms of the state, the fictional Coetzee-narrator outlines Hobbes's myth of the founding of the state, in which 'we' – its citizens 'historically and severally yielded up to the state the right to use physical force [...] thereby entering the realm (the protection) of the law. Those who chose and choose to stay outside the compact', he says, 'become outlaw' (Coetzee 2007: 3). Later, in a scene discussed in Chapter 3, Anya, the survivor of sexual assault, explains to him that he 'should' not feel shame or dishonour in respect of her sexual assault, or, for that matter, of the disgraceful torture of those at Guantanamo, because he is, as an individual, not responsible for either of these acts of violence. I cite the passage again:

> You have got it wrong, Mister C. Old thinking. Wrong analysis [...]. Abuse, rape, torture, it doesn't matter what: the news is, as long as it is not your fault, as long as you are not responsible, the dishonour doesn't stick to you. So you have been making yourself miserable over nothing. (Coetzee 2007: 103–105)

This is certainly the argument the law would take in its focus on individual responsibility. Yet when the author-narrator responds to Anya, as we have seen, he angers her intensely by claiming that he, contrary to her claim, feels dishonour in respect of her assailants. Further, he claims that she herself cannot escape that dishonour:

> No man is an island, I said. She looked blank. We are all part of the main, I said. Things haven't changed, mistress Anya... Dishonour won't be washed away. Won't be wished away.... Still has its old power to stick. Your three American boys – I have never laid eyes on them, but they dishonour me nevertheless.... And I would be very surprised if in your inmost depths they did not continue to dishonour you. (2007: 104–111)

In Chapter 3 I make an argument concerning shame and stigma – that in shame, following Agamben, the subject is instantiated – that is, becomes a subject – by 'virtue' of being seen in a manner that is entirely inconsonant with her sense of herself, and is thus prey to subjectification and desubjectification at one and the same moment. This means that the subject only becomes meaningful to others in terms of a reading of herself that she fundamentally rejects. The implication of my argument is that the healing of victim-survivors is, in part, dependent upon a society's true (as opposed to 'deaf') listening to the critique of its habitus both implied and offered by victim-survivors, and its subsequent reconfiguration of the speakable according to the inadequacies embodied in that critique. In this context, our author-narrator is not saying that Anya 'should' feel dishonour, but rather that it may be impossible for Anya to claim that she can free herself of such dishonour, as her constitution as a subject is not dependent upon her alone.

The myth the law projects is that Anya is in control of her instantiation as a subject; but no matter how proud Anya may be – and she shows considerable self-respect, authority and pride as a character – in her 'inmost depths' she is not free of her construction by others. This much is made clear when Alan, her boyfriend and the potential swindler of the author-narrator's (Coetzee's) bank account, gets drunk and embarrasses her in front of him. She is not to blame, but she feels shame, acute shame, nonetheless. In the case of this domestic contretemps, Anya is ashamed to *be* Alan's partner, and subsequently dumps him, leaving his apartment and also the service of Coetzee. The potential for her construction by others to have a negative impact on her is also indicated in her refusal to tell the Coetzee character anything further about the story of her sexual assault after she laid the charges. Whether her assailants were found, how she was treated subsequently, and the like, remain unknown: 'The rest doesn't concern you', she tells him, when he inquires of her what happened after the charge.

In this context, shame is not an assertion of responsibility, but a marker of the subject's acute discomfort with her (de)subjectification within a given circumstance. Also at work is a notion that the law may assume subjects to be independently responsible, but some subjects – the Coetzee character, say, and the women who indicated concern about the breakdown of marital relations for reasons that exceed their individual safety and security (Boyce, Jolly et al. 2003–2006) – imagine, construct and represent responsibility as a communal attribute. In this view of things, it would appear that the construction of shame and the responsibility for the violation are mutually, that is, *socially* constituted. In the instance of shame, this is true both for the women we have met, fictional and actual, who find themselves 'outside' the law. It is also true for a character such as Themba, or public figures such as Mbeki and Zuma, whose various performances in public are calculated to engender respect and honour (as masculine).

If shame results in the stigmatization of the subject, we can see how the law can mark its Others as shameful in the context of post-apartheid South Africa – and other states where democracy is, so to speak, under development (arguably, all democracies). Those who fail to perform the law as the law intends rights to be performed by those subject to it, are treated as inadequate, or shameful, subjects. Certainly one gets a sense of this in the guilt expressed by women who are unable to act upon their rights. One can also see shame as a motivation for the assertive subject's attempt to make sure the state 'does right' by him: characters as various as Coetzee's Lurie, demanding that Lucy report her rapists, and Mahala's Themba, who uses the law to ensure that his aunt is arrested for her husband's murder, both appeal to the law, one could argue, in the wake of their shameful inability to enact their roles as proper male subjects. Lurie fails to protect Lucy and Themba sees his sexual alliance with his aunt as intensely shameful. In either case their appeal to the law can be read as a defensive hyper-performance of the role of citizen, one who knows to demand rights from the state to, in a sense, 'make him right' by obscuring the cause of the shame.

Poverty and the threat of poverty add an extra dimension to the experience of shame, in that those most able to command material resources are most able to harness the machinery of legal rights in their favour; those least able to do so are not often permitted to plead poverty as a mitigating factor in defence of their inadequacy before the law. This is true not only in terms of specific cases but also more generally, as in the case of women without access to resources who wish to renegotiate their relations with their partners but cannot, for fear of being thrown out should the partner respond with aggression. The narrative of 'Tauhali', cited at length in Chapter 3, is an example of this dilemma.

The collusion of law and poverty to produce shame is the subject of a recent fiction entitled *Shameless* (2008) by Futhi Ntshingila. In it, the protagonist, Thandiwe, collapses the distinctions between transactional sex on the one hand, and prostitution and employment for black women in affirmative action positions on the other. Arriving destitute in central Johannesburg after a childhood marked by the break-up of both her biological and subsequent adoptive families, she receives board and lodging in Johannesburg in exchange for helping Sipho, an advertising agency employee, develop storyboards for advertising campaigns. She is then offered a job by the white president of the company for which Sipho works, a man named Dickson, but realizes all he wants her to do is occupy a large corner office, attend an occasional meeting, and go on the books to make the company affirmative action compliant. She refuses to take the job, arguing that all he wants is, in effect, a black Barbie. Later, at a party where Dickson is present, he and Thandiwe have sex in his car, after which he throws bundles of money at her and calls her 'a bloody whore' (Ntshingila 2008: 81). She laughs at him and asks him if his wife knows what he is. He then becomes 'her second client' (81), setting her up in a house which is registered to her, exclusively, in ownership. Once he has realized Thandiwe will not let him 'own' her exclusively, he ends up referring her to his friends as a woman who provides sexual services.

Thandiwe does not distinguish between this sort of work and the work she continues to do for Sipho: 'More than ever it was a business transaction for mutual benefit. I sold my body, my time and my advice to men. I got paid in money as does any worker. My clients were not forced to use my services. Free will and physical urges steered them toward me' (83). Thandiwe's emphasis on clients not being forced to use her services suggests that under affirmative action compliancy law, black women are constituted in practice as prostitutes, and their employers as their clients.

Underscoring this analogy is the fact that Thandiwe undertakes to tell her story to an ambitious filmmaker, another young black woman named Kwena. Thandiwe points out to Kwena that the string of mentors Kwena has had over the years while trying to work her way up in the film business speaks to the fact that Kwena is in no different a situation than Thandiwe would have been had she in effect sold herself to Dickson's company. Furthermore, Thandiwe firmly rejects the marketing disguised as advocacy that Kwena voices when she solicits Thandiwe as a potential subject for the film. Kwena tries to point out that she is doing Thandiwe a favour by offering her 'a voice', especially when she could be dead before long, like thousands of other sex workers in Johannesburg: 'I am giving you a platform to tell your story', she argues (27). Thandiwe responds vehemently:

> 'Hold it right there! Who said I need my story told? Do you think anyone cares about whether I live or die? You came here because you knew the story of a prostitute would be your platform. I am giving you the platform, that is, if I choose to!' (Ntshingila 2008: 27)

Thandiwe makes this stand just after she has a violent quarrel with Dickson, who has become obsessive about her since his wife has become ill. She is trying to 'wean' him off her by refusing to see him, but he does not accept this situation, getting furious with her for her rejection of him, then apologizing and pleading to be punished for his abuse of her. Thandiwe has indeed rendered her potential boss and current client abject. Her response to Kwena is an equally calculated negotiation: she allows Kwena to make the film, but only because she sees it to be a mutually beneficial enterprise. Eventually, Dickson shoots Thandiwe, because his wife is about to die, and she says she will take some time to think about moving in with him, despite his having (in his eyes) 'set her up' with house and income.

Thandiwe survives the shooting. However, the mood is hardly one of a celebratory reclaiming of agency, or turning the tables on clients of whatever kind. The narrator, Zonke, a childhood friend of Thandiwe's, accompanies her back to the village in which they were both born, where Thandiwe thanks her ancestors for having saved her. But they cannot find the ancestral graves, most particularly that of Thandiwe's grandmother, a much-loved figure of female defiance and pride in the novel. The river has dried up and the villagers' faces 'have lost any carefree quality and look almost haunted' (107). The demise of the river is attributed to 'the blood and tears of the victims' that have 'eroded the rich soil that used to be there' (107).

The narrative does not conclude on this sombre note, but with a slightly different scene: the viewing of the film about Thandiwe. Kwena is described by the narrator as 'beautiful' in her candidness about her life (108) – just as earlier her grandmother's old and large body was described as beautiful when the grandmother flaunted convention and bathed in the nude just after the death of her son, Thandiwe's uncle. Yet, this scene is no triumphalist celebration of reclaimed agency. As she introduces Thandiwe – in a wheelchair since her attack and present at the showing – to the audience, Kwena, the filmmaker, ends her speech with the epigraph with which Ntshingila prefaces the entire fiction: 'The shameless ones are free from illusions. They have mourned the loss of innocence. They choose survival in the periphery' (108).

*Shameless* suggests that the law plays no inconsiderable role in the subjectification of those at the periphery. More specifically, *Shameless* proposes that the legal provisions for affirmative employment perform a quintessential act of deaf listening: they may be intended to ensure racial and gender equality in the workplace, but their actual translation in practice produces black women as prize objects for sale and barter. Moreover, Ntshingila's fiction, and the narratives of women from rural KwaZulu-Natal participating in our research (Boyce, Jolly et al. 2003–2006) suggest that the law instantiates them as subjects, yet at the same time also desubjectifies them, as per Agamben's discourse on shame in the context of Holocaust survivors. The narratives of the men who demonstrate an abiding fear of being rendered abject as the motivation for (hyper) performances of masculine identity form the masculine correlative of this dilemma. Further, the response of adolescents to the traumatic imposition of gendered identities as a mark of adulthood can be read, from this perspective, as a reluctance to be instantiated as subjects subject to shame.

What does it mean for the law to position its subjects as present at their own defacement? In *Diary of a Bad Year*, the state is posed very much as Thandiwe positions other subjects in relation to herself. The state considers the actual lives of its subjects immaterial, to the extent that it confines its role to constituting them as subjects. In this context, human flourishing is immaterial to the state. Thandiwe says, in response to Kwena's appeal to her to allow her story to be told, that she is immaterial to the community at large: 'Do you think anyone cares about whether I live or die?', she asks. Similarly, the author-narrator of *Diary* points out that the state only 'cares' about its citizens to the extent that those citizens are subject-able to its dictates. It cares deeply about registering births and deaths, precisely because these construct an identity whose distinguishing feature is that of subjection to the state:

> We are born subject. From the moment of our birth we are subject. One mark of this subjectification is the certificate of our birth. The perfected state holds and guards the monopoly of certifying birth. Either you are given (and carry with you) the certificate of the state, thereby acquiring an identity which during the course of your life enables the state to identify you and track you (track you down); or you do without an identity and condemn yourself to living outside the state like an animal (animals do not have identity papers). (Coetzee 2008: 4)

The author-narrator, Coetzee, concludes bluntly, mirroring the phrase of Thandiwe: 'Whether the citizen lives or dies is not a concern of the state. What matters to the state and its records is whether the citizen is alive or dead' (5).

The quasi-subjects that I have attempted to trace in the course of exploring the engendering of human rights in South Africa – quasi-subjects rendered available for violation through their culturing as such – are spoken, as best they can be, through the vocabulary of the margins: 'survival' at the 'periphery' in Ntshingila's terms. I am not suggesting that the laws of the South African Constitution are wrong-headed, but rather instruments of deaf listening in a context in which a large number of the state's subjects are positioned as appealing for admission to, rather than commanding, the rights assigned them in law. In part, this stems from the state's over-dependence upon constitutional and other forms of human rights law to instantiate subjects as proper, without due attention to what theorists of the humanities call the conditions for a successful performative act in local contexts. This over-reliance is by no means confined to South Africa. What happens to community affiliations when the law is relied upon to play an overwhelming role in negotiating 'on behalf of' its subjects is evidenced by the fetishization of national security in the US, Australia and elsewhere. This is yet another expression of anxiety about those on the periphery.

When agency is reduced to that of the legal subject, its actual potential as a resource for change is limited by the very source of its currency within the public sphere, namely its investment in the individual as the primary categorization of the subject. Further, constitutional law cannot supersede the loyalties that preceded it.[3] The reasons for Zuma's popularity and success within the democratic framework of post-apartheid South Africa, I propose, lie precisely in his presentation of himself as an unashamed patriarch of a kind of community quite foreign to that constructed by the language of the contemporary, democratic state. If the state presents itself as capable of overwriting sustained histories of colonialism and racism through acts of constitutional law-making, a performance such as Zuma's appears to highlight the inadequacy of such laws in the eyes of the majority of the state's subjects.

Perhaps, however, this relative 'marginalization' of the law should not be viewed purely in a negative light. There is one subject who cares whether Thandiwe lives or dies: her childhood friend from the rural areas, Zonke, who narrates her story in a way that the spectacular lens of Kwena's camera, however masterful its operator, cannot. If shame is publicly constituted, in acts of spectacular violence in which the state is symbolically complicit, it is possible that the reconfiguration of shame may entail an un-censoring of dishonour – that most unspectacular of sentiments – as an outmoded form of acknowledgment. The admission of shame in such a scenario would not be limited to private moments, such as in Themba's embrace of the Bitch of Sekunjalo. It would extend to an imaginative community that seeks to register such dishonour as initiating innovative ways of envisaging acknowledgements of the authority of those who have, and do, suffer the violence of their unspeakability; acknowledgements that are commensurate with the demands made

---

3   I am grateful to Eve D'Aeth for this insight.

by that authority. Such an imaginative community is invoked in and by Futhi Ntshingila's *Shameless*. Perhaps, risking utopianism, we can consider that an outlawed concept of dishonour, precisely as an outlaw(ed) concept, may yet prove a resource for un-culturing that violence in which we are complicit, but by which we are nevertheless constituted, in Bourdieu's terms, as symbolic victims.

# Bibliography

Abrahams, N., R. Jewkes and R. Laubsher, 1999. '"I do not believe in democracy in the home": Men's Relationships with and Abuse of Women', *Medical Research Council*, August. At http://www.mrc.ac.za/gender/nodemocracy.pdf (accessed 19 April 2010).

Africa Strategic Research Corporation and the Kaiser Family Foundation, 2001. 'The 2001 National Survey of South African Youth'. At http://www.lovelife. org.za/corporate/research/lovelifeforus.doc (accessed 15 April 2010).

African National Congress (ANC), 1998. 'Submission of the African National Congress to the Truth and Reconciliation Commission in Reply to the Section 30 (2) of Act 34 of 1996 on the TRC'. October. At http://www.anc.org.za/ ancdocs/misc/trcreply.html (accessed 19 April 2010).

—, 2000. 'Statement of the ANC at the Human Rights Commission Hearings on Racism in the Media'. 5 April. At http://www.anc.org.za/ancdocs/misc/2000/ sp0405.html (accessed 20 April 2010).

Agamben, Giorgio, 1999. *Remnants of Auschwitz: The Witness and the Archive*, tr. Daniel Heller-Roazen (Cambridge: MIT Press).

ANC see African National Congress.

Arms Deal Virtual Press Office, The, n.d. At http://www.armsdeal-vpo.co.za (accessed 26 October 2008).

Attridge, Derek, 2000. 'Age of Bronze, State of Grace: Music and Dogs in Coetzee's Disgrace', *Novel* 34, no. 1: 98–121.

—, 2004. *J. M. Coetzee and the Ethics of Reading: Literature in the Event* (Pietermaritzburg, SA; Chicago: University of KwaZulu-Natal Press; Chicago University Press).

Attwell, David, 1998. '"Dialogue" and "Fulfilment" in J. M. Coetzee's *Age of Iron*', in *Writing South Africa: Literature, Apartheid, and Democracy, 1970–1995*, ed. D. Attridge and R. Jolly (Cambridge: Cambridge University Press), pp. 166–79.

—, 1993. *J. M. Coetzee: South Africa and the Politics of Writing* (Cape Town; Berkeley: David Philip; University of California Press).

—, 2002. 'Race in Disgrace', *Interventions*, 4, no. 3: 331–41.

Avni, Ora, 1995. 'Beyond Psychoanalysis: Elie Wiesel's "Night" in Historical Perspective', in *Auschwitz and After: Race, Culture and 'The Jewish Question' in France*, ed. Lawrence D. Kitzman (London; New York: Routledge), pp. 203–218.

Behr, Mark, 1995. *The Smell of Apples* (New York: Picador).

—, 1996. 'The Behr Truth, in his own Words: An Edited Version of Mark Behr's Speech, Made at a Writers Conference entitled "Faultlines: Inquiries around Truth and Reconciliation"', The *Mail & Guardian*, 12–18 July: 27.

Bhania, Deevia, 2003. 'Children are Children: Gender doesn't Matter', *Agenda*: 37–45.

Biko, Steve, 1987. 'Black Consciousness and the Quest for a New Humanity', in *I Write what I Like* by Steve Biko (London: Heinemann), pp. 87–98.

Bohler-Muller, Narnia, 2008. 'Reparations for Apartheid Human Rights Abuses: The Case of Khulumani', *AfricaGrowth Agenda*, April: 20–23.

Bond, Patrick, 2008. 'Can Reparations for Apartheid Profts be won in US Courts?', Khulumani, 6 July. At http://www.khulumani.net/component/content/article/ 10-Redress/243 (accessed 19 April 2010).

Boraine, Alex, 2000; 2001. 'The Language of Potential', in *After the TRC: Reflections on Truth and Reconciliation in South Africa*, ed. Wilmot James and Linda van der Vijver (Cape Town; Athens, Ohio: David Philip; Ohio University Press), pp. 73–81.

Bourdieu, Pierre, 1980. *The Logic of Practice*, tr. Richard Nice (Stanford: Stanford University Press).

—, 1991. *Language and Symbolic Power*, ed. John B. Thompson, tr. Gino Raymond and Matthew Adamson (Cambridge, Massachusetts: Harvard University Press).

—, 2000. *Pascalian Meditations*, tr. R. Nice (Cambridge: Polity Press).

—, and Loïc Wacquant, 1992. *An Invitation to Reflexive Sociology* (Cambridge: Polity Press).

Bower, Carol, 2003. 'The Relationship between Child Abuse and Poverty', *Agenda*, no. 56: 84–87.

Boyarin, Daniel, 1997. *Unheroic Conduct: The Rise of Heterosexuality and the Invention of the Jewish Man* (Berkeley: University of California Press).

Boyce, W., R. Jolly, A. Jeeves, N. Mngoma, S. Reid and S. Verma, 2003–2006. 'Transforming Violent Gender Relations to Reduce Risk of HIV/AIDS Infection Among Young Women and Girls – The Interviews', unedited, unpublished transcripts of focus-group interviews.

Butler, Anthony, 2005. 'South Africa's HIV/AIDS policy, 1994–2004: How can it be Explained?' *African Affairs*, 104, no. 417: 591–614.

Butler, Judith, 1993. *Bodies that Matter: on the Discursive Limits of Sex* (New York; London: Routledge).

—, 1997. *Excitable Speech: A Politics of the Performative* (London; New York: Routledge).

Buur, Lars, 2003. '"In the Name of the Victims": the Politics of Compensation in the Work of the South African Truth and Reconciliation Commission', in *Political Transition: Politics and Cultures*, ed. Paul Gready (London: Pluto Press), pp. 148–64.

Campbell, Catherine, 2003. *'Letting them Die': How HIV/AIDS Prevention Programmes often Fail* (London, Bloomington, IN, Cape Town: James Currey; Indiana University Press; Double Storey).

Cassiem, S., N. Mandla, N. Mankayi, and B. van Vuuren, 1997. 'Child Abuse and the Impact of Poverty', *Agenda*, 33: 43–48.

Chapman, Michael, 1996. *Southern African Literatures* (London; New York: Longman).

Chapman, Michael (ed.), 1989. *The Drum Decade: Stories from the 1950's*. (Pietermaritzburg: University of Natal Press).

CIETafrica. 'South Africa: Sexual Violence & HIV/AIDS'. At http://www.ciet.org/en/documents/projects/200621015051.asp (accessed 15 April 2010).

Clayton, Jonathan, 2007. 'Cleared of Rape and Fraud and Set to be South Africa's next President', *The Times Online*, 29 September. At http://www.timesonline.co.uk/tol/news/world/africa/article2554228.ece (accessed 19 April 2010).

Coetzee, J. M., 1980. *Waiting for the Barbarians* (London: Secker and Warburg).

—, 1986. 'Into the Dark Chamber: The Novelist and South Africa', *New York Times Book Review*, 12 January: 13; 35.

—, 1996. *Giving Offense: Essays on Censorship* (Chicago; London: Chicago University Press).

—, 1999. *Disgrace* (London: Secker & Warburg).

—, 2001. *The Lives of Animals*, ed. Amy Gutman (Princeton: Princeton University Press).

—, 2003. *Elizabeth Costello* (London: Secker & Warburg).

—, 2007. *Diary of a Bad Year* (London: Secker & Warburg).

—, and D. Attwell, 1992. *Doubling the Point: Essays and Interviews* (Cambridge, Masssachusetts: Harvard University Press).

Coetzer, Pieter, 2005. 'Rape in Contemporary South Africa: More Vexing and Vicious than Ever', *Journal for Contemporary History*, 30, no. 33: 169–82.

Colvin, C., 2000. '"We Are Still Struggling": Storytelling, Reparations and Reconciliation after the TRC' (*Centre for Studies in Violence and Reconciliation*). At http://www.csvr.org.za/docs/trc/wearestillstruggling.pdf (accessed 19 April 2010).

Congress, African National see African National Congress (ANC)

Consitutional Court of South Africa, n.d. *The Bill of Rights: An Overview and the Text*. At http://www.constitutionalcourt.org.za/text/rights/bill.html (accessed 19 April 2010).

Culbertson, Roberta, 1995. 'Embodied Memory, Transcendence, and Telling: Recounting Trauma, Re-establishing the Self', *New Literary History*, 26.1: 169–95.

Das, Veena, and Arthur Kleinman, 2000. Introduction, *Violence and Subjectivity* by Veena Das, Arthur Kleinman, Mamphela Ramphele and Pamela Reynolds (Berkeley; Los Angeles: University of California Press), pp. 1–18.

Dempster, Carolyn, 2002. 'Rape – Silent War on Women', *BBC World*, 9 April. At http://news.bbc;co.uk/2/hi/africa/1909220.stm (accessed 19 April 2010).

Dike, Fatima, 1998a. 'Interview with Fatima Dike', in *Black South African Women: An Anthology of Plays*, ed. Kathy Perkins (London; New York: Routledge), pp. 23–25.

—, 1998b. "So What's New?" in *Black South African Women: An Anthology of Plays*, ed. Kathy A. Perkins (London; New York: Routledge), pp. 23–46.

Eckstein, Barbara J., 1990. *The Language of Fiction in a World of Pain* (Philadelphia: University of Pennsylvania Press).

Finlayson, R., 2002. 'Women's Language of Respect: isihlonipho sabafazi', in *Language in South Africa*, ed. Rajend Mesthrie (Cambridge: Cambridge University Press), pp. 279–96.

Fromm, Harold, 2000. 'Coetzee's Postmodern Animals', *The Hudson Review*, 53, no. 2: 336–44.

Gilman, Sander, 1985. 'Black Bodies, White Bodies: toward an Iconography of Female Sexuality in late Nineteenth-Century Art, Medicine, and Literature', *Critical Inquiry*, 12, no. 1: 204–42.

—, 1991. *The Jew's Body* (New York: Routledge).

—, 1993. *Freud, Race and Gender* (Princeton: Princeton University Press).

Goldblatt, Beth, and Sheila Meintjies, 1996. 'Gender and the Truth and Reconciliation Commission', *Truth and Reconciliation Commission of South Africa: Human Rights Violations Hearings & Submissions*, May. At http://www.justice. gov.za/trc//hrvtrans/submit/gender.htm (accessed 19 April 2010).

Goodwin, Christopher, 2000. 'White Man without the Burden'. *Sunday Times News Review*, 16 January: 4.

Gordimer, Nadine. 'The Idea of Gardening', *New York Times Book Review*, 18 April 1984: 3–4.

Gorra, Michael, 2000. 'After the Fall', *New York Times Book Review*, 5 November: 36.

Graham, Shane, 2003. 'The Truth Commission and Post-apartheid Literature in South Africa', 34, no. 1: 12–30.

Graybill, Lyn, 2002. *Truth and Reconciliation in South Africa: Miracle or Model?* (Boulder, Colorado: Lynne Rienner).

*Guardian Weekly*, The, 2008. *The End of the Rainbow*, Editorial, 30 May.

Hamber, B., N. Mosikare, M. Friedman and T. Maepa, 2000. 'Speaking Out: The Role of the Khulumani Victim Support Group in Dealing with the Past in South Africa' (Brandon Hamber Publications), 17–21 June. At http://www. brandonhamber.com/pubs_papers.htm/ (accessed 19 April 2010).

Head, Bessie, 1974. *A Question of Power* (London; Nairobi; Ibadan: Heinemann).

Henri, Yazir, 2003. 'Reconciling Reconciliation: A Personal And Public Journey Of Testifying Before The South African Truth And Reconciliation Commission', in *Political Transition: Politics and Cultures*, ed. Paul Gready (London: Pluto Press), pp. 262–75.

Heyns, Michiel, 2000. 'The Whole Country's Truth: Confession and Narrative in Recent White South African Writing', *Modern Fiction Studies*, 46, no. 1: 42–66.

Himonga, Chuma, and Craig Bosch, 2000. 'The Application of African Customary Law under the Constitution of South Africa: Problems Solved or Just Beginning?' *South African Law Journal*, 117: 306–341.

Hirschowitz, R., S. Worku and M. Orkin, 2000. 'Quantitative Research Findings on Rape in South Africa' (Pretoria: Statistics of South Africa).

Hoad, Neville, 2005. 'Thabo Mbeki's AIDS Blues: The Intellectual, The Archive, and the Pandemic', *Public Culture*, 17, no. 1: 101–127.

Hope, Christopher, 2006. 'Strange State of Terror', The *Guardian Weekly*, 19

May. At http://www.guardian.co.uk/theguardian/2006/may/19/guardianweekly. guardianweekly11 (accessed 19 April 2010).

Horowitz, Elliott, 1998. 'The Vengeance of the Jews was Stronger than their Avarice: Modern Historians and the Persian Conquest of Jerusalem in 614', *Jewish Social Studies*, 4, no. 2: 1–39.

Human Rights Watch, 1995. *Violence Against Women in South Africa* (New York: Human Rights Watch).

Hunter, Mark, 2002. 'The Materiality of Everyday Sex: Thinking Beyond Prostitution', *African Studies*, 61, no. 1: 99–120.

James, Wilmot, and Linda van der Vijver, 2000; 2001. *After the TRC: Reflections on Truth and Reconciliation in South Africa* (Cape Town; Athens, Ohio: David Philip; University of Ohio Press).

Jewkes, R., R. Levin, N. Mbananga and D. Bradshaw, 2002. 'Rape of Girls in South Africa', *The Lancet*, 359, no. 9303: 711.

Jewkes, R., L. Martin and L. Penn-Kekana, 2002. 'The Virgin Cleansing Myth: Cases of Child Rape are not Exotic', *The Lancet*, 359, no. 9307, February 23: 711.

Jolly, Rosemary J., 1995. 'Rehearsals of Liberation: Contemporary Postcolonial Discourse and the New South Africa', *Publications of the Modern Language Association*, 110, no. 1: 17–29.

—, 1996. *Colonization, Violence and Narration in White South African Writing* (Johannesburg; Athens, Ohio: University of the Witwatersrand Press; Ohio University Press).

—, 2001. 'Desiring Good(s) in the Face of Needy Subjects: South Africa's Truth and Reconciliation Commission in a Global Context', *South Atlantic Quarterly*: 693–716.

—, 2007. 'For Northern Displacements: Understanding the Meaning of Madness in Global Constructions of HIV/AIDS', *The Global South*, 1, no. 1: 55–65.

—, and Alan Jeeves, forthcoming. 'Gender Equity, HIV/AIDS, and Democracy in Rural South Africa since 1994', *Canadian Journal of African Studies*.

Jones, Basil, and Adrian Kohler, 1998. 'Puppeteers' Note', in *Ubu and the Truth Commission*, by Jane Taylor (Cape Town: University of Cape Town Press), pp. xvi–xvii.

Kapp, C., 2006. 'Rape on Trial in South Africa', *The Lancet*, 367: 718–19.

Kayser, Undine, 2001. 'Interventions after the TRC – Reconciliation, Advocacy & Healing' (*Centre for Studies in Violence and Reconciliation*), October. At http// www.csvr.org.za/docs/trc/interventionsaftertrc.pdf (accessed 19 April 2010).

Kentridge, William, 1998. 'Director's Note', In *Ubu and the Truth Commission*, by Jane Taylor (Cape Town: University of Cape Town Press), pp. viii–xv.

Kippen, Lorelee, 2002. 'Transforming the Traumatic Space of Witnessing: The Limits of the Burlesque Monster in Jane Taylor's Ubu and the Tuth Commission', *Agora: An Online Graduate Journal*. At http://epe.lac.bac. gc.ca/100/202/300/agora/2002/v1n03/142.htm (accessed 19 April 2010).

Kossew, Sue (ed.), 1998. *Critical Essays on J. M. Coetzee* (New York: G. K. Hall).

Kottler, Sharon, 1998. 'Wives' Subjective Definitions of and Attitudes towards Wife Rape', unpublished MA dissertation (Pretoria: University of South Africa).

Krog, Antjie, 1998. *Country of my Skull* (Johannesburg: Random House).

—, 2000. *Country of my Skull: Guilt, Sorrow, and the Limits of Forgiveness in the New South Africa*, Introduction Charlayne Hunter-Gault (New York: Three Rivers Press).

Kruger, Loren, 1995. '"So What's New?" Women and Theater in the "New South Africa"', *Theater*, 25, no. 3: 46–54.

Lalu, Premesh, and Brent Harris, 1996. 'Journeys from the Horizons of History: Text, Trial and Tales in the Construction of Narratives of Pain', *Current Writing*, 8, no. 2: 24–38.

Leclerc-Madlala, Suzanne, 1996. 'Crime in an Epidemic: The Case of Rape and AIDS', *ACTA Criminologica*, 9, no. 2: 31–37.

Ling, L. H. M., 2002. 'Cultural Chauvinism and the Liberal International Order: "West versus Rest" in Asia's Financial Crisis', in *Power, Postcolonialism, and International Relations: Reading Race, Gender, Class*, ed. Geeta Chowdry and Sheila Nair (London: Routledge), pp. 115–41.

Lovelife, 2000. 'Hot Prospects, Cold Facts'. At http://www.kff.org/southafrica/upload/KFF-lovelife_a.pdf (accessed 8 February 2010).

Mahala, Siphiwo, 2007. *When a Man Cries* (Scottsville, South Africa: University of KwaZulu-Natal Press).

Mamdani, Mahmood, 1996a. 'Reconciliation without Justice', *South African Review of Books*, 46 (November-December): 3–5.

Mamdani, Mahmood, 1996b. *Citizen and Subject: Contemporary Africa and the Legacy of Late Colonialism* (Princeton: Princeton University Press).

Marais, Michael, 2000a. '"Little Enough, Less than Little: Nothing": Ethics, Engagement, and Change in the Fiction of J. M. Coetzee', *Modern Fiction Studies*, 46, no. 1: 159–82.

—, 2000b. 'The Possibility of Ethical Action: J. M. Coetzee's Disgrace', *Scrutiny 2*, 5, no. 1: 57–63.

Mbeki, Thabo, 1998. 'Statement of Deputy President Thabo Mbeki at the Africa Telecom '98 Forum, Johannesburg, May 04, 1998', *Department of Foreign Affairs of the Republic of South Africa*, 4 May. At http://www.dfa.gov.za/docs/speeches/1998/mbek0504.htm (accessed 19 April 2010).

—, 1999. 'Premier's Address', *Mpumalanga Provincial Government*, 19 December. At http://www.mpumalanga.gov.za/otp/speeches/archived_speeches/speech 19Dec99.htm (accessed 19 April 2010).

—, 2001. 'Address by President Thabo Mbeki at the Inaugural ZK Matthews Memorial Lecture', *African National Congress*, 12 October. At http://www.anc.org.za/ancdocs/history/mbeki/2001/tm1012.html (accessed 19 April 2010).

McGregor, Liz, 2005. *Khabazela: The Life and Times of a South African* (Johannesburg: Jacana).

Memela, Sandile, 2005. *Flowers of the Nation* (Scottsville: University of KwaZulu-Natal Press).

Memmi, Albert, 1991. *The Colonizer and the Colonized*, Introduction by Jean-Paul Sartre; Afterword by Susan Gilson Miller (Boston: Beacon Press).

Merchant, Carolyn, 1995. *Earthcare: Women and the Environment* (London; New York: Routledge).

Milojevic, I., 2002. 'Gender, Peace and Terrestrial Futures: Alternatives to Terrorism and War', *Journal of Futures Studies*, 6, no. 3: 21–44.

Mokgoro, Yvonne, 1996–1997. 'The Customary Law Question in the South African Constitution', *St Louis University Law Journal*, 41, no. 4: 1279–89.

Morrell, Robert, 1998. 'Of Men and Boys: Masculinity and Gender in Southern African Studies', *Journal of Southern African Studies*, 24, no. 4: 605–630.

—, ed., 2001. *Changing Men in South Africa* (Scottsville; London: University of Natal Press; Zed Books).

Moss, Laura, 2006. '"Nice Audible Crying": Editions, Testimonies, and Country of my Skull', *Research in African Literatures*, 37, no. 4: 85–104.

Mosse, George, 1985. *Nationalism and Sexuality: Middle-Class Morality and Sexual Norms in Modern Europe* (Madison: University of Wisconsin Press).

Motsei, Mmatshilo, 2007. *The Kanga and the Kangaroo Court: Reflections on the Rape Trial of Jacob Zuma* (Johannesburg: Jacana).

Mpahlele [Esekie], Ezekiel, [Bruno], 1989. 'The Suitcase', in *The Drum Decade: Stories from the 1950's*, ed. Michael Chapman (Pietermaritzburg: University of Natal Press), pp. 73–78.

Mpe, Phaswane, 2001. *Welcome to our Hillbrow* (Scottsville: University of Natal Press).

Mtwa, Percy, Mbongeni Ngema and Barney Simon, 1990. *Woza Albert!* (London: Methuen).

Ndebele, Njabulo, 1991. *The Rediscovery of the Ordinary: Essays on South African Literature and Culture* (Fordsburg: Congress of South African Writers).

—, 1992 [1983]. *The Prophetess*, adapted by Chris van Wyk (Johannesburg: Viva Books).

—, 2007a [1992], 'Recovering Childhood', in *Fine Lines from the Box: Further Thoughts about our Country*, by Njabulo Ndebele (Roggebaai: Umuzi), pp. 34–43.

—, 2007b [2006], 'Jacob Zuma and the Family: How Zuma's Bravado Brutalized the Public', in *Fine Lines from the Box: Further Thoughts about our Country*, by Njabulo Ndebele (Roggebaai: Umuzi), pp. 230–32.

Nel, Cecile, 2006. 'G-strings burnt at Zuma trial', *News24*, 4 April. At http://www.news24.com/News24/South_Africa/ZumaFiles/Gstrings-burnt-at-Zuma-trial-20060403 (accessed 19 April 2010).

Niehaus, Isak, 2005. 'Masculine Domination in Sexual Violence: Interpreting Accounts of three Cases of Rape in the South African Lowveld', in *Men Behaving Differently: South African men since 1994*, ed. Graeme Reid and Liz Walker (Cape Town: Double Storey), pp. 65–88.

Nkosi, Lewis, 1966. 'Fiction by Black South Africans', *Black Orpheus*, March: 48–54.

Ntshingila, Futhi, 2008. *Shameless* (Scottsville: University of KwaZulu-Natal Press).

Nuttall, S., and C. Coetzee, 1998. *Negotiating the Past* (Cape Town; Oxford: Oxford University Press).

Nyatsumba, Kaiser, 2000; 2001. 'Neither Dull Nor Tiresome', in *After the TRC: Reflections on Truth and Reconciliation in South Africa*, ed. Wilmot James and Linda van der Vijver (Cape Town; Athens, Ohio: David Philip; University of Ohio Press), pp. 88–93.

Oliver, Kelly, 2001. *Witnessing: Beyond Recognition* (Minneapolis: University of Minnesota Press).

—, 2004. 'Witnessing and Testimony', *Parallax*, 10, no. 1: 78–87.

Orr, Wendy, 2000. 'Reparation and the Healing of Victims', in *Looking Back, Reaching Forward: Reflections on the Truth and Reconciliation Commission of South Africa*, ed. Charles Villa Vicencio and Wilhelm Verwoerd (Cape Town: University of Cape Town Press, pp. 239–49.

'Palesa', 1996. Interview by Miriam Tlali, 15 May.

Parry, Benita, 1998. 'Speech and Silence in the Fictions of J. M. Coetzee', in *Writing South Africa: Literature, Apartheid and Democracy, 1970–1995*, ed. D. Attridge and R. Jolly (Cambridge: Cambridge University Press), pp. 149–65.

Pitcher, Graeme J., and Douglas M. G. Bowley, 2002. 'Infant Rape in South Africa', *The Lancet*, 359, no. 9303, January: 274–75.

Plant, Judith (ed.), 1989. *Healing the Wounds: The Promise of Ecofeminism* (Toronto: Beyond the Lines).

Plumwood, Val, 1994. *Feminism and the Mastery of Nature* (London; New York: Routledge).

—, 2002. *Environmental Culture: The Ecological Crisis of Reason* (New York: Routledge).

Pollock, Lori Dawn, 2000. 'Embodying Identities: Black Women's Writing in South Africa, 1970–1995'. Unpublished thesis (Kingston, Ontario: Queen's University).

Posel, Deborah, 2005a. 'Sex, Death and the Fate of the Nation: Reflections on the Politicization of Sexuality in Post-apartheid South Africa', *Africa*, 75: 125–53.

—, 2005b. 'The Scandal of Manhood: "Baby Rape" and the Politicization of Sexual Violence in Post-apartheid South Africa', *Culture, Health & Sexuality*, May–June: 239–52.

Province of KwaZulu-Natal, Office of the Premier, 2006. 'HIV and AIDS Strategy for the Province of KwaZulu-Natal 2006–2010 (Draft)', KwaZulu-Natal Provincial Government, 25 September. At http://www.kwazulunatal.gov.za/whats_new/Edited_HIV_and_AIDS_Provincial_Strategy.pdf (accessed 19 April 2010).

Ramphele, Mamphela, 1997. 'Political Widowhood in South Africa: The Embodiment of Ambiguity', in *Social Suffering*, ed. Arthur Kleinman, Veena Das and Margaret Lock (Berkeley; Los Angeles; London: University of California Press), pp. 99–118.

—, 2006. 'Reconciliation is not Enough', Speech to the TRC Ten Years After Conference held at the University of Cape Town in November 2006, Mail&Guardianonline, 1 December. At http://www.mg.co.za/article/2006-12-01-reconciliation-is-not-enough (accessed 19 April 2010).

—, 2008. *Laying Ghosts to Rest: Dilemmas of the Transformation in South Africa* (Cape Town: Tafelberg).

Rampolokeng, Lesego, 1999. *The Story I am About to Tell Indaba Engziyixoxa*, directed by Robert Colman, performed by Khulumani Support Group, 11 June. (Johannesburg: Wits Theatre).

Ratele, Kopano, 2006. 'Ruling Masculinity and Sexuality', *Feminist Africa*, 6: 48–64.

Reid, Graeme, and Liz Walker, 2005. *Men Behaving Differently: South African Men Since 1994*. (Cape Town: Double Storey).

Robins, Steven, 2006. 'Sexual Rights and Sexual Cultures: Reflections on "The Zuma Affair" and "New Masculinities" in South Africa', *Horizontes Antropologicos*, 12, no. 26: 149–83.

Ross, Fiona, 2003. *Bearing Witness: Women and the Truth and Reconciliation*

*Commission in South Africa* (London: Pluto Press).

Said, Edward, 1994. *Culture and Imperialism* (London: Vintage).

Salverson, Julie, 2001. *The Haunting of Sophie Scholl*, directed by Anne Hardcastle, performed at The Rotunda Theatre, Kingston, Ontario, Canada, November.

Sanders, Mark, 2000. 'Truth, Telling, Questioning: The Truth and Reconciliation Commission, Antjie Krog's *Country of My Skull*, and Literature after Apartheid', *Modern Fiction Studies*, 46, no. 1: 13–41.

—, 2007. *Ambiguities of Witnessing: Law and Literature in the Time of a Truth Commission* (Stanford: Stanford University Press).

Scarry, Elaine, 1985. *The Body in Pain: The Making and Unmaking of the World* (Oxford: Oxford University Press).

Schadeburg, Jurgen (ed.), 1989. *The Finest Photos of the Old Drum*, Bailey's African Photo Archives (London: Penguin).

Seroke, Joyce, 1999. 'Presentation to the Conference on "The Aftermath: Women in Post-War Reconstruction"' held at Johannesburg: University of the Witwatersrand, 20–22 July.

Sesanti, Simphiwe, 2008. 'The media and the Zuma/Zulu culture: An Afrocentric Perspective', in *Power, Politics and Identity in South African Media*, ed. Adrian Hadland, Eric Louw, Simphiwe Sesanti and Herman Wasserman (Cape Town: HSRC Press), pp. 364–77.

Sideris, Tina, 2005. '"You have to change and you don't know how!": Contesting What it Means to be a Man in a Rural Area of South Africa', in *Men Behaving Differently: South African Men Since 1994*, ed. Graeme Reid and Liz Walker, pp. 111–38 (Cape Town: Double Storey).

Simpson, Graeme, 1992. 'Jack-asses and Jackrollers: Rediscovering Gender in Understanding Violence' (Centre for the Study of Violence and Reconciliation). At http://www.csvr.org.za/index.php?option=com_content&task=view&id=778 (accessed 19 April 2010).

Sitze, Adam, 2004. 'Denialism', *South Atlantic Quarterly*, no. 103.4: 769–811.

Sooka, Yasmin, 1999. 'Keynote Address to the Conference on "The Aftermath: Women in Post-War Reconstruction"', Johannesburg: University of the Witwatersrand, 20–22 July.

Soper, Kate, 1995. *What is Nature? Culture, Politics and the non-Human* (Cambridge: Blackwell).

Stanton, S., M. Lochrenberg and V. Mukasa, 1997. 'Improved Justice for Survivors of Sexual Violence? Adult Survivors' Experiences of the Wynberg Sexual Offences Court and Associated Services' (Cape Town: University of Cape Town and Human Rights Commission).

Steinberg, Jonny (2008). *Three-Letter Plague: A Young Man's Journey through a Great Epidemic* (Johannesburg; Cape Town: Jonathan Ball).

Supreme Court of Appeal of South Africa, 2006. 'Judgment in S V Shaik and Others', 6 November. At http://www.justice.gov.za/sca/judgments/sca_2006/2006 (accessed 19 April 2010).

'Tauhali', 1996. Interview by Rosemary Jolly, 15 February.

Taylor, Charles, 1989. *Sources of the Self: The Making of Modern Identity* (Cambridge, Massachusetts: Harvard Univeristy Press).

Taylor, Jane, 1998. *Ubu and the Truth Commission* (Cape Town: University of Cape Town Press).

Taylor, Mike Earl, 2002. 'HIV/AIDS, the Stats, the Virgin Cure and Infant Rape', *Science in Africa*, April. At http://www.scienceinafrica.co.za/2002/april/virgin. htm (accessed 19 April 2010).

'Thandi', 1996. 'Written Life Story (for Rosemary Jolly and Miriam Tlali)', 31 May (Soweto, South Africa).

Tlali, Miriam, 1998. 'Interview with Miriam Tlali', in *Writing South Africa: Literature, Apartheid, and Democracy, 1970–1995*, ed. Derek Attridge and Rosemary J. Jolly (Cambridge: Cambridge University Press), pp.141–48.

TRC see Truth and Reconciliation Commission of South Africa

Truth and Reconciliation Commission of South Africa (TRC), 2003a [1998]. *Truth and Reconciliation Commission of South Africa Report*, VII vols. (Cape Town: Juta).

—, 2003b. *Amnesty Hearings and Decisions*, 10 April. At http://www.justice.gov.za/ trc/amntrans/index.htm (accessed 19 April 2010).

—, 2003c. *Human Rights Violations Hearings and Submissions*, 10 April. At http:// www.justice.gov.za/trc/hrvtrans/index.htm (accessed 19 April 2010).

United Nations Office for the Co-ordination of Humanitarian Affairs, 2006. 'South Africa: Sexual Assault Hidden in Culture of Silence'. *IRIN Africa*, 2 March. At http://www.irinnews.org/report.aspx?reportid=58305 (accessed 19 April 2010).

van As, A. B., M. Withers, N. du Toit, A. J. Millar and H. Rhode, 2001. 'Child Rape: Patterns of Injury, Management and Outcome', *South African Medical* Journal, 91, no. 12, December: 1035–38.

Vetten, Lisa, and J. Dladla, 2000. 'Women's Fear and Survival in Inner-City Johannesburg', *Agenda*, 45: 70–75.

—, 2001. 'Violence, Vengeance and Gender: A Preliminary Investigation into the Links between Violence against Women and HIV/AIDS in South Africa' (Johannesburg: Centre for Studies in Violence and Reconciliation).

Villa Vicencio, Charles, and Wilhelm Verwoerd, 2000. *Looking Back, Reaching Forward: Reflections on the Truth and Reconciliation Commission of South Africa* (Cape Town: University of Cape Town Press).

Wachtel, Eleanor, 2001. 'The Sympathetic Imagination: A Conversation with J. M. Coetzee', *Brick*, no. 67: 37–47.

Walaza, Nomfundo, 2000. 'Insufficent Healing and Reparation', in *Looking Back, Reaching Forward: Reflections on the Truth and Reconciliation Commission of South Africa*, by Charles Villa Vicencio and Wilhelm Verwoerd (Cape Town: University of Cape Town Press), pp. 250–55.

Wang, Joy, 2008. 'AIDS Denialism and "The Humanisation of the African"', *Race and Class*, 49, no. 3: 1–18.

Waters, M., 2001. Speech by M. Waters in Parliament on Child Abuse, 14 November. At http://www.parliament.gov.za/live/content.php?Category_ID=119 &fYear=2001&fMonth=11 (accessed 19 April 2010).

Wilson, Richard, 2001. *The Politics of Truth and Reconciliation in South Africa* (Cambridge: Cambridge University Press).

Wright, T., P. Hughes, and A. Ainley, 1988. "The Paradox of Morality: An Interview with Levinas', in *The Provocation of Levinas: Rethinking the Other*, ed. Robert Bernasconi and David Wood, tr. Andrew Benjamin and Tamra Wright (New York: Routledge & Kegan Paul), pp. 168–80.

# Index

The letter n indicates a footnote.